ART OF LIVING

TIMELESS WISDOM IS IN HEALTHY AND JOYFUL MIND, BODY, SPIRIT

Tadeusz Nowicki

BALBOA. PRESS

A DIVISION OF HAY HOUSE

Balboa Press books may be ordered through booksellers or by contacting:

Balboa Press
A Division of Hay House
1663 Liberty Drive
Bloomington, IN 47403
www.balboapress.com.au
1 (877) 407-4847

Because of the dynamic nature of the Internet, any web addresses or links contained in this book may have changed since publication and may no longer be valid. The views expressed in this work are solely those of the author and do not necessarily reflect the views of the publisher, and the publisher hereby disclaims any responsibility for them.

The author of this book does not dispense medical advice or prescribe the use of any technique as a form of treatment for physical, emotional, or medical problems without the advice of a physician, either directly or indirectly. The intent of the author is only to offer information of a general nature to help you in your quest for emotional and spiritual well-being. In the event you use any of the information in this book for yourself, which is your constitutional right, the author and the publisher assume no responsibility for your actions.

Any people depicted in stock imagery provided by Thinkstock are models, and such images are being used for illustrative purposes only. Certain stock imagery © Thinkstock.

Print information available on the last page.

ISBN: 978-1-5043-0971-4 (sc)
ISBN: 978-1-5043-0972-1 (e)

Balboa Press rev. date: 08/28/2017

CONTENTS

ACKNOWLEDGEMENTS

This book is my debt to all human ancestors, their survivors, and ageless nature wisdom. I give a special recognition to all who were and are freethinkers. They are the leading forces for evolving humanity. In creative, stimulative, and tragic struggles, many things, ideas, and books can be born. I give limitless thanks to those who have protected, influenced, and helped all freethinkers in the past and present. Most important, I send my love and special recognition to the killed masses in the name of religions, politics, wars, race, and insanity. It is an immense shame for all humanity, and it's a collapse of rationality. How could the love of life change into hate towards life?

Humanity is in the beginning of understanding its origin. With curiosity, learning, and knowing more about its responsibilities, humanity is constantly growing.

I wish to acknowledge the great world of wisdom created and collected by many serviceable thinkers. That is the first and the last resource leading to the survival of good humankind.

I acknowledge my editor at Balboa Press, and the co-workers, for improving every page, giving care, and guiding me to create better book.

I thank my wife, Anna, and our daughters, Joanna and Samantha, for their unlimited love and encouragement, and our fruitful life cooperation. I was very often surprised that Anna, a physician, would find information that was persuasive and needed for some segments of the book.

I want to particularly thank my 'second mother', and guardian, Irena Willim-Szewczyk, for her extraordinary influence.

The highest gratitude with love is for my mother, Helena Willim-Nowicki. She died at the age of ninety-one in 2010. Mostly with her own with help of our grandmother, she raised my older sister, Hanna, me; and my younger brother, Andrzej. My mother gave us essential and natural knowledge about life, as well as love and passion for living a healthy life. My father died too early at the age of forty-seven because he forgot about taking proper care of his mind, body, and spirit.

My deepest thanks to my life for everything what I have experienced, and for being able to see a little wonder in this magnificent and enigmatic journey.

INTRODUCTION

A long time ago, I started a fascinating and unique journey of learning. My intention was to start a journey through the universe, the inner microcosm and outer macrocosm. I become hooked on finding an extraordinary and true knowledge, a wisdom usable for me and others. The collection of information became the main source for this my book. I searched for essential extracts that can stimulate our minds to understand ourselves and our mysterious lives, and that can make it more fruitful and more enjoyable. Sometimes truth is amusing, and sometimes it's difficult and distressing. Truth in the end is the true winner. Everything depends how we understand it and use it to become more helpful, informative, wiser, and well.

The old title was *Understanding Man, Life, and the Universe*. As I changed with time, I changed my book. I realised that nobody would understand enough on such a broad subject. No philosophy, no religions, and no education will come closer. This process of learning for all of us will be forever. I also realised that not everything would be practical, or useful enough, or the best way to live life. I search for knowledge, which is serviceable straight away. These never-ending processes of life are help us be functional as we constantly learn how to survive and live with the joy of life as individuals and as a species. Without proper understanding of ourselves, nature, and life, we cannot escape from strictness, harshness, and false ideas of existing. Life is all we have, and not much is explained. Life is too intricate, and it's beyond the scope of my book or any book.

We are beyond the real scene if we cannot see the wider spectrum of life and inside of ourselves. We should seek more conscious living experiences, and we should suffer less. Conscious living is contemplative living. We cannot survive and advance properly without all of the above. True wisdom is the outcome of life's contemplative journey. When I started study and steadily collecting the knowledge for myself, it was chaotic and not always focused on important information. However, I was lucky to become addicted to curiosity, which led me in right direction. With passing time, I realised that I should share it. I studied more to better understand life.

I considered that I did not understand enough to publish. I preferred to search for more truthfulness in life, rather than finish my book. I was calm and enjoyed being submerged in new facts. However, after conversations with many friends and strangers, discussing some life issues, they suggested that I finish my book. There is a never-ending river of information about life. It is true that life is enigmatic, and there are complex matters which are beyond the scope of my book or any book. Our life is a glimpse, and by exchanging glimpses we can see more. We will understand new things, and we will enjoy other wonders of life. If we will combine our exploration and understanding, then we will enjoy more of the enigma of our existence. Our lifetime is the only way we can explain it and enjoy it. However, I think that life can be only explained by itself.

I have written for humans who are inquisitive with a desire to find order and meaning in life. By mixing my thoughts with the reader's impressions and ideas, we should obtain original hybrids of concepts and effects. I believe that it will be helpful to stimulate positively some deeper levels of the mind. I try to supply various readers' needs via summaries of some human important concepts, which include the scientific and proscientific validation, as well as ancient and modern wisdom.

Some information that I include in this book come from ancient times, and it has not changed for many thousands of years. However, human exploration of all that is will never be final. I have striven for objectivity. I had hoped to avoid the subjective through interpretation that would hold the left and the right, the negative and positive. I believe my book wanders on the middle way and presents various type of knowledge in recognisable forms for most people. I offer a combination of information from several subjects about the mystery and mastery of life.

I use the word *wellness* as the wide term of philosophical, psychological, and physiological sense and concepts, in order to define our states of mind and body. Wellness exists in a variety of emotional states and is an individual perception. It is about living the life in the natural way, discovering and creating its meaning. Wellness needs a certain order of important factors and timing to exist. Wellness is so enigmatic and obvious at the same time.

We are on the way to raising our personal consciousness, which is increasing the collective consciousness and awareness of humanity. Additionally, conjoining with all people and cooperating with whole environment is the only way to enhance our chances to survive as a civilization. I am very deeply grateful for my existence, and I like that I can study some of the immense ocean of information and insight. Furthermore, I hope my book will be useful for you. Out of my humble service, positive sensations, and excitement, I offer my thoughts.

I wish you conscious wellness with the proper care of your body, mind, and spirit. All the best in enjoying your lifetime as you have and enjoy what you need.

Tadeusz Nowicki

"Love the world as yourself, then you can truly care for all things."
—Tao Te-Ching

Where are you going?
You are the phenomenon of the life.
Are you reflecting enough on the ways of your life?
Do you have a conscious, good, and balanced life?
Remember
That your journey through life is the
Journey through knowledge about life,
The universe, man, and your inner self.
Essential knowledge creates more
Freedom, wellness, and fulfilment in your life.

CHAPTER 1

TIMELESS WISDOM

> True wisdom comes to each of us when we realise how little we
> understand about life, ourselves, and the world around us.
>
> —Socrates

Timeless wisdom comes from life, nature, truth, and ancient and modern times. It is wisdom about the principles of evolving energy and matter in the single atom and the entire universe. Timeless wisdom comes from loving life, acquiring nature's truth every day, and understanding yourself and life. Universe information and life forces are the matrixes of nature wisdom. Timeless wisdom connects what seems unconnected.

Timeless wisdom accepts completely the gift of life, rectifies each day, and creates the balance, joy, purpose, and wellness of existence. Wisdom is unified with the continuity of conscious living, which interacts with the whole of nature and the universe. Wisdom comes from honouring and absolute truthfulness to life and yourself. Self-honouring will prompt the honouring of all living in harmony, honesty, and wisdom. You are already wise if you know what you don't know, and if you also know you will never know everything.

Our minds, hearts, guts, and biofields (auras) are the processors and recollection of our internal and external realities. We must be careful what kind of gut microbiota we have. We should act through our food, bodies, minds, and spirits before an imbalance happens. We are powerful generators of energies, influencing and creating reality around ourselves. The goal is to put wisdom and virtuous life into the attitudes of nations and civilisations. Wisdom explains itself and is the way to embrace life, the universe, and many civilisations. Wisdom is the only fortune that will never lose its greatness. The timeless secret of wisdom is living the essence of nature truth in nature's way. Wisdom's secret is timeless, and it's unified with the continuity of conscious humanity living and surviving in the way of nature.

The Power of Wisdom Comes from the Universality of Truth

The power of wisdom creates envy in others, but all of humanity has an equal right to retrieve information and learn. All goodness comes from good information stored and used by the mind, spirit, and body. To know that old things are stores of information is great, but knowing that ancient wisdom brings illumination is much more important; this is the base of everything in our lives. A worthy life is available only for a learned, inquiring, open mind.

> Nature's way is simple and easy, but men prefer
> what is intricate and artificial.
>
> —Lao Tzu

Wellness is the outcome of true, useful information; positive thoughts; ideas; and actions. In modern times, we must also find natural, unspoiled, nutritious food. Without it, we cannot function properly on any level. A good life needs regular exercise and enough rest and sleep. Let us create consciously, better, and with pleasure, knowing that we create a new thing in each moment. You can trust only Mother Nature, who never cheats and always supplies true information.

Truth is nature's conduct; it is the way of life. The ultimate truth is alive in nature. The conscious human lives the natural way, learning from life's endless manifestations, which lead to oneness and the unity of truth. The truth, with its consequences, guides itself and arrives at reality. Truth and wisdom speak for themselves. Search for wisdom as you would search for food and security. Everybody uses different ways to search for the truth, and all roads are good or necessary for different individuals.

If we respect the truth and wellness of life, the rest takes care of itself.

Life asks you to make a choice for reliability, to live and speak with truth. Elevated thinking creates equilibrium, love, and a beautiful life. Peace comes to those who appraise and follow the truth. Humanity is the effect of the many fusions of the truths, so consciously grow and stand for all. The universe and life are waiting for you to create your good life. Do not wait for things you ought to create through wisdom and right actions.

Ancient and modern wisdom collect life essence. Find the extract of ancient and modern wisdom to create your life wellness.

Ancient and Modern Wisdom for the Present

- First, learn how to learn.
- Learn to ponder.
- Learn by asking questions.
- Questions are sometimes more important than the answers.
- Learn by listening, reading, observing, and taking notes.
- Learn by sharing and exchanging.
- The more we give, the more we receive.
- Use relaxed, unhurried, modest, constructive ways to explore life.
- Meaning is temporary on the road of life.
- All ways are temporary and endless.
- If there is change, there is life.
- With peace, balance, joy, and wisdom, you can grow; maturing is acquired.
- Your best home is where the mind, body, and spirit are at peace and in balance.
- Respectful harmony with the nature creates a prospering whole.
- Closeness with nature rebalances our lives.
- Alignment with nature's cycles maximizes wellness.
- Greatness starts with self-control and acceptance.
- In difficult times, the inner self becomes wiser and stronger by whispering with the universe.
- We can find the light of wisdom in human faces. Predictably, virtue follows the light of wisdom. Wisdom, with wonder and love for the life, leads to wellness.
- Knowledge and wisdom are included in nature.
- The love of nature is a natural preparation for wisdom and fulfilment.
- Nature is the best teacher; we can obtain knowledge we understand.
- We can imitate nature and reflect the truth.
- Nature and truth are present all the time in everything. Each of us has a separate mind and different levels of understanding, so we have different needs. We are the form of life's complexities; we have different clarities, visions, and limitations.
- Knowledge cannot be locked up. It is cosmic and open to every thinker. Knowledge is limited only by one's curiosity, ways of searching, and intellectual ability.
- Wisdom includes sensitivity and compassion that is widely learned and accepted by all.
- Do anything to be close to serenity and balance.
- Collect thoughts of truth endlessly so that your mind will become full of wisdom.

- The ruler of life, science, art, and wisdom is the truth, screened by the flood of ordinary things and events. The truth made the way a proper one, freer and more joyful.
- A little insight opens whole wisdom. If you will not understand it, you cannot use it, and you will never remember it.
- The ocean of information overloads us. We need to make proper selections.
- The art of living is being in balance and being useful to one's family, one's social circle, and humanity.

How to Acquire Knowledge and Ageless Wisdom

1. Develop a reliable mind-spirit-body and love for life.
2. Provide optimal whole care for the body-mind-spirit.
3. Consciously and constantly connect yourself with life and nature.
4. Discover yourself.
5. Collect true information from the past and present.
6. Learn about life's mastery and ways.
7. Actuality, truth, nature, and life create wisdom.
8. Every inquiry is designed and restricted by your knowledge.
9. Logical thinking on the basis of reason becomes knowledge, or wisdom, for people with higher consciousnesses.

Additionally, we need:

- the desire to know and honestly work on it
- a positive, rational attitude towards everything
- to be unafraid to think
- proper thinking, seeing the world, and creating our lives
- all kinds of useful information and understanding of ourselves and our world
- to concentrate on the most important subjects; study yourself, others, and life
- accessibility to information
- to be fully submerged in the present
- mindfulness united with the intellectual insight and improved awareness and consciousness about nature and its beings
- progressions of knowing, storing, and processing information

- to develop and control practical circumstances, which secures balance, peace, gratitude, and contentment
- to go to the past only for valued memories, information, joy, and teachings
- to not dwell on regret, grief, disillusionment, defeat, and indecision
- to unlock unlimited potential in order to attain maximum performance during life
- to know we are not always right, but we have the chance to evolve
- to grow through an exchange of the old for the new, of the good for the better; the great news is that possibilities are truly endless
- to know that we can design our destinies and live the lives of dreams
- the processes of creative endeavours with an extensive vision beyond the human body
- to avoid depending completely on any belief system, but to incorporate our own views
- to increase awareness of the real power of our minds and remodel ourselves and the world

One who will not respect life or think constructively and positively about life does not deserve it. Life itself composes the power of attraction in quantum levels to create life and spread it in the universe. The universe and conscious life are in the eternal process of becoming.

How many people can produce new ideas, innovations, and unique ways of creation? Not the majority. A small number of people achieve the highest flights of intellect.

Ancient and modern wisdom complete each other to obtain easier wellness and enlightenment, and to create sustainable existence. Wisdom comes through the balance of perception, acceptance, reflection, and serenity. Most ancestral wisdom is collected in the subconscious memory. All known sages, thinkers, and philosophers are merely transmitters of earlier knowledge. Nobody knows where and when the human mind was awakened and started to consciously collect information and produce original thoughts.

The natural life is the outcome of the universe's law and its energy. Wisdom is the discovered, understandable truth from the natural life.

We are here to learn, share, and combine our forces. It's our duty to discover and develop all that is best in us. Discover something new every day. Even a little bit will make you more content as you crave more knowledge. Realizing your dependence on knowledge, learning, and action will make you freer. These aspects start with curiosity. Seek the source of the mystery and wisdom. Stop and listen, think about life and the universe, concentrate, and understand the truth.

You cannot control yourself and have a pleasing existence until you understand yourself and correct all that's inexcusable.

Mastery of wisdom starts with knowing ourselves. Knowing all kinds of relationships with nature and humans is the way to reach fullness of life. Mastery knows the simple fact that sometimes we are in control, and we must accept when we are out of control. Mastery is about controlling our attitudes. Regarding what we can't control and do not understand, we should accept it with smile and humility. Mastery of wisdom offers an extensive understanding of the changeable reality, constantly inquiring into its unpredictability with a positive and respectful attitude. Knowing that there is no end towards mastery, but being on such a journey, is the ultimate, joyful destiny.

Mastery asks you to use willingness in order to gain control over the fears of the unknown and the unknowable.

Wisdom is the difference between man's insignificance and human greatness. Can you open the book of nature to learn the truth? Wisdom can saturate only the open heart, mind, and spirit in a lifetime of exploration.

All life is about myriad good, bad, neutral, and extraordinary experiences. Experience it, expect it thankfully, and live joyfully with all. Your life is about understanding more raising your consciousness. Dwell on the essence of life and truth, matured from ancient time; it will bring the best of life and the best of you.

Ask yourself honestly, "What is the most essential issue for everybody? What is the first, most important responsibility?" The answers to these questions are inseparable from each other. In order to have a good quality of daily existence, we need health, so we should take a proper care of our body-mind-spirit every day. The universe exists only through mind, which is the foundation of human individual existence and existence of outside world. For the searchers and for the man of wisdom, the best way is the mind practice. Mind is an effect of computing gathered information by mind-body universe. Mind power is enormous; it creates our daily existence and relations with the external world. However, it relies on healthy gut microbiota and good natural nutrition.

The Quintessence of Knowledge Creates the Immortalized Words of Wisdom

The best way to have more pleasure from the disease of curiosity is by asking more questions and studying more.

Ancient philosophy realized the vital ability to see the world and ourselves. We are rediscovering natural, universal wisdom and its application in the daily routine of our lives.

It is an art to create a natural way towards wisdom, securing our harmonious existence with ourselves and nature. With ancient and modern wisdom, we all will be able to live and dance amongst the stars. Many answers will change in time because we change, and our knowledge will change too. Vast, collective wisdom started in ancient times does not change. Ancient, ageless wisdom and the modern era of the digital world saturate each other. Wisdom supremacy lies in constantly exploring the mysterious and the familiar. Living with wisdom finds that everything is connected, and living without wisdom isn't worth the effort. Living without the light of wisdom is living in darkness. You can learn from ancient and modern wisdom that our attitude is more important than reality. Ancient wisdom mixed with modern, true information can secure our future. This blend can work for the world goodwill towards proper human relationships and cooperation. The more consistent, harmonious, and correct with the natural law human life is, the better quality of life and joy that will emerge. Imagination, inspiration, and intuition are the language of wisdom through which man and the universe communicate. Collective subconsciousness is our inner wisdom; it is the universal awareness, which is unique for every man. Subconscious information stored within man is unlimited because it stands for not only him but also all his ancestors. Subconsciousness connects all humans and higher animals.

Love and Wisdom Create the Wellness of Life

Pursuit of wisdom means creating a wiser, healthier, and more joyful mind and body. The most fulfilling travel is discovery within our inner selves

In order to discover anything, we need curiosity, and then knowledge will develop, saturating and guiding us. In our confused world, we need true information, and then true knowledge can develop. We will be on the way towards life with real wisdom.

True wealth is the wisdom in healthy mind and body; it involves exchanging our energy, love, friendship, knowledge, compassion, cooperation, and favour. We can become a better civilization by using ancient and modern wisdom from all cultures, all traditions, all nations. With respect for nature, life, and ourselves, through wisdom we can secure all and create all.

Love and wisdom, with the right actions, build completeness in conscious being. Wisdom exists beyond the choice of information and knowledge; it is a living process.

There is a saying that those who do not learn from wisdom are condemned to be confused and repeat their mistakes. You are wise if you know what you don't know. Wisdom is so universal that it can easily predict. Real, usable wisdom is the highest empowerment. There is no measure for wisdom because there is no measure for ignorance. Conscious ignorance, negativity, lying, pretending, untruth, and disinformation are infamous human inventions, poisoning the mind, heart, body, and spirit. Unfortunately, the inferiority of humanity will never fix itself. Our power of the vision, knowing, and understanding can create balance and contentment. Enjoy it and love your life by loving your body-mind-spirit. Create your health and worldwide balance. Self-love and respect towards life will positively renew people and all life around the globe.

"Doing what you love is the cornerstone of having abundance in your life."
—Dr. Wayne W. Dyer

Wisdom recognizes the power of the human's extensive mind, which regulates our destiny. Our thoughts mark our lives' journeys. Therefore we will never be lost in our ways. Wise and constructive living is knowing and doing the right thing. Wisdom is vitalised from the vast fountain of collected mental powers. Part of true wisdom is knowledge from within.

It is an inner knowing, a collected wisdom in our genes. There is also the spiritual collective wisdom of humanity. In conclusion, we are a complex of information, like the universe. There is a lifetime lesson to find and develop our inner treasure, our wisdom.

True information leads to the true science and real wisdom. Wise men don't dwell on any belief system—he carefully creates his own.

Wise men first become sensible thinkers and astute observers. A sage man shares his wisdom in an elusive way. He is here to serve. He is quick to praise and encourage, empower others by making them aware about their unique abilities, act responsibly, and cooperate in conflict-resolving ways. A wise man gives wisdom to command destiny. Leaders must have wisdom before they can command the destiny of others. Wisdom never hurries; it lives in completeness of life with profound peace, joy, simplicity, and love, embracing all.

Scientists tell us that we live in sea of universal wisdom. Psychologist William James supported such universal wisdom. He considered this as a deeper level of the mind. He taught that along with a conscious and subconscious mind, man also has a deeper level of the mind in which exists an infinite intelligence that longs to work for and through man. By recognising it, giving it your attention, and directing it, you release this super-wisdom within. The old masters practised prayer, reflection, concentration, and meditation as methods for contacting wisdom within them. Their meditation and concentration practices have now come to the attention of the Western world, which is fascinated by the power and practice of meditation. We should be encouraging the ancient method of attaining wisdom through meditation. We build upon the foundations laid by others, and our own work, if valid, serves in its turn as the level from which others build. Many things in this world need collective association and dependence. We are taking part in decades, centuries of manual and mental efforts against ignorance. The sacrifice we make to share this wisdom is minor in comparison to the efforts put forth by the many who made this knowledge available to us. We must realise that we are travelling the path of the wise ones. We are the ignorance and wisdom of our ancestors.

There is no measure for wisdom; there is no measure for anything at all.

—Anna Zofia Nowicki

In the beautiful mystery of the life, there are myriad things to explain. All I know is that life is superior when we are engulfed in collective wisdom. Knowledge, wisdom, and enlightenment are about understanding, inspiring confidence, and having insight into the possibilities and creations of the right path, as well as acquiring what we expect and deserve. The deepest drive for all people is the search for meaning, and what to do in life to reach happiness.

There is the a mighty, never-ending cycle of matter, energy, intelligence, and consciousness. Everything is one in a never-ending cycle.

Matter - Energy -> Biological Powers -> Natural Intelligence -
Vitality of life -> Consciousness -> Energy - Matter

Who We Are

Man, the rational mind, is the highest manifestation of life, which creates everybody as a unique individual. We are the matrix of conscious energy interacting with everything that exists. The more we are conscious and virtuous, the more we create with our unique influence and the signature of our minds, spirits, and genotypes. Your life is needed as the uniqueness; share it, and you will enrich all.

Our lifetime, health, and wisdom are the most precious combination to create useful existence, promote humanity, and add something to the universe. Our physics will plant the new dimensions and the new concept of a universe and man; after that, the new man will be born with a new comprehension. To get information about a mind potency and application, we must step into the unknown world of the mind and inner universe. From the abundant universe, we start the limitless journey of the universal life. We are like a universe in the constant, eternal change and creation. We are the smaller universe in service to larger universe; we are one of the smaller parts. The universe of change embraces even its tiny parts.

Who Am I? Where Am I?

If you do not know who you are, you do not know whom you wish to become. How can you recognise what you do not know? Answer that question, and you will know what to do. You create your own life, mind, and body, together with nature. Man exists through contemplation. The mind is excited by stimulating ideas. Human thoughts vibrate without limitation in the universe, and maybe that is the reason that the universe creates us as one of its extension. There is the illusion of the separation from each other and from all that is. If you are able to see, feel, and understand, then you will see interconnectedness in everything and the usefulness of everything.

> To price me for my contemplation for authority,
> Fate make me an authority myself.
> To punish me for my contempt for authority,
> Fate made me an authority myself.
>
> —Einstein

Our thoughts are our unseparated travelling friends, or our enemies constantly chasing us. Thoughtlessness and the lack of a reflective mind will produce disintegration, the true mental death.

Einstein changed the world. He said, "You had to cram all this stuff into your mind for the examination, whether you liked it or not." The above is about the disadvantage of our education, which still exists. We still need to memorize more rather than think independently. What our students need is first stimulation and freedom; then true and original curiosity of inquiry will grow and last. The old system deters and trashes the potential of Einstein. During the school years, the present education system is not stimulating enough, and it even discourages interest amongst all kind of students. Moreover, the digital age becomes Russian roulette for a large percentage of students. Uncaring society corrupts the best of us, but a concerned society can change the worst of us.

Abundant Life of Virtue—One's Self-mastery

Few things have surprised me completely, and nothing has pleased me more than the ultimate fusion of ancient and modern wisdom. Wisdom and virtue through the millennia are consistent with tranquillity, harmony, enlightenment, and a fruitful and enjoyable existence. They can secure our virtuousness in personal existence, as well as our survival as a civilisation.

Our life is the manifestation of our knowledge and wisdom, which is the best tool to deal with nature's concealed possibilities. The safe and the proper way is to trust only nature's virtue. Love and wisdom create balance with nature and human relationships.

One must first completely accept the gift of life, learn to dance with the scales, and use a balance. The greatest joy of all is to simply be. It comes from the joys of everyday life, not from briefness in ecstasy, euphoria, or orgasm. Life is the journey of learning, understanding, and proper acting in the life. Life itself is the best teacher because it constantly offers extraordinary opportunities which we should discover. Life is a journey mostly inside our minds; it is a constant updating survey of all our ideas. We rebuild ourselves through every moment of our lives. We become the outcome of our ideas.

Human life is an oscillation between happiness and misery. Unfortunately, we seek it outside us. Humans cannot live in constant happiness because it is always a state of relative perceptions and changing realizations.

Our duty towards ourselves and our civilization is to apply the truth, justice, and virtue to everything connected with us, as well as with the earth and the universe. It is about great service to life, suspended on a tiny speck in the universe.

"One can have no smaller or greater mastery than mastery of oneself."

—Leonardo da Vinci

If you understand more, you will worry less.

Knowing yourself is mastering yourself. It is a great wisdom, and there is no end in mastery. The inner game of life mastery shows how to perform gracefully and fearlessly, not worrying about mistakes. All good teachings for the mind-body-spirit lead to mastery. We cannot rely on anyone for our personal mastery except ourselves. All goodness is an effect of the mastery of choice, not the ignorance in selection. Living with virtue in life will endlessly reward us. Having mind in the state of virtue is more important than having a technology in the state of art. True information, wisdom, virtue, and love will rediscover heaven on the earth. Civilization and the single man should only fear their own ignorance.

Wisdom and virtue are ultimate, as are the universal commodities, which are transcendent through material, intellectual, spiritual, and all life existence. Such forceful influence and transfusion in all is obvious, because all of us hold it deeply.

In the fragmentation of the daily life, we can only partially pay attention. We contribute and benefit from it.

Art of Living a Life of Virtue: One's Self-mastery

The art of living is an awareness of being part of nature. Feel and know life and its order. We can achieve it by being in nature, with nature. The conscious mind creates the essential life and focuses on knowing and controlling yourself, which is the base for wisdom and the art of living.

The art of living represents the ability to be grateful for being alive, even in the wide spectrum of reality, with positive and negative in the same moment. It is our choice to focus and create more positive or negative. The art of living is the art of admiration of life and the world, and of appreciating ourselves. Ask and seek knowledge, and you will find it. All that stimulates your thoughts extends your joy of life. Hundreds of years pass with little progress in spiritual and intellectual advancement; man thinks about acquiring knowledge but finds he is only acquiring skills. The skills make a better material world, but they do not make man advanced enough mentally and spiritually. Knowledge of skills and mechanical techniques does not help man know about himself and his purpose on earth. Development of different sciences brings order in understanding nature's chaos.

Appreciate life, yourself, others, and the whole of nature. Acknowledge what you see and learn about it properly. You are becoming integrated, and all is inseparable in a changeable world. Become reasonable in every experience. Remember that possessions and luxuries will disrupt the essence of your living. A down-to-earth lifestyle supports a balanced and fruitful way of living. The less you need, the more content and free you are.

Thoughts unused are lost to humanity. Learning is a process, and the achievement of mastery is the end of it. We must study and have experiences in order to gain knowledge. Knowledge is relative, and our relationship with the universe is exploratory, with gradual experiments organised by nature. Self-improvement is the best investment you can make, because you are investing directly in yourself, and it will offer you dividends forever at no extra charge. To be good riders of life, we must gain first proper knowledge about man's body-mind-spirit and the governing laws of the world. It seems that we will never know enough about ourselves, so the finest art is to know oneself thoroughly but never cease modelling the body-mind-spirit. This is the first step if we want understand the things of our inner universe, and we should not waste our time and energy. All of us want to know about it in a separate setup. If we approach life with a balance of nature, we will obtain more and varying opportunities to survive.

Life is the best teacher. The best student will study to the end of his life. Real wisdom comes from nature. We should control our search for truth because there are too many ways that do not lead to a greater understanding. Our lives are misguided today and lack the wide spectrum of knowledge and duty to make a balance in ourselves, in all nations, and in the world's ecosystem.

We treat the ancient philosophy with no respect, and we underestimate the importance of its influences on concepts of life and the earth. Every original idea and concept is based on a predecessor; all evolutionary minds are derived from older civilizations, our ancestors. Most of the present ideas came from ancient sources. We pass on a much bigger mass of knowledge than we inherit. Education includes knowledge of the past, and everybody should know the basics of history regarding his own family and country, as well as humanity, earth, and ideas about the universe.

The natural, rational system of learning is based on the principle of sharing. All our children and students start to learn the knowledge of life, which is prepared by parents, teachers, and all of us. What we will save from history is what we will put inside their brains, like freedom, tolerance, and humanness. It will make them suitable to create the future of civilisation. Many old books declare that all knowledge is in the self. Personally, I think that we can find in the self a lot, but not more than from nature and by exchanging with other humans. By using nature as a guide in developing the right moral, ethical, and intellectual qualities in our young, we will build a good future for humankind.

Mind-body-spirit wellness is improvement to the unending journey to achieve the continuum of humanity. Grains of the knowledge come from the small pieces of comprehended information, which comes as crumbs from the nature and universe. The masses have always ridiculed, frightened, and rejected the unusual and the new. I was fascinated by the idea that we are relearning principles that humanity has known already, but we've disregarded these ideas for millennia. It is about principles that may have been brought here by those who were chasing the prospect of longevity. All our incorrect information and mistakes were corrected by life and became priceless treasures. Intellect is the offspring of innumerable changing causes; it is the combination of forces which are never repeated. We should try to put our ideas and principles constantly on the safe middle way, and our philosophical systems will stay on logical, rational ground. Originality in thinking is highly visible when somebody has enough talent and inner power to express himself.

What Is the Essence of Consciousness?

Accumulated knowledge is united with consciousness. Human consciousness is the offspring of our genes and is immeasurably unknown, and it's constantly changing the causes and effects from a combination of forces that's never repeated. Thoughts are part of quantum processes and its possibilities. Patterns of quantum energies have great significance on the level of human consciousness. In our lives, we must deal with this polarity of reaction all the time – positive and negative, yin and yang. It is a polarity of mind and the whole of the universe. The negative and positive elements are obvious in physical nature; we can find them in the attraction and repulsion patterns of neutrons and protons. To think one thing, we must now exclude other things. Each thought is an interpretation, which is an effect of connections with other elements. The more elements in composition, the higher the levels of vibrations and the denser the stream of information. Information as a form of energy will never die.

Through space, the universe stimulates to evolve in unique ways. Human existence is the tiny spec and activity in universe. Humanity is the quest on earth only, so we should behave properly and not devastate the ecosystem. Human evolution is the progressive understanding of life, humanity, and the universe. We are in the dream of unity in humanity, all working together to evolve into galactic space and create a new life and better ways. We need each person's uniqueness for better understanding and exploration of the world. There is no limit in the limit. There are only different circumstances.

Any kind of real knowledge is good; only misusing the knowledge or misunderstanding it can produce the wrong effect. The power of real knowledge and its utilisation reflects human reality in life. In the enormous universe, human energies can cooperate with matter and life forces. Our intellect and contemplation are the best tools to interweave human existence with boundless life. The power of intellectual creativity of the mind is the greatest fertile power.

There is Brain Memory and Body Memory

The brain-to-body memory storages are connected through hormones messages and as holograms stored in peptides. Many scientists think about memory as a diffused continuum in the mind and in the body. They recognise interacting complexes of the human brain, heart, gut, and biofields as cooperating processes. Primal forms of memory and cognition in a hereditary part are the basic sources to develop ideas, words, and images of the present civilisation. We are the parts of the evolutionary transmission mechanism, and we are remodelling what has been remodelled. There is a strong correlation between a person's memory and his intelligence. However, people can lose their memory and intelligence. Our lives give us logical information and everything that is very meaningful. Such long-life experiences and information build the biological computer's ability.

Humans as omnivores eat plants and animals. Cannibals eat their enemies' flesh, hearts, and brains. They believe that if they eat the brain, it will provide them with extra knowledge and skills. There is a chemical basis for memory, supported by D. J. Albert, who extracted the protein from trained rats and injected it into untrained rats. The injected rats learned to do the same tricks more quickly.

The Art of Living in Internal and External Ecosystems

The highest art of living is about controlling and knowing yourself. Everything that you know, understand, and use in your life creates your mind-body-spirit and describes you adequately.

Self-exploration and self-understanding are the basis for the art of living. The art of living is to be in harmony with the nature of the internal and external universe. It is about the celebration of life by the harmony of one's internal and external mastery. The art of living originates from wellness, which is verification of virtuousness, accumulated integrity, and proper distribution. It includes attuned goodness composed by harmoniously flowing life, a sense of vitality, tranquillity, confidence, and healthy and joyful body-mind-spirit. It artlessly, naturally supports wellness on all levels of living.

The art of living celebrates life via a wide and deep spectrum, and it contributes enormously to the global community. The art of living also encompass the celebration of aging. Many people think of others as old, and the true is because all of us are aging daily. The art of living improves with age; it is the essential time to share the wise way of living for a better future. The art of living is about having control over the controllable. We can become down-to-earth beings, reach a better quality of life, and live longer. The art of living explains itself enough, but we cannot understand it absolutely. Choose to live now and enjoy study of the life. Our knowledge and attitude can change our reality. There are no schools on how to design proper living. We have the Academy of Arts, but not one about the art of living.

If there is change, there is Life. The art of living relies on constant adaptation to change. The art of living worships love. Love was created by life as the reassurance to evolve. Love bonds everything, and it starts on the molecular level as an attraction between plus and minus. When we are in love, love acts itself and grows. The superiority of love overcomes worry, hate, money, and authority, and it confronts all things.

With love, we create a constructive evolution. Love is inseparable from an evolving life. Love create more life. You can't receive, send, and understand real love without loving truly. We are all equal in our ability to love and create love. While loving others, we should not forget to love ourselves.

The art of living uses all our thinking and actions to be in balance between the positive and the negative, conflict and peace, worry and love, adoration and hate. The art of living faces the future with excitement, not with distress and worry. It is about loving your life and thinking with passion and respect throughout the world. All life and the world will appreciate you back. Love and respect yourself because you are alive and participate in the life experiment. It is a privilege to be aware, creating your best prospect. You are the part of the superb, enigmatic universe. Your existence is about honouring, wondering, and cooperating on all levels of life, and becoming a responsible entity. You are on the way to developing your full potential on all levels of your life, and so far you are the highest developed known form of life.

The art of living is an effect of our understanding of the self, reality, and our actions. It means living, enjoying oneself, and doing everything possible to enrich life at all levels. Interact properly with complex of the mind-spirit-body towards wellness, and have a long, enjoyable journey. We are the cosmic particles embodied in the body-mind-spirit. A single atom, the whole of you, all living creatures, the whole earth, and the entire universe have the same laws of energy-matter transformation.

Everything operates within the universal laws in the never-ending sequence. We are part of the entire universe, which unite the microcosm and macrocosm into one. Each of us daily creates his life by thoughts and actions selected by his understanding and choices. Our daily activities and collections, thinking, drinking, eating, family, friends, hobbies, and interests originate from our levels of life wellness. It is a privilege to be able to select the best options and actions, which are constantly connected with our dreams, goals, potentials, courage, and chances—but not connected with ours fears. Every day is the best gift; enjoy it truly. The art of living means accepting whatever is now in our lives. It means accepting its disappointments, recognising one's achievements, and acknowledging the limits of existence. Accepting what happens is the first step towards improvement if it is needed. Only a forgiving, open, and balanced mind can properly explore life. Its beauty and a unique wellness arise from a content and peaceful mind. The majority of people take better care of their cars, gardens, houses, and vacations than the body-mind-spirit.

The Art of Living Is a Unique State and Comes from a Healthy, Skilful Mind-Body-Spirit

The art of living is the positive summary of interactions between many components and circumstances.

- Physical, mental, and spiritual health
- Balanced gut microbiota
- Balanced temperament and personality
- Good relationships
- Enjoyable work
- Sensible philosophy of life and nature

The art of living means being able investigate our own minds and bodies, trying to improve them endlessly. In modern time, we have a tendency to have less time and energy for our often-ignored body-mind-spirit. We must realise that health must be the first and best, if we want to truly live the greatest way of life. The art of living promotes daily contentment. The law of life and the art of life are inseparable. Take proper care of your life from start to finish.

The art of living in the complexity of the life encompasses the art of life, which started more than five thousand years ago; it's known as Ayurveda knowledge. It involves expanding and conserving the harmony within ourselves and nature. We should seek exploration through the mind; we become enriched and will enrich others. Accept the continuing process of birth, nurturing your own growth. Hold gifts of the passing days; you decide who you are, so make it all good to share. Improve the celebration of aging. Create powerful intuition and an inclination to condense information. Decipher the truth quicker than other practices. Enjoy the fact that life makes sense; whoever doubts it is not ready to live. The universe and life are ultimately complex. Life creates love, and love creates life; both are in an inseparable circle. Your life is your meaning, becoming intention and creation. Life's existence and nonexistence are the cycle, and both become your meaning. Each decision interplays with good and bad, changing with the changes of life. All that we know for sure is that change will be forever in such a process. Change and exchange interplay between the eternal yin and yang. If there is a change, there is life. All life and the whole universe come from changes in atoms. Use changes for life as cultivation in the mind and body. All that you have is your life in the present time. Life is too short, so extend it with quality. Everyone must discover by himself what the goodness of life is. Each moment of your life is connected to your ability to originate another possibility. Each day creates a new you, so try to become better. An advanced mind has no fear of the unknown, which is a skill of curiosity and resilience. Selecting information, friends, and lifestyle becomes your way of life. Only fine and intact ethics, meaning, principles, and serenity will establish a whole life. Reflection with closeness to nature will renovate your sense of life, and its joy. We have many phases in our lives, and virtuosity makes the next one better. Some people are distressed by a challenging and incomprehensible life. Following the reality of nature will lead to a legitimacy of being. Before learning, we should study what we need to know.

The Art of thinking originates from the art of life, the limitless joy of life. It's a link to dreaming, meditation, making correct decisions, and a truthful and conscious path. Think more deeply in order to discover the means of life's pleasure and its insatiable ways.

The nature of life is simply that we win some and lose some. The art of life is to win important things, and it's okay to lose the restrictive and inadequate things. The art of living develops a personal, internal balance, as well as an external balance in society and the ecosystem. In the modern world, many people compete by impressing others with mostly futile achievements; they focus on personal advantage but not on honesty, courtesy, compassion, selflessness, altruism, knowledge, or wisdom.

The Art of Living Creates Ways for a Balanced Life

1. Known yourself, and create yourself to become a serene, self-aware entity
2. Strive for true knowledge
3. Accept the inevitable unpredictable, like aging and death
4. Accept yourself, like yourself, and be honest to yourself
5. Acknowledge life, nature, and the universe
6. Be confident and true for yourself
7. Be flexible to many beliefs; adopt open viewpoints
8. Stay open and non-judgemental, keeping a sense of discovery and love
9. Attitude is key for everything, so think positively
10. Set yourself realistic goals, dream freely, and make life more usable
11. Talk out your problems
12. Balance work and play
13. Enjoy all that nature makes enjoyable
14. Enjoy the good, and endure the lows
15. See the positive, even in the negative

16. Discharge your personal resentment towards anything
17. Plan time for family, friends, and events
18. Do not waste your and others' time on the web or social media
19. Think about physical activities to lift your energy level
20. Take a little relaxation, a little time away
21. Your healthy diet works for you as natural medicine; health is your great wealth
22. Create a rational time schedule
23. It's never too late to start again
24. Learn to say no
25. Have communication that is open and honest
26. Balance in human relationships, and in nature, is created by love and acceptation
27. A balanced life creates abundant and wise choices
28. Good life is balanced life; be grateful for it.
29. Life is change, so go with change
30. Your thoughts and love create your life; share your substance with all
31. Become curious, learn endlessly, and imagine constantly

The Art of Living Combines all Other Arts

- The art of any good action starts here and now
- The art of refined personality is constantly improving, not worrying
- The arts of positivism and wellness are contagious for individuals and society
- The art of nutrition is what to eat, how to eat, and when to eat
- The art of a healthy body-mind-spirit complex
- The art of straightforwardness, with modesty, creates power and leads to wisdom
- The art of wisdom creates good life, quick reaction, positive attitude, more freedom, overcoming difficulties, and joy of life

Awarded Lifetime

1. Be the change
2. What you think, you become
3. Where there is love, there is life
4. Learn as if you'll live forever
5. Your health is your real wealth
6. Have a sense of humour

7. Your life is your message
8. Actions express priorities
9. Our greatness is being able to remake ourselves
10. Find yourself in the service of others
11. If you fail, smile; it is a good lesson
12. Don't give up—try again
13. Love your life and world; they will take care of you

The art of living is promoted by Buddha's seven rules for a better life.

1. Never hate
2. Don't worry
3. Live simply
4. Expect a little
5. Give a lot
6. Smile
7. Live with love

Some people do not remember a single day when they were bored. They travel in their minds with enormous enjoyment and with deep gratitude for the miracle of life. Many people show that their wellness comes from an internally and externally balanced life.

The Art of Living Creates Wellness in the Mind-Spirit-Body

The art of living includes a creative response to changes, using change as the trampoline for our advantage to achieve desirable. It combines all virtuousness, which overdrives all temporal conditions. Happenings with love are the perfect amalgamation, reinforcing and embracing the whole life. Wellness realization affects everything around us. It is the process of completeness, leading to unity of ourselves, humanity, and nature.

There is no wellness without a healthy mind-body-spirit, which arises from understanding the principles of life and the reasons to become healthy. It is about the proper connection with itself and the whole life, finding what is vital for our daily body-mind-spirit performance. It is the supreme virtuosity. Wellness is a decision, being consistent and responsible for one's own thinking and actions. Wellness is not about short moments; it covers the whole life. Our frame of mind, its spectrum of personal values, and understanding life are the major factors creating our wellness in a wide range and its continuum. It can start from many things we want, because wellness values all that is good and concentrates on positive aspects. Wellness in life usually has a satisfied ending, and its summary confirms it. Living is about dreaming, planning, and habits in daily actions leading to fulfilling our goals. Life constantly supplies the facts, which we can use to improve our lives and interactions with others. We do not have many individuals with the readiness, time, and discipline to withdraw from ordinary life and awaken to stimulated living. Nurse your open mind to become curious about all. What make your life more meaningful, healthy, wise so that you're able to grow and share?

Many of the Best Things in Life Are Free

In order to live a whole life, we need to be healthy so we can experience the goodness of existence. Enjoy the best adventure in your life, which is exploration of the inner self and the world, as well as collecting the treasure of wisdom. Wisdom is the base of daily life's satisfaction.

Air, sun, water, the body, the mind, ideas, and health are free. It is very hard to replace all that is free. It is much easier to replace what costs money.

An attitude of love towards life, with a daily appreciation of our existence, is the best resource for creating quality. Life evolves through movement towards quality. The moment when we acknowledge this, we will realise that we have everything. Living each moment well is the miracle of our lives, and it's an art. That's the summary of us, and it's the composition of many factors that produces the moment of now.

There is no more important concern and responsibility than your life. The nature of the human's mind energy and vibration creates a negative or positive reality. An optimistic attitude with creative actions towards one's life is the outcome of nutritional mental, spiritual, and physical states of the whole human. The intensity of wellness depends of how much true information, good emotions, and beliefs we give against the self-destructive thoughts, ideas, and negative emotions which we accumulate and transfer into our reality. Our end of the day is the beginning of everything. Realise that right now, you are the result of your past.

The starting point of everything is becoming aware and doing one by one the sensible and healthy things with a positive, encouraging attention and constructive energy. Therefore the benefits of health increase over time. Take the best care of your best friend, yourself. Your life is a service for yourself, others, and nature. Keep in mind that you should enjoy every day of your life. Goodwill and compassion can see the wider spectrum rightly with the heart, with all requirements to unite, cooperate, prosper, and survive as an individual and as humankind. It is a necessity for proper human evolution. To evolve is our birthright. In order to live, we must be with nature and be nourished by it.

The art of living creates better ways.

- Become healthy in the mind-body-spirit
- Use good information
- Change and improve our information set
- Maintain a positive attitude
- Improve life by wisely choosing our friends, place of living, lifestyle, interests, and hobbies
- Ask ourselves, "Who am I around? Where am I going? What am I going to become?"
- Realise that all changes in life depends of how we will change
- Know that wrongdoing on any level of life sooner or later becomes harmful
- Know that a wrong way of relaxation can undermine a whole good life
- Become knowledgeable enough to use good advice straightaway
- Be aware of information, or even of delicate remarks, to not change our good way of living
- Know that we cannot understand what we do not mentally grasp
- Know that any virtue is the tip of the iceberg of the wisdom
- Be aware that we create our misery through our ignorance
- Know that there is serenity, contentment in every day, and joy to share with others
- Know that discord will pass into a concord in the life of the man who loved harmony
- Know that there is a very harmful, common saying: "Everything in moderation is okay"
- Know that such ways kill slowly; do not expect to be healthy and enjoy longevity. There is no logic in the phrase "Within allowable limits"

Living longer is the aim of many people, but living longer with good quality of the mind-body-spirit is only available to those who take good care of what is the most important: their health. The majority of people rely on drugs which manage only the symptoms, not trying to cure the reasons for such conditions. The kind of food we select creates the body-mind-spirit complex; moreover, it also creates the future of our global environment. Life can never be well until the body-mind-spirit and the ecosystem are well. Nature and life express themselves perfectly.

The first step towards a better life is the need to find out who you are. The next step is to find a constructive relationship with yourself, nature, and the universe. Understand that nature works better with lovely, sensible care, and that when left undisturbed by wrongdoing, you will become true human beings. The results speak for themselves: there is very serious ecosystem degradation, as well human degradation. Globally, most money-orientated activities create unbalances and pollution.

There is a way to get out of ignorance and foolishness. It is the way of ancient and modern wisdom. Only through wise and truthful ways do the environment and humanity have a chance to survive, as well as many still unknown species.

Instead of following nature, many humans try to make nature follow humans. The duty to ourselves is to have good understanding and a healthy mind and body. We should be pure in mind and body. Nutritional imbalances in the body are the reason for aberrant behaviour. Our present ways do not lead us to the stability and longevity we seek. Wrong foods set up the wrong gut microbiota, which will make us become dependent and negatively controlled by them, living miserable lives. Wrong food gives improper elements and expenditure of incorrect energies, which leads to laziness on the physical and mental levels. A lot of inner energy is needed to shift bad habits, the taste for easy living, and low energy living, which are limiting our freedom of choice.

To be alive, we need constantly live constructive ways. It is our responsibility for the miracle of life. The law of the universe is that everyone is making his own life, his own reality, and his own interpretation of it. We're expressing the joy of living in our own ways, taking responsibility for ourselves, and becoming our own creators.

"Miracles in the world are many, there is no greater miracle than man."

—Sophocles

We are performing creation through daily work to the best of our ability. It takes years to create better individual lives, and it takes millennia to make a superior humanity. If you want to awaken humanity, then wake yourself first. The little things of everyday life build up to big milestones because all elements of life cooperate. If we want to be successful in our lives and understand everything important, we should work consciously towards wellness ways. Understanding and controlling yourself leads to a successful life. Living is an art in order to reach a rational understanding of the ultimate nature of universe. We are still unable to fully recognise and receive the abundance of the universe. Our best time in life is now, because we are still alive and can act sensibly. Health is the base of everything else a human needs. That is the reason why we need to fulfil the gap between the natural, technological, psychological, and spiritual worlds.

"In human interrelations, we influence one another unconsciously;
we are members of one huge colony, one organism-human
civilisation. Everybody is partially responsible for what happens
on the earth, what happens in each individual universe. Human
state is never static, it is in evolution, which itself try to understand
the process of life, try to get the highest degree in life."
—*The Beacon Press,* 1954

Only the mind can embrace nature and the universe, and only the mind can make us victims. Our whole lives are the result of our constant daily interactions with reality. Therefore we are dependable only on our minds, which should use ancient and modern wisdom. We are under orders to live with nature, and only sensible cooperation—not the mechanical reactions to the forces of nature, but the balanced interaction between man and nature—can result in wellness and survival. Human beings are constantly changing, moving, and interacting through the universe. We are part of nature, which supplies everything so that we can share our existence and advance. Modern man is not free in the earthy environment; he is still dependant on it. He is worshiping a modern god, money, which makes consequences like pollution and man-made destruction of nature. We should realise that modern man lives more and more in environments changed by humans; moreover, we live in the world of our abstractions, conceptions, ideas, and symbols. We live in a joint entity, opened to sensible and serviceable humans.

Do you understand many things that are important in your life? It is wishful thinking, a fantasy, and you will never be able to understand everything, but you can use your lifespan to collect vital information and use it wisely. After realizing what is important in our lives, we will know that the better or the best is partially now, and more will come. We can learn from ancient wisdom, and the present has very useful knowledge, as well as how to concentrate only on important and wonderful things. There are no miracles; there is only selection of positive possibilities, dreams, and ideas which can become significant realities. Bad things can happen as a result of ignorance and negative concentration on material things in life. Worrying is a form of sabotage for us, others, and life. Stop and think about the most important aspects in your life; that way, you will not lose time, energy, and opportunities. It is the best way to concentrate on the long-term goodness for us, our planet, and our ecosystem. Right values and balance make our everyday living joyful and secure our humanity. All words and thoughts live forever. The purpose of existing is to create the best life. The simplest and the most effective way to secure the best in life involves all actions to obtain and maintain the wellness of the mind-body-spirit, along with the never-ending process of collecting true, reliable, usable information. That knowledge correctly processes wisdom and actions to obtain balance, peace, love, and compassion. Each of us should participate in the creation of the balance, peace, and protection of the world's ecosystem. Cooperation with and appreciation for each other results in the wholeness of humanity and planet. Each day of our lives is a way of empowering our potential on all levels. United and expanded global consciousness will improve ourselves, others, and the ecosystem. There is an urgent need for positive human consciousness in order to create a more balanced, global population. Man is the measure for himself.

Every man's molecules have already been in the past in various forms of life, and not always as organic elements. We have memories about the past through all our elements, which remember the previous bonds, interactions, and various complicated forms. We have the archetype ability to look properly for our minds and bodies to thrive now and in the future. All of us are in the whole universe because we are all interconnected. Therefore, man's imprinted memory and reasons are part of the universal law. All material and non-material particles of living beings separate at death and start other cycles of immortality and possibility. Progressive life is eternal. Life is existence, built by change, motion, and infinity. Nothing is final, terminal, or absolute. Nothing in the changeable universe is permanent. All things, problems, and people change.

What Is Life?

Life is the most precious sensation. It is too elusive, difficult to define, challenging to grasp, hard to hold, and inconsistent with time. All life starts with the interaction between the energy and mater vibration, as well as the consciousness in the quantum plane.

"Life is worth losing."

—George Carlin

Life is a form of the matter-energy presence. Life itself is the great energy initiator. It is the inherent power in creative life, the power to change itself by successive progressions of form. Everything in life works towards a biological purpose, which is the universal need, and so coming, being, and passing away are inescapable parts of life. The meaning of life is included in nature, and for many it seems incomprehensible. The nature of life explains itself by never-ending change and chance cycles. Life in the biological sense is an action. It is a dynamic, rhythmic, and balanced interchange of processes where nature's law has command over material forces. Life and the mind are both dynamic processes. Life always works together with mighty change. The good and bad are included in change. Each moment is a mixture of good and bad, only our attitude creates positive or negative interpretations of the change. We will change our beliefs by changing our perception. From such change will come our best possibilities. We will improve our values if we will expand our understanding.

We can distinguish life through the human senses (human reality), and true life is a free action of a natural element—the actuality of the universe. Actuality, or true knowledge, is one of the stages of the universe. The unity of man and life are differentiated by our ordinary sense-experience. By our observations and analysis, we apply our energies, which trigger many changes now, some noticeable and changeable by us. Correct and intensive observation becomes part of creation and its after-effects. Scientific methods lead to the trinity of time, space, and matter, which are human abstractions and conceptions. Life is always ready to give us its secrets, if we only known how to ask and seek it. Life is a beautiful and magnificently stimulating journey. All that we know is that the universe is beyond knowing, is beyond shape and form, is not knowable. Living joyfully is a never-ending learning process. Successful humans are open and alert, and they constantly analyse their performances as they systematically try to find new ways to improve. We are learning throughout all our lives by gaining and losing. What conquers you becomes your best teacher.

If you want to improve, first overcome what is upsetting you. It is not important how many steps we make in our inner universe. It is important how many good steps and things we make under sound consciousness, which enriches everything in both universes. We travel in our inner universe and other people do not have access to it. We do things that other people will never understand. What is the real you? It is your change. Changing your personality for better regularly can take longer then all your education time. When you are already here, it is your life duty towards all your ancestors, who tried to lead you to this point of your life. Reflect on it and enjoy being in the world. Life is masterly woven via the events of every day. Make sure to provide the majority of joyful compositions of life. Life itself is a miracle, a complex union, a relationship on myriad levels where the exchange of information and cooperation is honest and strict according to the universe's ways.

The Potentials of Life

Thinking, ideas, choices, and creations are potentials in your life. Open and inquiring minds collect knowledge and good sense. Curiosity with truth and the pleasure being will create a wonderful life. You will enrich others by enriching yourself, and you will never put yourself down. Becoming yourself means that you are ready, strong, and free. If you allow bad, impure ideas to dwell in your mind, then expect to lose your way. Some men create their own prison cells to falsely feel safe. It is much harder to change others then oneself. True information, wisdom, virtue, and joy are the best ways to rediscover yourself and the better life on earth.

By loving your life enough, you will love nature, and then you will protect the whole ecosystem. Te power of loving life unites and improves everything. There is no limit to the power of the human mind; the deeper concentration is, the more energy of reality and the segments of possibility we can use in one's life. Life makes good things for itself in order to preserve life. Life is the effect of the significance of cosmic miracles. Life is the effect of the quantum process and its individual consistencies. It is uniqueness, it is a quantum process creating events, with the starting and final points becoming one. That is consciousness. Consciousness is the effect (product) and cause (creator) of everything.

Consciousness is the information, the vibrational and refined energy wave, able to enrich itself from the wide spectrum of an electromagnetic wave. Consciousness is the synchronized energies' evolving form of contemplative sensation. Time is not the condition of consciousness. Consciousness as energy vibration is timeless. Our consciousness decides whether we will live in a random, meaningless, indifferent universe, or whether we consciously select and create connectedness with the whole. Consciousness is not singular; it is non-local. It is trance-time and universe-wide; it is omnipresent and eternal. Its source is a matrix of energy and information. The collective subconsciousness is the collection of all human knowledge based on psychological knowledge, material and physical knowledge, and spiritual knowledge.

Humanity should unite the minds of people who are open, tolerable, accepting, and flexible. Everything is about improving the collective consciousness. We should remember that consciousness is the primary path; without it, we could not be aware of the outer world or of other worlds' existence. We can think about our lives and search to find out what is life and who we are. Where are we going? What we are doing here? Eventually, we will face questions as we attempt to find and understand our human connection with our ancestors, nature, and the universe. We are lucky enough to experience the wonderful, enigmatic miracle of life, and so our duty is maximum participation in all processes of life. Life is the complex of all forms of life with superb instructions on how to live and evolve. Life is the living medium, living instructions; it is the conscious information matrix.

"If it's true that our species are alone in the universe, then I'd have to say that the universe aimed rather low and settled for very little."

—George Carlin

On the Way of Life

Life lives as an awesome mystery, so find the meaning of life for yourself. Create your own story, enhancing humanity's future. Find advice in the silence and reflection. Build the space to dwell in the doors to everything that is important to you. With this enormous privilege, define yourself in the present. Follow the wheel of life, living in a balanced way. Good life is in the repetition of good things. Constructive thoughts and actions lead to a wholesome and honourable way. Do not look for too much pleasure, mistaking one thing for another; it turns into pain and loneliness and undermines your existence. Life is an infinite collection of interconnected energies and their transmissions. Such an enigma evokes images, thoughts, and emotions in all of us about who we are. To those who do not understand it, it can bring confusion. Those who are aware of it will be illuminated.

Be constructive and transform yourself beyond fulfilment. Love your life as your own self; that is the entry point. Your lifetime is worthwhile only if you are conscious and creative. You are all your body's cells and bacteria. Use your mind, body, and spirit as the essence of all accumulated awareness. Wisdom, peace, and joy are only found in a healthy mind-body-spirit. Wisdom recognizes reality as interacting contrasts. Enjoy every day with awesome pride; it is the greatest achievement. Create your tomorrow, and the future of humanity. You are welcome in the whole.

Nature—Matter—Energy—Vibration—Information - Space—Time—Life—Consciousness

"We don't know yet about life; how can we know about death?"

—Confucius

There is a certain rhythm in the working of life forces. There is a period of progression and a period of regression; both are normal proceedings of life. To be a good rider of the life, both knowledge and the ability to act are necessary. The constant challenge of life is to see more opportunities and create more freedom. Disconnectedness from life and nature are the reasons why many people have an imbalance. If a man becomes more conscious of the infinite deterministic forces in his life, he becomes freer explorer. Matter is a condensed source of forces, and it is a focus for other energies. Space, time, and matter are not measurable periodic media in the universe. Space and time bind everything, but from a human viewpoint, they seem to divide everything because human life is restricted and finite.

The Basis of Life Is Vibration; Vibration Is Creation

Vibrations are unique compositions of universe. Absolutely everything arises from the vibrations. The science of vibrations was known to ancient man. In the future, more people will become aware of the harmonious flow of the earth's energy, as well as the hidden energy of the universe. Every few millennia, civilizations were destroyed, and the next generation had to learn about earlier knowledge, rediscovering parts of what our ancestors knew. Body electricity produces vibrations, which affect every person and every object with which one comes into contact. The human body is a medium that produces vibrations and reacts to all forms of matter in the universe. The vibrations from the billions of electrically charged, subatomic elements build our bodies.

The universe exists as a vibration and oscillatory spectrum, which forms and alternates between matter and energy. The whole universe is full of life filled by different waves that supply great energy, such as electricity, gravity, sound waves, colour, smell, and more. Vibrations from the galaxy and the planets interact with all forms of animated and non-animated life. Terrestrial electro-gravity and magnetic currents vary with solar and lunar rhythms. Every living and non-living element originates from a vibration (wave form) in the universe. All things exist in the cycles; things and phases come and go. All cells in nature are a complete, galvanic battery. Each living creature produces distinctive products and emanates original energy.

Purpose of Life

"Life is about sharing the best, what we got. Life excels through uniqueness of everything in anything. Treat every failure as the valuable experience, and the stepping stone for success. The Only Sure Way to Avoid Making Mistakes Is to Have No New Ideas."

—Albert Einstein

If our purpose of life is to become useful for us and everything else, then it is an ultimate purposefulness. Purpose of life is contained in the law of matter, which is orientated towards rationality, cooperation, and harmony. Matter, energy, and space move endlessly on the wheels of change.

Life gives total meaning only for itself. We can find more meaning and principles in the never-ending exploration of life and ourselves. Evolution has its own purpose. The purpose of the life exists through our minds and genes. Our individual lives' purpose is to acquire knowledge of the self and nature, and also to take part in creation of life. The purpose of life is living in order, which comes from the laws of matter. The purpose of our lives is to survive and satisfy ourselves with a balanced existence. The purpose of life is to become useful to ourselves and others. The purpose of life is explainable partially through our individual levels of understanding. Our process of growing enhances the purpose of life, making it wider, deeper, and more practical. If life's basics are good enough, the next level is an improvement in the way of living and thinking. Our life is an enormous complex striving to fulfil our dreams and abilities. Everything that improves understanding the purpose of our lives is fundamental to the whole of humanity.

The purpose of life carries its own plans and actions. Life forces us to participate in our own journeys. True information in our genes, our collected knowledge, and our actions with immagination and couriosity will create our lives.

The purpose of life is to create a good future. We need to become wiser and more useful. The purpose of life is experiencing it, being able to find worth and a sense in it, and leaving something that can be improved and that survives us. The purpose of life is the ability to set up effective links and cooperation between all spheres of being and awareness, which offer harmony in the mind, body, and spirit.

The reason for living is embracing the nature of events and things, as well as doing everything to become accepted and supported by nature. The only way to describe purpose of life is the intention and action with nature. Life is about purposeful movement. We need to be active mentally and physically. The principle of life is an internal and external coexistence with everything.

Exploration of life requires investigation and management of the ultimate factors: your lifetime of mind, body, and spirit. Every man create his life according to his understanding. In the end, he will get what he deserves. The primal purpose of human life is to enhance consciousness by true information, and to create humanly our realities. The function of life is to find purposefulness in living, grasping essential wellness in our existence.

Knowing about our imperfections is an honest asset and indicates wisdom. Our wisdom describes and designs the quality and longevity of our lives.

Nature Decides Everything on the Earth

The purpose of all living humans is to reach and support the best potential of the body, mind, and spirit.

1. Your lifetime is the outcome of mutual purpose and respect of your overall mental, physical, and spiritual performance. It is an interacting complex.
2. The mind's purpose and performance depends on your attitude, the quality of your information, and the efficiency of processing information.

The purpose of life is a long, useful, functional journey that will sustain itself through nature and a healthy mind-body-spirit. The main purpose of living is to learn and understand as much as possible about the intricacy of life in order to improve our existence and enjoyment. Human purpose of living is a search for a more enormous complexity of life and nature to learn more, to understand more, and to cooperate more with everything. We make purposeful living if we start doing all things which are important, useful, and interesting for us and others. Meaningful living is purposeful existence, which lifts our self-control and self-worth and provides significant life. If we have life without enthusiasm, goals, and purpose, then misery and worry will arrive. Intensive and fulfilled living creates a sensible lifetime journey. New ways of thinking, doing what we love, hobbies, and new passions will change us and enrich our lives. Most important, it will uncover more of the purpose of life.

Nature creates all things after already existing forms, patterns, and laws. Everything known must operate as a duplication of the natural elements. Nevertheless, nature likes variety, and this is the reason each person is a unique living creature. The healthy frame of the mind and body is the key to how we will operate in this world. A man who has read widely and developed an open mind has no problem with the extraction of ideas, impressions, and rational conclusions. Such a man is ready to enter a different world. His inquisitive mind becomes the creative device which one day will originate the inner space of invaluable treasures. A life without a purposeful mind and things to live for is like a vessel without a rudder: its course is being continually changed by the conditions to which is exposed.

After collecting the basic needs in life, it is time to create a more sensible and healthy life. All creative activities which will bring joy will make life more complete and content. We need self-control, and we need to accumulate self-discipline. If this will not become personal concern, then all life becomes hazardous.

The practical purpose of life is to free man from the misleading and gloomy world, and also to teach man to sense, create reality, and develop consciousness. We understand that according to our ability, persistence, and strong will, we have chances for different ways to live, to understand ourselves, and to find the secrets and purpose of our lives. Rational purpose of life speeds the process of wellness by knowing that wellness comes from correct, positive processes of thinking; a balanced philosophy of life; and the right attitude to life. We can see very clearly how important the procedures of being are. The purpose of life is unique for everyone, but generally it is about improving and extending life. Trying to find purpose of life is contributing to the world with a sense of direction. Some people find purpose and design in the material or spiritual worlds, via religious beliefs. Living creates enough reasons to be good for ourselves and others, to enrich humanity, and to help life evolve further in its intrinsic plan for the glory of life cycle. Purpose of life is the movement towards truth to create a long, unique, and excellent life. Purposefulness of life creates a healthy body-mind-spirit that's free from confusion. It is our fortune and happiness. Wellness is the natural outcome of a purposeful life.

My conclusions are that the working theory of life and its purpose are in a naturalistic view of the universe. All truths that exist in the life are interrelated, held together by the reality of life.

Our society is at a stage where we are losing order, principles, and honesty. Overpopulation, degradation of ecosystem, the introduction of deceptive information, the manipulation of life—these lead to extinction. All our actions and thoughts illustrate whether we are worthy as a human race to exist and progress to the next, higher state of being. Evolution in life is not based on money and economy, but on the wisdom, balance, peace, and love for the life, along with a willingness to cooperate with nature and others for the good of all.

> "But a man's true greatness lies in the consciousness of an
> honest purpose in life, founded on a just estimate of himself
> and everything else, on frequent self-examination, and a
> steady obedience to the rule which he knows to be right."
> —Marcus Aurelius

Life is in never-ending cycle of refinement. Refine yours by worthy purposes that enrich others on your path.

Purposeful living is about constant collection of information and events for one's improvement. Processing the vast amount of information in proper ways leads to pleasurable, purposeful life that's useable for humanity and nature. Living a purposeful life is a constant rationale. Our lives are wonderful opportunities to take part consciously in the purposeful creation of the varieties of oneness.

Understanding interconnectedness and oneness is the base of wellness and purposeful living on the personal and humanity levels. Life as a process selects itself in countless mosaic trials, where a life supports actions and events create the miracle of life. Humans are an extension of life that needs many obligations and support in order to improve and sustain life.

Everyone can find purpose, meaning, and beauty in daily living, and the feeling of connectivity with the universe is an extra bonus. A strong sense of purpose secures more satisfaction from a healthier and more purposeful life. Reliability of purposefulness leads to a flourishing life. Purpose is included already in each phenomenal and wonderful life. Each of us has the ability to see the beauty in necessities for living and the magnificence of all. The ability to see the beauty of the world makes us younger and more energetic, extending our lifespan. Each day starts with sunrise as we start a new life.

Problems and suffering are life's teachers, and understanding them enhances enjoyment of life. Many times we are not able to change the conditions around us, but we can change our attitude. That will create equilibrium in the mind-body-spirit. Staying with reason and in balance becomes the way of life itself. It is the purpose of living and the art of life. Your internal peace creates the peace in others. You will become a conscious part of the changing universe.

The purpose of life is consistent with proper ways of living. We can discover the purpose of life by having a good and healthy life. With every day, we will better understand the meaning of harmony and love in our lives, in humanity, and in nature. Enjoying life with love and gratitude will enhance wellness and intensify the celebration of the miracle of being. All of us dream individually; we do not dream enough as humanity, with the vision to advance with responsibility for the nature and our genes. The purpose of life is to realise where we have been, where we are, and where we are going. We should be accepting its regrets, appreciating all achievements, and respecting the constraints with the vision of the time. If you are not afraid to live, you will not be afraid to think. In life, everything is about to get more control, expanding autonomy in our existence.

Nature creates life. Life is the effect of nature's truth, and all proper actions moves towards the truth of nature's law.

The purpose of life is to know more about where it begins. Then we will realise that we have some responsibilities towards life and humanity. Life is the whole living complex, and we too must cooperate with society and nature. Human life will have a purpose if we use our minds and follow nature. After many years of our development being constantly affected by different factors, we become ready to understand that we are changing and are an alternate environment. We rebuild ourselves and should cooperate with nature in the creation of the new human.

> "Instead of asking 'What do I want from life?' a more powerful question is, 'What does life want from me?'"
> —Eckhart Tolle

When we observe, contemplate, and understand life, ourselves, and the universe, we should be aware of the enormous complexity in everything. Life sustains us and does not want to destroy us. We are hired to evolve more, to learn, and to create the good things for the best of humanity, the entire planet, and all of life. The more conscious life is, the more beautiful and rightful it is, and the more joyful it becomes. Wonderland is a state of mind. The most rewarding life search is the discovery of our inner selves. Explore yourself with joy. Each life is an individual, distinctive expression of discovery that can be more meaningful and become a contribution to humanity and life. Life is a never-ending creation, a constant and relentless change.

Human creation should concentrate only on the good things in order to preserve and improve one's lifespan. Also, collect new ideas and unknown facts of your life. Honour and love your life; it is the process of rising consciousness and meaningful creation. Take a break, think, and embrace all. There are so many more for you to enjoy, absorb, share, improve, and create. Travel on Synchronicity River. A lot of things, events, and people are there for a reason; we need them to appear. We need to experience balance, peace, love, growth, and learning with the joy to simply be. True knowledge is the best provider, and it's the quickest way to reach a profound level in order to secure a healthy mind-body-spirit with wisdom, which is our greatest wealth. Many of our friends do not want us to change because they are unable to change too and go with us.

We are privileged to live, yet some people purposely punish themselves with wrong information, food, drugs, and bad company. We own our minds and bodies and their proper maintenance, as well as gratefulness and gratitude. Many diseases are the effects of human ignorance, unnatural ways of life, and weak will. Many people subconsciously or purposely neglect their minds and bodies and their natural healing way; they react to stress and health problems in order to get attention, and they rely on prescription drugs. Changing and understanding ourselves is a lifetime of responsible activity. In every moment of life, all that is alive collects and processes information for survival, goodness, and the advance of all nature. For humans, our priorities should be about harmonizing with ecosystem. A well-balanced life includes the purpose of life with contentment. Only man through his existence creates the quintessence of life.

What is the most powerful force for people with little understanding? Money! Money becomes the god and superior power for little minds. Technology and money become modern gods. If we follow those new gods, we will be absorbed by artificial life. In effect, we will become more primitive and far from real life. What is more important than money? Your health and wisdom of the mind-body-spirit. What is also important to realize? It is the ability to understand, collect, and use true information at the right time. Your life is a clarification of your ancestors' accumulated states of the mind-body-spirit. We are walking on the footprints of our ancestors. We should be honoured to carry their proficiencies forward and create more understanding and skills. Recognize the sanctity of the healthy mind and body. Sooner or later, people will realize that everything they will ever want it is having a healthy mind-body-spirit; the rest is only extras.

Only the Human Mind Defines Man in the Universe

A blessing for human life is the existence of real scientists, philosophers, wise men, and honest people, who collect and pass on truthful facts and wise ways of living to society. We still have a chance to correct and modulate our species. If it happens in a rational and conscious way, then we can survive. Human life is mostly the constant struggle to survive, to collect information, and to have self-knowledge and understanding. The only way to change lives around us, and our own mind-body-spirit, is with our minds. Transform yourself, your life, and the world for the better.

Being alive and healthy in the mind-body-spirit with the right knowledge is a pure blessing. Health is our greatest asset, and our primal need is to live an enjoyable life. All of us exchange, cooperate, and create. All of us are suspended in no time zone, living our lives through our minds. Contemplation will find more daily moments that fulfil us and better ourselves. We will learn more about ourselves. The outer and inner life will be in harmony, enriching each other. A contemplative life will teach us who we are and how to live our essential truth. A contemplative life is an evolving life. By getting in the flow, we can contribute much more to life and to our wellness. Some men focus on physical, mental, emotional, and spiritual transitions. Others take their responsibilities to their family or friends. All of us are finding the purpose of humanity.

Life is about creating a sensible journey that's satisfactory on the physical, mental, and spiritual levels. Your values create the path to a purposeful life, serving and protecting you and others. Life's purpose is to progress, preserve itself, and advance towards more control in the never-ending process. Nature teaches the best ways to succeed and advance with a unique life's purpose, along with unknown adventure and destination. We will search throughout our lives, and we will not know everything.

What Is Our Civilization's Purpose?

All of us dream individually. We forget to dream as humanity in order to advance with responsibility for nature and our genes. Living without purpose is futile. Ingratitude, dishonesty, selfishness, and egotism lead to humiliation and self-punishment. It's about creating a sensible life with satisfactory mental, spiritual, and material levels. The spaceless and timeless universe makes it impossible to know everything. Certainly it's similar for all earlier civilizations. Everything is about to enhance our existence by using all ways to become a fully conscious extension, with all balanced forces dancing with the beauty of the eternal change. Life is never ending and evolving as an individual and collective search for nature. Life is constantly learning to see and understand better, doing better for ourselves and others. Life is a collective event starting on the microbiota level, and human life is a cooperative experience to make life better for all. Our first duty is to become well, and then we will have powers to become useable for others. Humanity is a team responsibility. All of us create our individual futures and humanity's future.

Welcome to Our Related Fortune of Purposeful Life

The most valuable information about life and yourself is included in the present day.
Ask yourself sincerely,
Who are you?
What you think about your life and yourself?
Are you living without fear?
How is your quiet time?
Are you at peace with yourself?
Are you smiling with an inward sympathy and love for yourself?
Can you learn from the past, accepting it?
Can you enjoy the present and create the future with certainty?
Have you clarity in your dreams, with purity of intention?

What would you like to change?
Your lifetime is a mighty power.
Your life is a journey of self-discovery, finding meaning and purpose of life.
Insightful natural gifts uncover most outright.
Explore and support your inner self with curiosity and solitude.
With reflection, the outer world comes into order.
Life, sagacity, and love will beautifully explain themselves.
Life and love are as good as you are.
Our good living becomes their interpretations.
It is how we understand it, how we think about it, and how we act.
The quality within decides the quality outside;
The rest is the self-fulfilling process.
Life insight with appreciation leads to surviving longer and better.
Wholly fulfil your mission and role.
Find the sense of purposefulness in the ocean waves,
As well as in your existence with daily business.
Alternatively, change the life pattern of priorities.
Abandon senselessness of greed and jealousy.
Joyfully live through the boundless excitement of curiosity leading to wisdom.
Wisdom originates in resources of wellness—a joyful, healthy mind and body.
In the rapids of life's river, find the beauty of the raw elements.
Make a difference via the significance of your life's uniqueness.
Live in harmony with life and nature.
Live honestly with simplicity, in the grace of essence.
Truly passionate living and love are perfect in the same way.
You are welcome to reconnect with extra providence.
With the way of life, all victories are prepared,
Where peace and resourcefulness live together.
You are a social being without the possibility to survive as a man for yourself.
The ecosystem is one organism, a complete entity.
Fear from the ignorant mind destroys itself.
Unnecessary business starts meaningless activity,
Assembling a parody of living on the screen of life.
Exploring the outer world through a mass media–oriented existence,
Many are living far from a wellspring of wisdom,
With needy souls and empty minds of sense.

Absence of values destroys potential, driving life too quickly and recklessly.
Our senseless pleasure can flood the world of treasures.
Ignorance is the choice until we achieve burnout.
Ignorance misleads and results in misinterpretation.
Reorder knowledge and fruitfulness for the rest of your life.
Attract the art of life into the mind-body-spirit.
Then you will find the gifts in everyday, in every change,
Seeing the goodness of positive thoughts;
In each of them are the foundation of future events.
That's why it is time to recognise our purpose and longing.
Do not be ignorant of the wonderful secrets of life.
From the ruins of the antiquity, we can use knowledge.
The most illustrious and practical truths are supremely important.
Reach the whole thing to understand the mysterious nature and life.
How will life serve your life purpose?
Can you doubt your presence? Be content with whatever you have.
In the inevitability of the eternal, there is an interconnectedness of all.
Decide what is important and beneficial for you and others.
You will become the integral creative force for humanity.
Illuminated men have the privilege of many choices for the fulfilment of life.
We all travel by different ways, collecting life experiences for our unique growth.
The immense sea of matter-energy-information is alive; everything is interacting.
Atoms remember their evolution and earlier connections.
That is the mystery and power of the cosmic energy stream,
Fundamental for creation and life existence.
Your conscious life is a joint collection of information in segmental patterns of
Electromagnetic vibrations, creating physical, mental, and spiritual levels.

Secrets of Life

"To know all things is not permitted."

—Horace

The secrets of life are included in the attraction of yin and yang. Quantum magnetism is a core of the interplay competence. The power of attraction is between the positive yang and the negative yin. It is a primal love, the secret of life, embracing galaxies and the unknown.

We can learn from ancient wisdom that the secrets of life are included inside of us. Our information's emotions, actions, and thinking are the secret generator of the negative (destructive) or positive (constructive) energy vibration, which we send outside our bodies and minds onto the holographic screen of life.

Emotions travel with the speed of the light. Catch only the good ones and treasure them; they become the seeds of everything in order to live the wellness of life. The art of thinking creates the limitless joy of life. We should think deeply in order to find the means of pleasure and its insatiable ways.

On an ancient Greek temple were inscribed the words, "Love
tempered with wisdom is the secret of life."

The central part of wisdom is love for life, and together they create a bond with everything. The opposite factor of love is not hate; it is fear.

The secret of life is living according to nature's specifications. All other ways become violence, resulting in disintegration. The secret and sense of life is simply to be, trying to find the answers, and being in balance within yourself and the universe.

Understanding more will blend us with the collective consciousness. The key to the universe and life is our present consciousness. Life needs us to stay in the present. Life's essence is mostly held and continues in the present. The mighty flow of life's stream is in the now. We are parts of the truth, and so we are the keys for the truth. By taking responsibility for ourselves, we become co-creators.

"Always say yes to the present moment. What could be more futile,
more insane, than to create inner resistance to what already is?
what could be more insane than to oppose life itself, which is now
and always now? Surrender to what is. Say yes to life—and see how
life suddenly starts working for you rather than against you."
—Eckhart Tolle

The secret of life is something we should discover personally for ourselves, through our unique understanding. By understanding ourselves, we will understand all. Self-discovery and self-knowledge help us understand others, life, and the universe. Our unawareness will create a low-quality life, and our awareness will create an extraordinary life. Also, nothing beautiful, good, or useful can be gained without effort; success depends on persistence.

Flexibility is the right approach. Rethink what your goals will be. Remember the way that reconstructs the positive aspects of the past.

Each person's life has many fulfilling experiences as well as frustrating negatives. We can learn from past successes and from past failures. Each person has a unique way of existence, which is characterised by that person's method of dealing with life.

One of the Secrets of Life Is Omnipotent Change

Omnipotent change is life's law of necessity. We should treat change as the opportunity to improve ourselves. Changing, learning, and understanding yourself and life are lifetime obligations.

Change is self-propelled and sustained.
Change is adjustment by becoming a new form.
Change is the way of improvement.
Change is reorder and transformation.
All segments of cycles are evenly important.
They all improve equally from positive and negative properties.
Do not try to secure all that is designed to change and vanish.
Enjoy and maintain yourself through change, if you can.

Universal and Eternal Law Combines Two Multiplexes: on the micro scale (atoms) and on the macro scale (all galaxies). There are multi-faced forces—good and bad, light and darkness. Everything that exists has two opposite forces. We travel the way of nature, the way of probability and change, and we're propelled by yin and yang. Life is a constant change that offers more than the mind can absorb and process. We travel the route of our consciousness. The constant improvement of human consciousness is the only way to survive. In order to have good lives, we need to constantly learn and act properly. Travel through space and time outside and inside of yourself, with harmony and love for life. Soon the whole life will embrace you and offer new possibilities. The universe's energy is embracing all, and it is greater than the sum of its parts. The universe multiplies, and it is a state of being.

Each step towards real knowledge improves our existence, but we will never know enough. We will learn quicker from true history. All information on any level of life indicates that everything is connected by an amazing network of communication and energy. Insight comes with the condition of inner clarity and realization of the perfect oneness of mind essence with life and the universe. With this realization comes a different existence of super-sensitivity and intuitive understanding of nature and the universe.

The art of living is to be grateful for all what we have already. When we are happy, we share it with others and everything else. We can enjoy life more by seeing the waves of reality saturating the space around ourselves, others, and everything else.

Why does it seem that unhappiness is a stronger feeling and stays longer than happiness? Uplifting from winning is smaller than the downs from losing. We are programmed to compete, to win, to succeed. Know that all are temporary leads for the best strategy, which means not competing for every prize, and not gambling and wasting precious life. Play your game of life with the longest joy and the longest, healthiest performance. If you're spontaneous but wise, your mind-body-spirit will be always younger than your age. The greatest joy of all is to be healthy and conscious. It is the best success and wealth. A great state for the mind-body-spirit leads to a great state of life now and in the future. Our bodies, minds, and spirits create a sensitive whole in the arrangement to support each other.

Through simplicity we will find more true joy, gratitude, respect, and love. Winning means being healthier, enjoying more, and living longer. **The most important tool to secure your dreams and goals is you.** Studying the antiquity of serenity from multiple points of view creates a better picture of the past, however a deeper understanding of it starts a better future. Many people create their own emotional restrictions, which take them away from enjoyment and achievements in daily life. Moreover, they habitually are unable to find real, beneficial friends. Sometimes we have no friends around us, but it will be better to live without than to have false ones. People not willing to be grateful are not happy even with a great number of achievements. Plasticity is the best way to approach life. You can start well-being in yourself, in others and in your surroundings. It is the best merit that we can create. Any kind of wellness will give its seeds everywhere. Good are results of the right state of mind, the right attitude, and rational observance. Different life satisfactions are collected in different qualities from different people. A wider spectrum of awareness originates from appreciation, even from getting a small amount of what was expected; such a state will last longer.

Life Processes, Duality of Nature, and Polarity

There are active and passive dual principles of life, opposing forces, which balance each other to create a stable and enduring life. Yin and yang are opposite polarities within the circle of being. Everything has an opposed force, and they interplay within humanity.

Everything is in a temporary state, changing constantly. Confrontation of opposites is needed for the processes of life, which are dependent on change. The interaction between opposites is necessary to the expression of the universe. Nothing is permanently neutral. Change and movement are universal in the revolving processes of nature, and both are the manifestation of the indestructibility of the matter-energy-space-time system. Change is the essence of material, biological, and spiritual worlds.

Only the change is infinite. There is only the certainty of infinite movement and changes. Human life is never a simple one-way path, but it always involves no as well as yes. There's polarity of mind and polarity of matter. In our lives, we must deal with this polarity of reaction all the time. The human mind uses symbols related to binary opposition: one and zero, yes and no, positive and negative, left and right, life and death, light and dark. This negative and positive element is obvious in physical nature, in the attraction and repulsion patterns of neutrons and protons, but it assumes much greater significance on the level of human consciousness. Such realms are for us to explore. Our thoughts are created in the same way as atoms interact through the realms of matter-energy-space-time. That is why our thoughts create our reality.

The evolution of the mind is based on the extraction of two opposite polarities, two united sources of energy, one male (positive) and one female (negative). Motions (physical and mental) between polarities are fundamental for life and existence, which is constantly changing, even in our bodies and minds. We are in a natural swing between optimism and negativism, two poles of mood. Optimism is a powerful emotion, but it is a mighty and creative power when we mix it with action. We can clearly see synchronicity and dependence on each other in all levels of life and the universe. Everything is connected in the dance of superior, ever-lasting power factors. It starts in the smaller structures and then moves up to atoms, molecules, bigger living entities and un-living complexes, planets, and galaxies.

Look around. Nature created everything different, and nature wants us to use our differences. We must use our distinctions to cope with life.

Living and non-living components of the universe involve information processing devices of change. The human brain and body is a miniature of the enigmatic universe, constantly changing. The procedure of breakdown is change. Memory becomes our specific tool to remember change, to create time and space for our unique mental existence.

It is the law of nature that in the plants, animals, and humans, the levels never will be equal. Nature's aim is not equality; it is the very opposite of equality. The endeavours of all forces originate from equilibrium, on the way to variety and polarity. The inseparability of the essential law of attraction (the law of opposites), comes out in old sayings.

"The way up and the way down is the same."

—Heraclitus

We are the beautifully blended composition of leading forces in the universe. All our abilities, moods, and thoughts are stimulated by the universe. Every individual is part of the whole, and it's the consistency of the universal, natural law. All of that proves the oneness of nature and its multiplicity in the whole. Nature created the law of entropy, which governs the uniqueness and irreversibility. Nature originated the law of self-orderliness, constructing the higher living systems.

Life is a miracle and is precious. It is aliveness with variety, always changing from one composition to the next, with new designs. All of that stimulates wonder, joy, and love, being witness to those wonderful changes in everything around us and in us. We are looking for paradise, but we should realise that we are living in paradise now. We can live and create our wonderland on a daily basis, if we responsibly think and act.

Human needs are controlled by the body's bacteria system. Human life is a miniature of the enigmatic universe. Earth is a microbial planet with intelligent life, and we humans are only an extension of it. Bacteria are the most prolific organism on earth with social intelligence.

Evidence from palaeontology show bacterial microfossils dated to around four to six billion years ago. Even rocks are suitable to introduce life. Ancient microbial life, which was the base of 85 percent of earth's biospheres, evolved into mitochondria as a part of every living cell. It is a very useful entity existing in all cells of our bodies, able to produce energy for us from fat, carbohydrates, protein, and oxygen. Also, very significantly, they come with their own genetic code! Mitochondria appear only in advanced, more complex forms of life. Each human consciousness is a collective consciousness from all body cells' consciousness. Consciousness and intelligence are properties of life. They are the intrinsic property of cells.

We do not know much how bacteria advance, but we know that bacteria created life on earth—all plants and all living organisms, including humans.

Bacterial Computation, Microbial Consciousness

Shapiro is a scientist who studies bacteria genetics. He thinks bacteria are sentient. "Bacteria utilize sophisticated mechanisms for intercellular communication and even can commandeer the basic cell biology of 'higher' plants and animals to meet own needs."[1]

---

[1] http://shapiro.bsd.uchicago.edu/2006.ExeterMeeting.pdf

Human Needs

The triple nature of man exists on three levels.

1. Material
2. Mental, emotional, intellectual
3. Spiritual

Survival—Material Needs

All our material needs are temporary and include eating, sleeping, clothing, shelter, safety, mating, and transportation. Humans are born with material needs. It is good to remember about the supreme factor of time, which is destroying everything. There are needs to collect material issue and master the environment. In the same way, all needs are the same for animals and human. Needs for career and position are also practical responses in the material world.

It is time to ask yourself:

Who are you?
What do you have?
What do you want?
What do you really need?

We need a simpler life, which is a more peaceful life. If we have too much, it creates distraction. If we have the essentials, we don't have much, and we will realise we don't need much. Our freedom is more valuable than material things and money. Attachment to money as a symbol of power allows a certain standard of living. We need money as a medium, or we can create a new, less harmful, more universal medium. We live in a material world. Materialism is so desperately all-consuming in our world that only a selective life of wider awareness can bring higher intellectual, spiritual understanding and contentment. The exaggeration in the needs of material things and neglecting the intellectual and spiritual awareness reduce our sensibility and responsibility towards ourselves, society, and nature. Life is not about money-making cults. Most men create more desires than they can gratify. The very richest in our world cannot gratify every desire. There are limits to their needs, understanding, time, and health. There are limits to their desires and dreams.

There is a way to wisdom. First set up a healthy body-mind-spirit. Conserve life around you, enhance a natural connection with nature, and establish balanced living with interplay across all natural forces. Nothing beautiful, good, or useful can be added without effort. The more wisdom we know and use, the healthier and more favourable life we can have.

Intellectual Needs, Spiritual Needs

These two worlds are interrelated with needs in order to have value, a sense of meaning, wisdom, love, priorities, hope, creativity, life commitments, trust, joy, love of life, and oneness. Development of technology has heightened the increasing need for mental exploration and stimulation.

No one who ever lived has had enough power, prestige, or knowledge to overcome the basic conditions of all life. You win some and lose some. The very richest on this world cannot gratify every desire; there are limits to their time, strength, distance, and understanding. Our desires are a multitude, and those that we most gratify are but few. We have social, cultural, philosophical, and religious needs, as well as a need for acceptance. Life is very difficult, but it can be made the supreme adventure by one who is healthy, knows the road, and travels with the light of wisdom. Humanity unfolds very slowly because it acquires knowledge very slowly, and it also sluggishly applies the old and new wisdom. Do everything for wisdom; there will be no mistakes in reason and actions. All fears melt under the rational pressure of wisdom. We live in a world where we are exposed to very quick changes on all levels of life. As humans, we are not yet r yet to evolve in a balanced way. We are going too far from nature, from natural food, from close social interactions. We also are very far from old traditions.

Many people follow the material value system, forgetting that wellness of life and health is our real wealth. If we remember that statement on a daily basis, it will become our way of life. Many are lost, becoming distracted by mass media and by empty, artificial existences in the virtual world. Rediscover the bliss of family living, which was naturally integrated in the old times. One of the most important personal disasters is a relationship break-up. Finding a compatible partner gives a relationship the best chance. Good couples have similar value systems. By developing the intellectual level, we will become more alert with the desire to communicate, exchange ideas, and advance intellectual interests. On a psychological level, a deeper understanding with a more optimistic outlook on life will enhance expression of this level. A desire to understand the inner and outer worlds expand on this level and cover thinking, intuition, morals, ethics, rationale, survival, sex, and religion.

Wellness of Life

You are the creator of your wellness or misery. The secrets of wellness and humanity's survival starts within the collective consciousness of our gut bacteria, as well as the collective consciousness of all human body cells. Microbiota and the mind are the first and the only ways to wellness. It is the set, the key and the door into the world of wellness, into one's created reality. It is the outcome from a whole and good mind-body-spirit function, being healthy and content and having purposeful accomplishments.

Wellness is a holistic way of viewing health. It is the self-regulatory systems that interconnect the whole body-mind-spirit. Loving your life is about taking care of you body-mind-spirit and creating your wellness.

The secret of wellness is unified with the continuity of conscious living, living the essence of truth in the nature way. Wellness is accumulated or weakened each day. Living with wellness is your choice. Think well, do well, and live your wellness with gratitude. Illness does not manifest in one day or night. Many diseases develop through years of negligence of the mind and body.

Everything that you express by your mind-body-spirit describes you, even the states of equilibrium, vitality, and joy. Wellness is created by wise information, concepts, and actions. Health of the mind-body-spirit opens the door to wellness. Wellness comes from proper estimation and the selection of everything that is needed. Wellness as the complex is more than health, exercise, or nutrition. Wellness is also the state where positivism dominates negativism in thinking and actions. Wellness is the freedom from unbalance, pain, and clarity of the mind's designed destiny. Wellness needs long-term sustainability in individual life and in the planet's life. Mind wellness depends of the wellness of nature, so we must increase the global wellness of the environment. We cannot live long, joyful lives in an artificial nature. Our attitude towards everything is very important too.

The secrets to experiencing wellness is to expand our horizons and welcome people to exchange their information with love and appreciation. Wellness is harmony in the body and mind, and it depends on life's criteria. Wellness depends on a healthy body and a free, balanced mind. Continuous wellness is not realistic in natural consciousness of human. Wellness follows our balanced ways and proper actions with its own rhythms.

The shortest way towards wellness in life is your knowledgeable mind. True wellness is a creativity of the sensible mind focused on balance and peace. It is an extra perception for positive things. True wellness is the effectiveness of our love towards life, understanding ourselves, and the principles of life and the universe. It is about allowing acceptability, gratitude, and the joy of now. All other things will follow us in the favourable reality course of life and the universe. When we are happy, we share our good energy with others and everything else, and we enjoy seeing wave after wave saturate the space around ourselves, others, and everything else. Only nature and we humans can do this.

Many people think that wellness is created by fulfilling desires like money, material possessions, positions in society, and accomplishments. Wellness of life starts with daily wandering with curiosity, learning to grasp and use nature's essentials, which create, enhance our existence, and make it more useful for us and others. Living in such a way makes us more content, more harmonious, and wiser. Wellness is not strongly connected with levels of wealth. It is related to a healthy body-mind-spirit and the sensible, natural philosophy of life, nature, relationships, social connections, creative activities, personal sense, values, positivity, and religions.

In Latin American and Asian countries, simple communities reach higher levels of wellness than wealthy populations. Rational thinking doesn't make a connection between money and wellness. Positive attitudes with love towards life on a daily basis are the secret power designing our wellness. Consciousness and attitude change genes. Attitude is the precious commodity creating our whole lives; without it, our lives will fall apart. Think well, do well, and live wellness with gratitude. Wellness secures itself by truth and by understanding what is inevitable, unpredictable, and accepting. It dreams of a better life. Such a way makes our lives more enjoyable, more useable, and more interesting. Wisdom and wellness are coming every day from the ultimate source, which is the mighty nature-life complex.

We are the separate consciousness, the outcome of unknown quantum processes which give wellness, miserable existence, or tragic life. Wellness depends on one's own consciousness and one's health with practical wisdom. Wellness must be earned and secured by self-analysis, constant corrections, love, and courage to face life and fulfil ambitions and dreams. Life is the process of constant changes and choices about wellness in relationships, work, finances, and leisure. The true love for life wellness is hidden in all hearts, minds, and bodies, waiting with hope that humans will again live in harmony with nature and with themselves.

Daily positive actions are enjoyable and improve wellness, aging, and longevity. Laughter makes healthy physiological transformations, which extends one's lifespan. Love and wellness renew themselves and create and encompass everything else. Wellness is flourishing, living with gratitude, and achieving such a state to become very valuable. Wellness and suffering run in a circular motion, and they are part of everyday life. Man must look outward as well as inward for balanced life. Wellness is the full integration of mindbBodysSpirit-mature. We will balance our lives by taking good care of ourselves, our family, our friends, and our businesses. Wellness is unavoidable if we collect all that our body-mind-spirit needs in natural ways. Life wellness is about expanding and improving.

Our minds can work for us or against us. They work against us if they use false information, of if they work under the influence of drugs, bad food, and bad gut microbiota. Sometimes laziness, the wrong lifestyle, and ignorance will slow or degrade the mind.

We should find time for learning, thinking, and contemplation; then we should decide and act. More knowledge will create a more natural, simple, and peaceful life. Our knowledge is manifested in our lives, which celebrate itself via daily contentment, constant improvement, and enhancing others. As inner joy, health and wisdom are the secret system of extending youth and strength in any man. Wishing to reach wellness is just a starting point. We need to improve ourselves and fix features of our personality and character, which prevent us from entering contentment. Wellness comes from a balanced external and internal world. It relates to the balance in global society, nature, life, and the whole universe. Wellness is the lifelong way of living for quality. There should be a balance between material achievement and the improvement of mind-body-spirit.

Many people think that wellness is created by fulfilling desires like money, material possessions, positions in society, accomplishments. Does it matter how many material possessions we leave behind? Wellness can be enhanced through better understanding, and training the mind-body-spirit will uplift wellness even with modest material possessions. Life is not only about the money. If people think that more money will secure happiness, then they are wrong. Enjoy what do you have and don't worry about what you do not have. A concerned life will prize itself; an uncaring life will destroy itself. The choice is yours as to what you will get out of your life. Responsible use of abundance in one area of life can produce a proper supply in another area.

Wellness is the outcome of unified love, truth, wisdom, and health. Wellness is about being healthy, wise, and content. Wellness is about experiencing healthy adventure, where wellness is a journey without destination. Wellness is the outcome of holistic composition and interplaying factors. All joint goodness of wellness overdrives all temporal conditions and happenings.

Your inner work on yourself adds to your enjoyment of life. You can absolutely be the master of yourself. You will understand more and be wiser in your mind and body. You must learn about something valuable for the mind and for life.

We become distracted by mass media, losing the ability to contemplate. Everything is about true information, extra perception, and concentration on positive and proper things. Our knowledge and value system creates the quality of our life and wellness. True wellness comes from a natural life system, and the mind estimates what is needed and creates the healthy balance and peace. Wellness is in our minds, bodies, and spirits; it describes itself by harmony in the mind-body-spirit, not only being free from disease but also being full of life energy and expanding it with pleasure, greatness, and gratefulness. Wellness embraces mental, emotional, and physical well-being. We need to get enough sleep, drink clean water, eat natural food, and restore the mind-body-spirit. Wellness is about unfolding one's potential to be more alive, content, and beneficial. If we talk about wellness, we talk about a healthy mind-body-spirit, family relationships, and social connections.

Wellness is a good experience from physiological and psychological states. It is a sign of the fulfilment of our human capacities. The way of wellness is universal, uncomplicated, natural, and infinite. If all that we properly want and all that we get match, then we create complete wellness. Our wellness of life depends of how correct our understanding is, as well as the quality of what will satisfy our needs. Our life wellness is designed by us, and we need to use our wisdom, love, and compassion to obtain mind-body-spirit wellness. Wellness walks in the way of simplicity; it is the way of nature. Wellness comes from living the true way of life, which is orderly. This is the only way leading into wellness, and at the base of it is the unification of the mind-body-spirit.

What will happen to you if you will get what you want, but it is not what you need? Mother Nature offers a lot of free things which many of us do not appreciate promptly. When you satisfy your survival needs, it is time to improve and control your whole life. Learn to ponder and be grateful for the miracle of your life. Life becomes more enjoyable and balanced if you admire it daily. If it includes pure, strong intentions, then like directed consciousness, it will start preparing your future events. All creative life starts with the right question. Explore it, and you will find the right answers. Sometimes the question is more important than the answer. Your ultimate goals, needs, and duty are to understand yourself, your own mind, your interrelation with time and space, nature, and other people.

We can describe the pull of different interacting forces as attraction. Wellness is created by a balance between yin and yang energies. Everything is about functioning as one balanced whole; it is the essence of wellness in life that runs in a circular motion.

Wellness is the collection of information, positive emotions, and vibrations saturating everything around us. True wellness is the effectiveness of our love toward life, understanding ourselves, and accepting the principles of life and the universe with gratitude and joy. Wellness and gratefulness grow together, are inseparable, and enhance each other. Gratefulness should be applied as soon as possible after experiencing favourable events. Such an approach will enhance the wellness of life on all levels. The most important thing is to be thankful for the people who share their wisdom, positive emotions, friendship, and love.

Wellness in life is the result of understanding and correcting the healthy fusion between mind, body, and spirit. Our perception creates the present, and some of our insight creates the future.

Wellness is the personal state related to the concepts of life's values, goals, society, and people. The reality of wellness is that there are occasional variables under pressure of unseen circumstances. These are not rigid states. However, the human organism has the capacity for self-regulation in the body-mind complex, excellently leading and restoring what is needed. We can learn about true needs, simplicity, important goals, and doing good for others. We can change our horizons, approach, and way of living via our mastery of life. Love and appreciate your life, people, and nature; it will bring contentment.

Would you live differently after learning from other societies? Good life comes after good decisions and actions, which is a wonderland of our own creation. Learning, creating, enjoying, sharing, and helping result in goodness in our lives. Try to look inward and make this a habit. Ignore external distractions and remove the obstacles to create peace of mind for rational thinking and living. In this stage of evolution, humans cannot control or create everything; we can only follow nature and use already existing elements according to nature's law.

Understanding is the essence of the true, interrelated information. Some of our understandings create the future. Better understanding of ourselves, nature, and life leads to better harmony, and the synchronisation of our lives.

"You cannot be both unhappy and fully present in the Now."
—Eckhart Tolle

Life is a journey towards wellness, which will change the way we see ourselves. Whole wellness comes from conscious integration with the law of all life, the universal order. It is a perpetual rhythm of constant improvement.

Everything is about our perspective and attitude, so choose wisely. True wellness exists within man, but many people seek it outside of themselves. Take care of your body-mind-spirit and your gut microbiota; these are the only ways for real contentment. Life is an oscillation between happiness and distress on many different levels every day. The nature of life is simply that we win some and lose some. Right and wrong are man-made, and they're often temporary. Each person has unique skills and a unique way of being. Our uniqueness is very serviceable by intentions from nature. Uniformity is the way of death. Free yourself from senseless routines and rigid patterns; face a new dimension with immense horizons. Flexibility and dedication are the best ways to approach life. Wellness starts the moment we realise that life is a beautiful adventure of exploration of internal and external worlds. It comes from the effects of the connection with the whole in balanced, peaceful, and joyful ways. Wellness can become the never-ending joyful process that is independent of trivial things.

Indicators Leading to Wellness

1. Wellness is the never-ending exploration of itself and the universe.
2. A healthy mind-body complex is efficient and creates wellness and greatness.
3. A positive mind towards one's life is the first step to wellness.
4. The right viewpoint and the right mind-set are the principles of life.
5. The ability to show love, care, tolerance, and respect is the most important way to create harmony and wellness.
6. Wellness is not dependent on temporal circumstances and the environment.
7. A connection with the nature is a positive stimulus for a healthy mind and body.
8. A natural, healthy environment provides mental, spiritual, physical, and recreational benefits.
9. We should have good relationships with others and ourselves.
10. Laugh more! Laughter can have great benefits for your well-being.
11. If the feelings, mind, and heart cooperate, they create contentment and wellness.
12. Enjoy who you are and what you are doing for a living.
13. Strive for the essence of life and wisdom.
14. Wellness connects with social interaction and established values.

Only humankind can rediscover heaven and hell in the human world, and in itsself. It is very clear that we create the full spectrum of life, the hell and the haven. Wellness is not about sensual pleasures—it is about looking beyond them, and it is about balance in everything. Through working out, we can focus on the right direction. We can create many good things, values, love, compassion, sharing, and cooperation. We have an innate instinct to do well to others.

The true pursuit of wellness lies not in striving towards some material goal to satisfy our egos, but in a change in our attitude, way of thinking, and way of living. What is happening inwardly must reflect outwardly. Self-love is set up by life. It is true to life and itself. It is real, correct, and necessary for our existence, and it's essential for a genuine love relationship with others.

Lack of self-love and self-understanding creates an unhealthy basis, which often creates negativity, self-abuse, and drug and food addictions. Relationships and absorbing activities are important for wellness.

The love for others comes from the love of yourself and a love for life. Rediscover yourself. Enhance self-love and confidence. Compassion originates from self-love. If you love life, others, and yourself, then you have all what you need. There is no wellness without life balance and a vigorous mind-body-spirit complex. Wellness comes by being true to ourselves, others, and life, and by doing our best. Wellness and conscientious existence are based on naturalness. In addition, if we develop ourselves mentally to be in balance with nature and ourselves, we will have a naturally positive and easier life. Wellness is life's success, coming from balance, peace, and contentment. Exactitude, wisdom, enjoyment, and love of life, along with sharing, cooperation, and social interaction, create profound wellness.

Most Asian and Latin American countries, as well as some native communities, reach high levels of wellness without having a lot of material possessions. Once they are out of poverty, high levels of wealth and income make little difference in how happy they are. Income is strongly related to life satisfaction, but it's weakly related to emotional well-being, at least above a certain threshold.

Inspect daily the usefulness of your attitudes, as well as your thoughts about yourself, others, and life. Be positive about daily life experiences; they are your learning process to be content. Share the states of joy, love, and compassion with others; it is the shortest way to obtain a sense of wellness. Do not complain about life in general/ Think about how you can change your situation and then work on the solutions. Under difficult situations and the pressure of daily living, we often lose balance due to our own choices. An unbalanced, sick mind is confused with itself, cannot make the best decisions, and forgets about the body. That's why it is so much harder to correct the mind than the body. It is hard to smile while the world around you seems to be crumbling. However, keep in mind that times have been tough before, and we have recovered; therefore, we will recover again. Daily, insignificant imperfections and arguments are wasting your time. Everything else is in change. You should focus on real enjoyment and realization, which makes sense in your life. Realise that all things change, including you.

Who are you? Moreover, what do you want to blend and project into your future? On the way to the improvement of the mind-body-spirit-life qualities, we create the states of wellness, happiness, joy, and contentment, according to our values and abilities. We are hired as living creatures, and we are very important parts of everything that exists. Our existences describe society, the universe, and us. Some of the questions and issues are fundamental for our existence, so we try to find the answers. Our reality is that individual appearance is created by a wide spectrum of forces creating energy fields. We are the matrix of energies, and we decide what kinds of energies we will use and multiply. It is serviceable to examine the whole body's performance and our personal attitudes towards ourselves and life. The quality of life depends on the quality of live and all the body's cells.

Modern humankind can handle information better mentally and spiritually, and we should understand that we were born to create ourselves and take part in the creation of humanity. Modern humankind realises that the mind is an unknown universe, similar to the outside, whole universe. Our lives are an exploration of two worlds, and it had barely started. The internal universe of the single atom relates to all again. Space, time, matter, and energy are interwoven into one medium.

"Everything is enfolded into everything."

—David Bohm

The ancient wisdom said, "All are one." The mind has been designed as an instrument to be in tune with the universe and take part in co-creation. It is for all who have asked for an open mind. All of us are hired to share our energy and ideas, enriching each other for the advancement of human race and the world. All of us have a mission of cooperation to discover and create a new experience, interpretation, and outlook of the world with a new dimension of thinking. The time for us to improve our life towards a new, full, living society, securing survival of the human race, is not in the far future. With technology's advancement, new obstacles arrive; there is confusion and disinformation on the Internet and in other mass media. Dealing with this problem is not easy. Another issue is the relentless, shallow advertisement of new products and entertainment.

Senseless overconsumption promotes pollution and wastes the earth's resources. Superficial amusements become senseless and distractive, educating small-minded personalities.It's no wonder there is an absence of resolute cooperation and collaborative responsibility in decision making. In addition, we need a sound education, which can filter the flood of information and disinformation. True information is alive and vital. Good thoughts and things will hardly disappear; they hold essential truths. We need to examine how the Internet and electronic gadgets affect our lives. Nicolas Carr, in his book *The Shallow*, concludes that the Internet creates superficial understanding, fostering ignorance.

"If you change your thoughts, you actually change your biology."

—Bruce H. Lipton

Thoughts create their own reality. Realities exchange and unite for the goodness of the whole. A sensory conclusion in life provides only physical pleasure at the expense of not awakening talent and not refining the mind. It is limiting our possibilities for fuller life. In addition, exclusively gratifying sensual desires may be termed empty and selfish. The quality and quantity of your thoughts create your life, changing your genes and your body-mind-spirit. Select the values, ways, and happiness in life that will develop with the years and will be an unending source of satisfaction. To receive more, we need to give more. Do not cheaply spend your possibilities for happiness. Self-appraisal is vitally necessary to making life worthwhile. You will not waste yourself. Think beyond the moment. Things change, and so do you. Everything must diminish with the passing years. The necessity of evolving human race is to secure a unique and independent mind of all individuals, which composes the matrix of collective consciousness working as the Internet for humanity.

Challenges in Life

As they say, "It is the greatest manifestation of power to be calm." Sigmund Freud defined mental health as the ability to live and to work. Man creates one of most disastrous stresses by himself, and he also stresses about others in everyday life. If you control your mind, you govern the wildest territories in the world. Stress is needed in emergency situations, when we need to save our lives.

Certain actions of the central nervous system are involuntary and incoherent; this is the basic reason for unexpected, erratic reactions in human behaviour. Our ego, anger, and jealousy create attachment, and many unbalanced thoughts and actions hurt us and others. Attachment to objects, ways of living, and some people can cut our freedom, causing disharmony in the mind-body and around us. Negative feelings about ourselves are harmful to the mind and body. Disharmony in thoughts, emotions, and actions harm us and others by producing negative energy fields in our minds and bodies and around us, creating a wide spectrum for an unhealthy environment. The mind has a profound effect on the body, and the body has a profound effect on the mind. Things creating healthy and more permanent pleasures are highly valuable. As nature changes, its supply changes, our needs change, our pleasures change, and the meaning of life transforms. The intensity of wellness in life fluctuates. If we are mostly satisfied in life, we are living a good life. Realise that becoming absorbed by material wealth is mindless.

Living wellness comes from a wholesome body-mind-spirit. The current research indicates direct interrelation of the gut's microscopic living world with the brain-mind-spirit.

Our nutritional and mental ignorance creates gut distress and mental distress. A lack of internal balance between each species of bacteria, archaea, fungi, and floras is the main reason for a whole-body imbalance and gut distress. In more serious disproportions, there are predispositions to malnutrition, depression, suicidal desires, and schizophrenia.

Are we addicted to stress caused by chronic busyness? If we say too often that we are too busy, we set a trap of time by ourselves. It is also a trap of addiction to becoming busy. Very often there are no indications to being stressed, but we allow the hurried world to push us to overact. Constant despondency and melancholy influence the internal organs. Diseases, pain, and suffering are the result of the past unbalances, mistakes, and consciously failing to appreciate life. The organism is constantly striving to get in balance. Man must properly serve both in order to live in harmony in his mind and body.

The sooner you earn the value of a natural life, the better you will be able to harmonise with life, nature, and people. If we have a happy frame of mind, we can keep the body creative and in fine form to old age. Recognize the sanctity of the healthy mind and body. Sooner or later, everybody will realise that all they really want is to have a healthy mind and body; the rest is extra. Many people subconsciously or purposely neglect their mind-body and natural healing ways. They react to stress and health problems to get attention, and they rely on prescription drugs. Not having a natural way of life and not pursuing natural treatment will produce disharmonic vibrations between the mind and body. Harmony in the body-mind-spirit system depends on its condition, the way of living, and life criteria. We are privileged to live, yet some people purposely punish themselves by using the wrong information, bad food, drugs, lifestyle, and bad company. We owe our minds and bodies proper maintenance and gratitude. Take control of what controls you. Everyone can get better; you need to want it and take proper action.

Whenever we get what we want, we are still vulnerable to fear, grief, and anger, which can generate the experience of unhappiness. The best way to avoid this is to enjoy what we do have and not worry about what we do not have. The wise man says that true wellness exists in the mind. The inner space of our minds can lead us to discover never-ending possibilities. It can lead to possible ways of exploring the unknown world and experiencing the beautiful adventure of our lives. The wrong ideas and attitude in our heads make us unhappy. Thought has a great power to create a happy or unhappy state of mind. Negativity from the past and in the present creates a miserable life.

If we want to improve our lives and the world, we should know that right and wrong are man-made maxims. We should follow nature. Nothing beautiful, good, or useful can be gained without effort, because success depends on patience. Our calm reaction and wise attitude will reach personal fulfilment. Flexibility, moderation, and the middle way are the right moves to reach our goals. By channelling our life through routines and rigid patterns, we will enter a new dimension with immense horizons. Inflexibility is the shortest way to an imbalanced, harmful life.

Desires designed by powerful fights and futile ambitions are the way to self-destruction. If it is the love of a possession, it is momentary. The pleasure settles down, the things quickly go, and one is forced to pursue some other longings.

True success only comes from proper selections and the pursuit of useful results. Any satisfaction within us should aim to become longer and purposeful to quickly vanish, irritate, or harm. It is good to be a constant dreamer, but never be satisfied. You will discover as much beauty in the world as you have inside you. Also, the meaning of life to a youth, to one of middle age, or to the aged is often quite different.

All kinds of relationships, bonds, and associations are forms of exchanging energy, information, and kindness beneficial to each other. Overall, they're improving the expression, meaning, and quality of life. All effort to achieve success, and all success achieved, enrich each other. Our mental, spiritual, and physical energy stores until we are ready for success. Conscious life is the best teacher. The mind is programming and creating itself. Our wants and desires are governing us and creating illusions. The wrong idea in our head makes us unhappy. "Good luck" can be invited by wider, deeper understanding, and with action and determination, it creates opportunity. All attempts become positive and powerful forces. Then we will see clearly and wisely enough to come up with effective and positive ways to interact with people and situations. A small number of words starting understanding, smiles, good wishes, love, and peace means much more than the masses of senseless, negative, hurtful thoughts, words, and actions.

> "Science and technology may be in part responsible for many of the problems that face us today - but largely because public understanding of them is desperately inadequate (technology is a tool, not a panacea), and because insufficient effort has been made to accommodate our society to the new technologies."
> —Carl Sagan

It is nature's law that always includes the positive and the negative. Human existence relies on the paradox of bipolarity, and it is a continuum of positive and negative. The true form of mental training is to evolve to an equilibrium.

Positive and negative forces or evaluations are about each other. It is impossible to judge one event as positive without seeing other events as negative. Positive thinking is a similar kind of mental activity as negative thinking; it is the other side of the same coin and thus inextricably linked to it. Let it be; let it happen. These are golden sentences, and these phrases refer to a deep acceptance of the fundamental processes inherent in life.

To be upset over what you don't have. Is to waste what you do have. Our desire multiplies so much faster than our capacity to satisfy them. Nothing outside of ourselves lasts long enough to satisfy completely. Continuous happiness is not realistic. Right and wrong are man-made precepts, and these have no basis of stability beyond the earth. There is one very important and difficult task in human life: it is about adjusting the Mind-Body-Spirit to the trinity of time, space, and matter. In the universe of the mind, there is no time, no space. Our main task is to find harmony with whatever you have for the attainment of health, wellness, and peace. Joy and wellness are the indicators of balance in a human structure. Practicing love develops a non-critical attitude towards life and people. Love brings more contentment than competence.

The opposite factor of love is not hate; it is fear. Love that is not expressing itself and growing with more freedom will die. Almost every person feels a longing for companionship; union is the beginning of growth as individual and as a unit.

Marriage makes the most sense when two conscious beings are in a fusion of minds and bodies. There is stimulation and enrichment. Marriage companionship is a great path for development; a soul mate is a complement to the self. Marriage helps each other at the physical, mental, and spiritual levels. Acceptability (the first level of love) improves the interactions of individuals and groups. Staying true to yourself empowers you. One's own self is very difficult to subdue. It is easy to be a bad man; what is positive and useful is very difficult. Controlling oneself is much harder than controlling others. You must try to grow mentally and spiritually. If your mind is well balanced with plenty of experiences, life will be lived to the full, securing happiness and success. A healthy mind and body are the results of your constructive thoughts and choices. Good thoughts will produce good action and happiness.

Self-analysis promotes happiness with the courage to face life and the will to fulfil dreams and ambitions. Happy people live in "no time." If you allow the bad, impure ideas and thoughts to dwell in your mind, then expect to lose your way. Also, we should understand that it is more important to be the honest person than to find the desirable person.

Being able to remove wrong thoughts and ideas is more important and challenging than removing tumours and abscesses. The majority make themselves suffer. Long travel in the right direction is more productive and enjoyable then a short trip with delight. Great rewards usually only come from great efforts. No one can expect to succeed the first time.

Progressions of small success in a variety of things are more fruitful than achieving one overwhelming desire. We cannot get joy from an unbalanced life. We must learn how to achieve the state of balance in our own nature. Acquiring real knowledge is the existential necessity; it leads to wider perception, deep consciousness, and the right choices in our life. Life is the best teacher.

Lack of love for life is responsible for most of the discontent in society, as well as lack of communication, world conflicts, and world pollution. Love brings more pleasure than friendship or skill. Love fulfils quicker and better than a respectable life.

We need to remember that we cannot justify ourselves in becoming selfish, angry, jealous, resentful, scary, or greedy. The sense of life game is to emotionally accept the unacceptable. Regardless of whether we get what we want, we are still vulnerable to fear, grief, or anger, which can generate unhappiness. Through understanding we lose fear, we start to take control, and we are more positive, meaningful, and creative. Man's destiny is to develop constantly and consciously on all levels, with more freedom and greater expressions of life. It will work if you work honestly and with the right knowledge.

You have unique things to share with the world. You must use your originality and your uniqueness, if you want to be happy and successful. Our thoughts, words, and actions manifest our understanding and creation of our lives. Our actions and ideals conform to the self. Life means producing unique forms of fulfilment in life. Everyone makes his own life, and each person has a unique way of being in the world. The enchanted man is very dynamic, very generous, and conscientious of all men. A healthy man enjoys his prolonged existence and vitality. Any lack of joyousness prompts body-mind disintegration. Men creates one of the most disastrous stresses: stress on each other in everyday life. Through the rat race, man acquires a frosty and ruthless outlook on life. He is going far away from the real enjoyment, the real achievements, the real meaning of life.

Nature is change; nature wants us to use our uniqueness to cope with our lives. We should enjoy life while we are here, taking all joy from each day. The secret of a good life must be the general harmonious and wellness of life. Think realistically about your life possibilities; do not exaggerate it out of proportion. Accept what is irreversible. Accept yourself. Worry does not help. Cooperation is better than competition. Set up high-quality relationships with people you trust and with whom you can be yourself. Try doing things that are new to you. Challenge yourself by starting some new hobbies. Go to places you have never been to. Do not be afraid to think, use your own knowledge, and make your own conclusions. Know what you want and take care of yourself, other people, and the universe.

Enjoy openly the accomplishments of others. Improve the quality of life. Take the short way; do not waste time and energy. If you start something, finish it.

The spectrum of understanding describes our freedom. Ignorance limits concerns about life, restricts our experiences in it, and changes the dimensions of the truth. The law of life is that pain and joy, conscious and unconscious, are in equal measure in the meaning of life. Everything is mixed with positive and negative, good and evil, agony and wellness. The law of life takes proper care of life. Nothing can change the law of life, the law of nature, or the law of matter and energy. Life offers in all its moment the number one law: change.

Sensible Living

We dream to fulfil our dreams, to be without unceasing prayer.
To be without somebody's will and mercy. To be without limitation of our potentiality.
Life is about privileges of choices, the fulfilment of life.
Expand endlessly the quality of your life.
The most important and deepest crusade is the search for meaning.
Do not be afraid to think.
Start one of the longest journeys: into yourselves.
Learn about yourself and your limitations so you can improve endlessly.
Learn to see yourself. Stop, look, listen, and think.
Find your real inner truth and be in harmony.
Pay attention to the present; do not dwell in the problems from the past.
Learn how to find your new way. Use the best path of your life.
Actions originate fortune. The true happiness is to fulfil your potential and abilities.
Do not expect too much wellness in too short a time. Allow yourself to be well.
Nature makes variety; use your differences to create a unique life.
Find your unique differences; they can make you to prosper.
Too often we sacrifice our individual way of life because we are afraid to be different.
Don't waste yourself—use your time properly. You are your most precious resource.
Create time to become not your master but your ally.
The best time to learn about illness is when you are well.
Suffering and joy are cooperating teachers.
Do not waste your time with excessive TV watching.
Do not watch rubbish TV, porn, or violent movies; do not play
destructive and addictive games. They will deviate your true self.

All things that we have via wickedly cravings will sooner or later become damaging.
Challenge yourself by starting new hobbies. Try doing things that are new to you.
Go to places you have never visited.
Take proper care of your mind-body-spirit.
Look for quality relationships and friendship.

The quality of a relationship's time is more important than its duration. Defend your personal freedom. Recognise good housework and mothering as real accomplishments. Self-expression of your uniqueness enriches everybody. Do not strive only for material achievement; improve yourself mentally and spiritually. The real achievement is not recognized by money, but by usability for the nature and people around the world. What will justify losing yourself for chasing money? Workaholics will become invalidated mentally and physically. A happy mind produces cheerful thoughts in those who are around him. Select friends; avoid aggressive, ignorant delusions. Submerge yourself in creative pursuits like music, art, writing, science, and more. A life without things to live for is like an empty vessel without a rudder. Every man is a potential perfect state with natural ability; with experience and practice, he can create a beautiful and unique life. Even very happy people have problems, but they've learned how to control complication and accept the inevitable. Even a little positivity will improve your future. After many millennia, the primal human characters do not change. Still, we have the good ones, the average and bad ones. Take proper care of yourself, people, society, and the ecosystem. Remember to be grateful for every moment in your life, which is also the farewell for the previous one.

CHAPTER 2

EMPOWER YOUR MIND

"Every atom of matter is intelligent, deriving energy from the primordial germ. The intelligence of man is the sum of intelligence of atoms of which he is composed. Every atom has an intelligent power of selection and is always striving to get into harmonious relation with the other atoms. The human body is, I think, maintained in its integrity by the intelligent persistence of its atoms, or rather by an agreement between the atoms so to persist. When the harmonious adjustment is destroyed, the man dies, and the atoms seek other relations. Man, therefore, may be regarded in some sort as a macrocosm of atoms agreeing to constitute his life as long as order and discipline can be maintained. For life, I regard as indestructible."

—Thomas Edison

The mind is a hub, and everything circles around the mind. True ideas about the mind will change the whole world. If all atoms configure themselves towards balance, then the atoms in our body and brain will produce balance too. From this point, we are on the way to being fulfilled and happy in our lives. Moreover, we should help atoms and energy waves to not fluctuate in the wide spectrum of changes. All your mind and body feelings, your consciousness, are fragmentary and temporary. Research and life have proven that the mind's and body's greatest potential are unlocked by the effects of proper nutrition, regular sleep, exercise, relaxation, and stimulation. They are the universal keys of true health and harmony for a happy and successful life. Be a positive thinker; enjoy yourself and your life. Invest only in things you love. Love yourself enough to create your life.

> "If you do not love yourself totally, wholly, and fully,
> somewhere along the way, you learned not to. You can
> unlearn it. Start by being kind to yourself now."
>
> —Louise Hay

There are some rules about right thinking: how to act, rules for the right ways to use time, and rules about reward and punishment. The more mental you are, the more wellness you create. You deserve all that you and your love create. You create the powers to serve you, and they will serve you if you use and respect them. Self-esteem is the result of a relationship that you have with yourself, and it is randomly formed during childhood.

Good luck can be enticed by accepting opportunity. Action will send you to the success you most desire. Men of action are favoured by the goddess of good luck. Where there's determination, the way can be found.

A conscious and independent mind believes the following:

1. Everything is possible.
2. Flexibility and openness means no yeses or nos.
3. There are no authorities or boundaries.
4. Natural curiosity means starving for knowledge.
5. Self-reliance from the body is supported by good gut microbiota.
6. Free will is supported by good gut microbiota.

Human and Life Problems

Every human being must confront problems because they are indispensable to evolution. It is impossible to evolve without having problems to solve and difficulties to overcome. Control your emotions not by repressing them but by understanding them. All of us will experience dark periods in life; they are the fate of every human being. For the wise man, they are stimulating inner challenges and opportunities to evolve. Face them responsibly; then you can overcome them, and they will hasten your evolution. Don't live in the irritations or problems of the past. Focus on what is happening now.

All our media should stimulate, educate, enlighten, and guide people about real problems and real enjoyment of life. Most of media changes people's sensitivity, awareness, morals, and ethics. They open the way for artificial values, voiding all kinds of motivation. Everyone should follow the conduct of the wise and honourable man, but instead the masses follow the shallowness.

Very often we overlook and misuse our gifts by ourselves or through the persuasion of others. Do not mix yourself with miserable people, which sabotage their own lives, or else you will start feeling low yourself. Do not over-strain or try to save too much money. Never accept money from people unless they are willing to give it to you. Take time and distance; they increase the significance of words and will increase your certainty of the willingness of others to help you.

We can learn far more from pain, disappointment, failure, and loss than we can learn from prosperity and success. Now, it will be good to contemplate on Andre Agassi's statement.

"Winning changes nothing ... A win does not feel as good as a loss feels bad, and the good feeling does not last as long as the bad. Not even close."

—Andre Agassi

The more I think about it, the more I think it is correct for the human mind to become the centre of everything else. Everything is promising, if we do not lose harmony between the fundamental psychological, spiritual, and physiological systems.

One day we can find that without consciousness, all becomes an enormous void. Take out the consciousness, and everything disappears, including us. Consciousness is the vibrating waves of energy and matter; it is information. All information saturates space and all forms of consciousness. All forms of consciousness affect all forms of energy and matter.

Many thinkers support the statement that the mind is both the projector and the screen. The human mind becomes a miniature of the universe. The connection of neurons in our brains expand like the universe. Nature plus the mind equals the micro universe. The human biofield interacts with everything around it.

Matter <-> Energy <-> Information <-> Consciousness <-> Matter

"I doubt all things and am certain of nothing."

—Descartes

If you truly doubt all, can you doubt of yourself? What can you expect from life? What do you expect from yourself? Become conscious of your thoughts, ideas, and dreams. Make them better with constructive imagination. Doubts and worry will restrain or conquer your progressive dreams and visions. Do not let problems dominate you, but instead let them stimulate you. They always include occasions that you can convert into new circumstances with sensible opportunities. Enhance the creation of your own life by resourceful flexibility, by better solutions and prospects. Permanently visualize your future with joyous expectation, and forever take care of your hopes, ideas, and wishes.

Correct and full concentration every day will prepare you for the next day. Your life today holds factors creating the magic of tomorrow. Your thoughts, desires, and dreams create your future. Thinking is the extraordinary ability to analyse, create, see, and reflect on the new visions of reality. Throughout the consciousness, we discover hidden things and the human ability to become co-creators of the universe.

As we venture through our inner lives, some of us become enemies within the self. It all starts with deception to the natural social instinct, which is about honest interactions. How does it happen that we created a society where people act dishonestly? When the first white men arrived in Polynesia, the natives could not understand what lies and dishonesty were. Today we need integrity, honesty, and political and religion tolerance as our quest for the future survival of humanity.

Working of the mind changed drastically in the digital era. We refined some of the mind's ability in processing the huge amount of information, but usually it's not related and without patterns. We are paying too big a price for it; we lost the depth of concentration. The depth of our understanding depends on our preconceptions and our ability to think deep and long.

The digital era clearly creates shallowness in our minds. Can we redesign it? Yes, we can. We must come back to handwriting again. There is a mysterious connection between writing, concentration, memorising, and seeing the whole world with a wider and deeper perception.

> Chinese characters do not constitute an alphabet or a compact syllabary. Rather the writing system is roughly logo syllabic; that is, a character generally represents one syllable of spoken Chinese and may be a word on its own or a part of a polysyllabic word.

> The Chinese writing system is the unique phenomenon in the modern world of alphabet scripts. Instead of a few dozen letters, it has developed thousands of complex signs or "characters" that represent morphemes and words.[2]

---

[2] https://en.wikipedia.org/wiki/Written_Chinese

The oldest and the longest used written system in the world is Chinese. It began about 3,500 years ago. Chinese writing is sophisticated and became an art. The complexities of Chinese writing need more neurons to memorise it, understand it more deeply, and create extra space for personal interpretation of what one can see, express, and understand. It is one of the reasons that Chinese students excel in universities around the world.

Ignorance is our worst enemy and **will l**ower life performances. Pity and humanity's disaster were created in the past, which wasted evolving time and a treasure trove of information in burned books, demolished art and buildings, the killing of wise men, and much more. The mind is an effect of computing gathered information by the mind-body-spirit. Where it starts and finishes is a mystery. The mind's power is enormous; it creates our daily existence and our relations with the external world.

If humanity is divided, then more problems will arise, undermining our future. There is the ancient teaching about humans' origin from sunlight. We are the children of the light, describing and exploring ourselves and the universe by continuously expanding our consciousness. For the conscious being, the universe becomes the home.

Our understanding and consciousness are telling who we are, where we are going, and who we will become. Our interpretation of reality is the reason for contentment or excavation to collapse into extinction.

Not living consciously harms us, others, humankind, and nature. Life wants us to exchange our life energies. We are the refiners of energy. Fear is the negative life force. Love is the positive life force. We are the life, and we are the change.

Can Consciousness Be Unconscious about Itself?

Be aware of your thoughts. If you are in the company of difficult, harmful, negative people, then change company, otherwise you are going to lose too much of your energy and time. Create your own affirmations and gratitude. Pessimistic streams of energy are taking a lot of lifetime and energy, leaving us not acting properly and often powerless. Optimistic streams of energy are constantly charging our bodies and minds with surplus life energy, pushing us to a courageous variety of action. A personal sense of existence is not enough to be happy and be in balance, embracing the universe. We need to live with a sensible approach, and then content life will start.

Realise that we know and understand nothing of everything and something of nothing. However, it is the only way to progress. It is amazing that 99.9 percent of everything that exists around us is unknown.

Thinking about complexity, philosophy is an essential and continual work of human minds. We need an association between philosophy and various sciences in order to see clearly the whole of life and nature. A proper understanding of a relationship between properties of nature and man depends upon a synthesis of statements and suggestions made by all sciences, particularly by natural philosophy as a mother of sciences, an essence of knowledge, or a honey of knowledge.

Why are we here?

Why are you reading this? This is not a coincidence! In the universe of energies, there is no coincidence; there are fields of interplaying forces. There are forces of interconnection and synchronisation in all. What happened happened because of interconnection with everything. Life originated from nature's principles. The mother of science rose from rational contemplation on nature. Human thoughts and the whole body are in constant interaction with all vibrations that exist in nature. If we cannot understand and talk with ourselves, we are lost in the two worlds, the inner and external. These two worlds are essential to obtain the highest form of consciousness, contentment, and peace. Don't lose your chance; respect your origin, your life, and all that you are.

We are here to learn, rectify our energies, rise our consciousness, exchange energy, and improve. We're meant to find some wise thoughts to widen our understanding. We are here to experience the goodness of life. We are here to enrich and empower each other, to give and take. Life wants us to be united, to use our unique abilities to create a better now, to build together the enormous organism of vibrant humanity. We need each other. We all are the conglomeration of single cells, but we are connected, and we are in the constant process of developing humankind. We can succeed and survive if we use honesty, friendship, love, and cooperation.

"Intellect is the satellite of Deity."

—Archytas

It is much wiser to take under consideration that something can be true, than to reject any information without examination. Who relies on authority and memory only? Sooner or later, one will be confused by misleading information. In the mind is the constant battle between light and darkness, wisdom and ignorance.

What is your real ability and chance? Regret becomes a double loser. He who knows himself lives a more effective and enjoyable life. You only live once as a unique appearance, so enjoy it and make the most of every minute. Remember that the power of inner peace is the highest competence.

Civilisation needs natural philosophy and higher thought, which design new way for humankind to come closer to and cooperate with nature. Natural philosophy is the union between nature, thoughts, matter, energy, and vibrations. Higher consciousness creates higher contentment and a tranquil mind, which are the supreme prize in life.

By contemplation, our brains can find relationships and regularity in accidental irregularities. The results will often come as flashes of intuition, glimpses, hunches, ideas, sensations, and sparks of imaginations. On the basis of philosophical reflection, we will start our search to generalise human experience and knowledge about life. We search for meaning in human existence by rational methods of analysing and understanding human life. We are the citizens of the great state-world.

Try to live a good life with all your effort (mentally and physically) in order to get the best possible outcome, by properly looking after yourself. If nature will send you away from your existence after many years, what you can say? You should be happy that it happened to you. You are the owner of a moment, going to meet all in the void of non-existence, which are other moments of continuation in quantum levels. Thinking without concentration or reflection cannot bring illumination. Freethinking is a research of everything in anything. We will gain nothing on trust and doctrine. Freethinking is a thinking of probabilities, chances, and prospects. Freethinking is open to doubt and reason; therefore, true thinking is positive, efficient, powerful, flexible, provisional, temporal, and infinite. Freethinking is a living, unfolding thinking. It is a progressive and evolutionary thinking. Such thinking at the beginning needs many attitudes, outlooks, and possibilities.

"Man's true nature is to be citizen of a free state."

—Aristotle

Wise men choose freethinking as a non-limited style of life, where tranquillity is the guard of a balanced, harmonic life. There are certain problems that any philosophy must seek to solve, such as nature, the mystery of creation, the nature of life, and the destiny of man. Understanding comes from a system of differential diagnoses, logical deductions, and intuition on a number features. Intuition is the brain's shortcut, running above the speed of the light. In the end, we create our own destiny. The attempt to explain the unknown universe via scientific explanation is mostly unsuccessful; we need more facts and basic information about everything. In general, we may say that if we grow together with scientific knowledge, at the same time the universe will grow by space, by time parameters, and by unlimited new phenomena. All scientific concepts in the past and present are developed by changing facts and information, a new approach, and new understanding.

"Ideas have consequences."

—Richard Weaver

Anthropic Principle: The Universe Is Compatible with Life

Physicist Freeman Dyson said, "The Universe seems to know that we are coming." By rational education, we can generate a new way of life and create resourceful criteria of life to serve men's needs. We must make certain drastic changes in the educational world. Conservative movement formalises and institutionalises all kinds of education in such a way that masses do not need information and do not feel an urge for inner development. The average man is in a crisis to process various information.

To know and understand the universe, we should be a collaborator and rival. After that, we have a chance to participate in a relay race of consciousness and intellect. You should understand that you need only use all your time, energy, and opportunity to collect knowledge that comes your way. Many parts of knowing create understanding, which becomes a part of wisdom. The people from the east have long known that true wisdom lies within the individual, and that it wells up from within when given an opportunity to do so. Wisdom provides fuller wakefulness and a wider spectrum of reality. Prosperity reflects the wisdom concept. Everybody needs a principle of selection for his own life, and such a questionnaire will guide him through the world of perception, knowing, and understanding.

We do not know how the atomic consciousness supports itself to prove the operation of its interior and cosmic actions. You can invite this infinite intelligence to solve any problem that concerns you. We are all on the way to discover who, what, and why we are. How dramatic the effect will be for the majority of us if we realise what is going on between the man's world and the whole universe.

The knower of truth is far above the mind and its complication. The mind is always in motion if the brain is alive. Action in the mind is where we live our lives and where we create our future. Ancient knowledge supports the myth that we are our own creators, we are pure consciousness. The main, fundamental nature is our open, rational minds; this is the essence of being human. Did not Aristotle define man as a rational animal?

In our world, we should recognise the inadequacies of the present scientific method for a study of man, nature, and life. It leads us to find a new, pre-scientific, and sometimes very ancient methods that will be more adequate for revealing the nature of man and life.

> "Listen to the mustn'ts, child. Listen to the don'ts. Listen to the shouldn'ts, the impossibles, the won'ts. Listen to the don't haves and listen to me. Anything is possible, anything can be."
>
> —Shel Silverstein

Everything Is Possible for Humans

Everything is possible for humans. Everything is perceivable by the mind and is a product of the mind. We should realise that the majority of phenomena in the universe are not perceivable by us. The mind brings us quicker, closer, and safer to the truth of life, and it helps us understand more of the designs of the universe. If we will not live with a balance between man and nature, eventually we will be under the mercy of the environment, and then we will have no choice and less control. Many scientists predict humanity's fate, but many leaders and the majority of the population do not listen enough and are not aware enough.

The duty of all philosophers is to restore a gradual change in human minds in a direction that will set up a balance between the mind and body and a balance between man and nature. Every sensible step in everyday life is a practical contribution; it is a summary of wisdom from the whole life. To develop in the right direction, we must take into consideration the knowledge and conception of all earlier civilisations. We are here to learn and leave more for the next generation. We are still travelling a road that has been the same for past civilisations; they were (and we are) profoundly seeking a solution to life's mysteries. We are struggling to discover who and why we are. Moreover, we discover what science has sought after and is still seeking. All science stimulates and remodels our lives, and for this reason, science is too important to be left entirely to the scientists.

> "I do not create: I only tell of the past."
>
> —Confucius

All our next changes are the next creation. Life, the universe, and the future are constant creations of change. We exist with those who now create our society, and with those who will emerge. What we do, and what we learn and create, not only offers pleasure to us but also adds to the source from which others may originate gratification. We try to learn more about ancient civilisations—things we hardly knew. We all respond to environmental conditions in a similar way, so our basic feelings and responses are mostly the same as our ancestors. In the era of quickness, we have less time for reflection than our ancestors had. Our present civilisation has developed so much technology that in order to survive, we must learn from the past. We find the cycles of civilisations and cultures: they decline and disappear, and therefore we want to explore how information and ideas are passed from one civilisation to another, and how essential knowledge disappears through ignorance, fanaticism, and madness.

All people share the same earth and have the same desire to live, and to live fully. We travel on our lives' experiences, so our psychological, sociological, spiritual, and philosophical fundamental needs are different. Such needs will grow up in quality if our mental faculties intensify. Exchange of information between men should be freely available, and the honest Internet is a good way. However, lack of rational human interrelation and communications have become a common failing, and now we are too competitive to cooperate and trust. Information in many resources has become infected by disinformation.

We live in a human jungle. We live in a new era characterised by rapidly accelerating changes, deviations in behaviour, and lower human values. I think that overpopulation, unhealthy food, drugs, and addictive digital gadgets are the main negative factors creating isolation, competitiveness, aggression, racism, and a lack of tolerance. We need to improve communication and consciousness. All of us are living elements dependant on coexisting together.

> "A perfect civilisation is one in which art, science, religion, and industry
> are equalised as the result of balanced thought and action."
>
> —Walter Russell

Many people are in ignorance and insensitivity because they depart from quality, beauty, and well-being to a self-indulgently destructive lifestyle. They can miss the superb and beautiful experiences of life. In order to be unique beings, as nature creates us, we need great courage, which is our duty to life and Mother Nature. True courage puts first the ethical value in all our actions; it is controlled and empowered by reason and truth. We can see the external world only after it is filtered by our minds, hearts, and guts. That is the reason why healthful, generous, kind, wise, peaceful, and rightful people are the last to worry, hate, and be afraid.

Mind Destiny

"Destiny is not a matter of chance; but a matter of choice. It is not
a thing to be waited for, it is a thing to be achieved."

—William Jennings Bryan

You create the greatest treasure, which is your own mind destined to become the universe itself. The mind's creation of destiny depends of what kind of information is ruling the mind. Different information creates a different destiny. We exist in the world of our creation. Enjoyable life in this world is the effect of proper understanding and correct daily action. The mind's destiny is a way to contribute in the scheme of things. Its destiny is the self-realization and the mission to enrich, enlighten, and inspire. Different kind of media create different destinies and special forms of dependency. Information controls the mind; true information secures the best destiny. Unfold the best in your mind with real knowledge to secure the best future. We envision a world that encourages expression of the highest self, resulting in peace and prosperity for all. Manifest your dreams by attracting what you deeply desire and setting powerful intentions. Our dreams are a result of the nature of our character, which knows our ways. Our lives are within a dream, subconsciousness, and reality.

"All that we are is the result of what we have thought; it is
compounded of our thoughts, made up of our thoughts."
—Buddhist scriptures, the first verse of the Dhammapada (Pali Canon)

Rethink your life and make a proper, positive choice. It is a great act. If you do not make a choice, it is a choice anyway. However, too often it's not favourable for us change. Nature and human change constantly. We can use change in desirable ways. The best life is one we design ourselves. The best first investment is to invest in ourselves. Your most precious commodities are your health and time. No one can escape from time and change; they compose uncertainty of our individual lives and the earth's life.

The art of life is living in the moment with virtuous conduct. The art of life it being aware of the magnificence of life and enjoying it on a daily basis. In modern society, the individual mind's destiny is not clearly defined. Modern humanity needs to declare and commit to rectify changing ideas and values. The most important are issues about love, work, family, leisure, environment, and humanity's future.

Too many leaders of education, politics, and the economy do not have high enough standards of values, ethics, and morals. They lack commitment to the goodness of society and the environment. Their purely materialistic approach is the reason for the destruction of the ecosystem. We need more social, ethical, humanistic-orientated leaders to secure humanity's survival.

If politics, the power of money will use coercive ways to achieve control and profit. These people risk being left in the dark ages. The pressures of technology, automation, the digital age, and the always hungry economy are too big and not balanced with humanity's needs and future. With the lack of balance, society's mind is not quite ready for change, especially when everyone is facing overpopulation and an increased degradation of the environment.

Humans are like modern monkeys and are living on the branches of the tree of life. They forget that what we are doing to the tree of life will affect us too.

What is an intention? It is bigger than a wish and more intense than a goal. An intention is the force that combines the power of your mind and spirit. These forces with determination travel through the universe, collecting matter and energy. Then they create and manifest the images from your mind and spirit. Pure intention in the human world is very precious. It is invisible, but it's able to change or improve many visible and invisible realities. What you currently have in your life will reveal your previous thoughts and actions. Your present and future depends on your current state of the mind-body-spirit, you ability to make a selection via the quality of information.

Change your intention and change your life. Concentration and decency of intention determines the effects and worth of actions in life.

Autonomous Mind

"Man is a reasoning animal."

—Seneca

If your mind is confused, your life is nowhere to be found. The majority consider that we are our minds, but it is a myth. We are a collective consciousness of all our body cells and microorganisms living with us. We are a complex of information that contains our own experience and collective information.

Man is conscious of his existence and should know that he was created by nature; its laws are as an organic machine. Nature and matter share some conscious existence with the man and other life forms. Consciousness of the all that existed, exists, and will be existing is the collective consciousness of nature and the universe.

There are some similarities and consistencies between the emptiness of 99.999 percent of the universe, all atoms, and the human mind. Also, our senses can register only glimpses of reality and what is around us. Factually, we can experience it only in 0.001–0.01 percent, and the rest are not accessible by us. The good news is that an open, curious mind will never become bored and will forever will be learning, amazed, and stimulated, living in the ecstasy of discoveries of unknown wonders.

All life is about the creation of consciousness, the essential outcome of life, and the factor to create all.

Outline of the Growth of the Human Mind

The start of a new way of growth means that many new resolutions will be made. By using the mind and knowledge, we will become one with the whole universe. We can find a new way of using the mind in a rational and universal manner, to search for a proper place for man in universe. Every man's mind is less than a fraction of an atom from the entire universe complexity. Human consciousness is the energy complex of a mostly unknown structure, a spectrum of electromagnetical waves, which are also in the forms of conscious intention and subconsciousness. Such sensations imprint change in living and non-living systems, from close to immense distances. The waves of humans' and animals' consciousness in experiments are held in submarines deep in the oceans, as well as in cosmic space. They indicate that conscious waves in positive, meditative, ecstatic, panic, or tragic circumstances travel enormous distances, transferring information to change the reality in the sender and receiver places. There are also brain-body complex changes. The waves of individual and collective consciousness can circle far from our planet. Consciousness as information is imprinted on the spectrum of waves beyond the accepted four fundamental forces.

"The history of the world is none other than the progress of the consciousness of freedom."
—Hegel

The uneducated man sacrifices most of his freedom. Consciousness is one of the most delicate, almighty, and creative forces of the mysterious matter-energy. Consciousness is connecting energy-matter and all forms of consciousness by unknown forces that are present universally.

Consciousness is an outcome from processing available information, creating different mental levels. The lack of reflection and meditation indicates a lack of communication between consciousness and subconsciousness. Human consciousness is powerful creative device of nature interacting with all that exists, by quantum and morphogenetic fields and interconnectedness. Humans and all other animals store their info not only in their brains but also in biofields around their bodies. Morphogenetic fields include human and animal body fields. Human biofields impact all and are organized by other biofields from all living organism, and by electromagnetic vibrations and information from non-living matter. There is a connection between collective memory and collective consciousness, as well as with quantum and morphogenetic fields. The varied spectrum of waves carries their own information on all previous interactions with the nature-universe elements, and they become enriched by our conscious or unconscious thinking.

http://www.sheldrake.org/research/morphic-resonance/introduction

Bioelectromagnetochemical forces saturate the whole universe, and the matrix of such composition connects everything that is. Consciousness interacts constantly with bioelectromagnetochemical forces. The more you use your subconsciousness and consciousness, the faster will be your improvement of understanding yourself, life, and the universe. Super-consciousness is the multiplex of intuitive perception, intellectual processes, coded information in the genes, collective memory, collective consciousness, and quantum and morphogenetic fields. If these elements melt together, then there will be a possibility to use all systems for universal consciousness. Higher consciousness or super-consciousness is the only way to find and understand the sense of human existence in the universe, and therefore such states of consciousness should be demanded by our society. Super-consciousness tells us how far we have gone and what possibilities we have. Consciousness can be aware of itself; let it be. Realising this goal is within the capabilities of all of us and is not the special privilege of any elite. Many have been widespread and illumined, have been touched by higher consciousness, and have had a momentary influx of sublime wisdom, but such experiences do not necessarily transform one's life or oneself. Many men have just reached a new phase of consciousness, but they've not had time or opportunity to exploit or master it.

A man with self-consciousness may sink in morals and intelligence below the higher animal with simple consciousness, merely so a man with universal consciousness in certain circumstances can be a little (if at all) above another. There is a great universal force that has come from deep within us to guide us and encourage others. Our skill is an art, an inborn gift that has been polished by suffering and constant learning. These abilities and, sensibilities lie dormant within everyone. You are more close to these if you understand yourself. Anyone can use it, and everyone does in times of great emotion, often without realising. Man, with lack or distorted awareness of oneself, can block his awareness of others.

Discover your true potential by constantly learning and increasing your level of consciousness. The subconscious and conscious accept whatever we pretend is real and will use it to create outer reality. Collective subconsciousness is spaceless and timeless, and it has wide influences in our lives—personal, social, and global.

The universe is a collective entity and collective consciousness. Cosmic consciousness is the collective consciousness. Collective knowledge, collective consciousness, and the subconsciousness are the base for human wisdom. Personal wisdom of consciousness chooses and clarifies the amount of information provided by the universe.

Our essential nature is to become carriers and transformers of the individual and collective consciousness. We can ask ourselves whether it is possible that consciousness is the unintended by-product, as the composition, or an output of one stage of unconscious matter.

All previous civilisations lost themselves through the ignorance of leaders who lost the ability to think with the deep vision, and alternatively without responsibility and goodness for all.

> "All things flow, nothing abides. You cannot step into the
> same river twice, for the waters are continually flowing
> on. Nothing is permanent except change."
> —Heraclitus

The first law of the universe is a constant change. It is so ultimate that it cannot change itself. You are change. It is our right and our duty to be never-ending change. Human life is a purifying process; it is endless development. Humans should work properly to become needed by nature, because through us the world should become a better one.

> "Make visible what, without you might perhaps never have been seen."
> —Robert Bresson

The energy of our intention and interaction, with all-around energies, creates now. Acceptance of now creates a balance with everything and ourselves.

Behaviour reflects the quality of the inner self. Wisdom, contemplation, peace, and joy refine life. In sunny and rainy days, as in hot or cold, we should realise that life is the most precious gift. We should be grateful dreamers, living in the never-ending, stimulating entertainment of life, because we can see more beauty and more loveliness in our lives.

Dreams become the vehicle to move freely through space and time. From dreams, we can create our future.

Life endlessly travels through space and time with harmony, passion, and attraction. The whole of life will embrace us. We are here to become integral participants of everything that is. Our existence describes the reality of everything. The universe is you. The mind is the collector and processor of information. You are the unique matrix of information. The universe's speech is our collective consciousness.

Where does everything come from? The whole of nature and life is unanswerable and unexplainable.

What is the purpose of thinking human? Think and you will discover and create. A thinking human should first try to find what is the purpose of life, as well as of thier personal life. If you study deeply and with passion, you will be ready to choose the best ways and useful things for your individual life. Each of us has the right to choose his or her own way in life, but in such ways that they will not negatively affect others. We are social, collective organisms.

What you think, what you understand, your meaning of life, and your value systems will control the development of your mind-body-sprit. You will create your individual levels of performance and wellness. To live on the high level of a formed life is the supreme opportunity and privilege, but it's also a great responsibility. We have the responsibility to take care of ourselves. Joyful connection with the inner self and positive relationships with those around us is the starting point for prosperous life. Wisdom creates ways for our best performances, and we also create our own doubts and ignorance.

"The chief function of the body is to carry your brain around."
—Thomas Edison

Science develops so quickly that the average mind cannot easily understand it. Desire for knowledge becomes an addiction and will be never satisfied. It is a never-ending process. Hunger for knowing increases with knowing more. There is a never-ending task to find the identity of all things.

Certain knowledge opens the door of the unknown, beyond the capacities of the average human mind and beyond the limit of instruments and machines. Antithesis creates the enigma. Truth starts and finishes the inseparability of good and evil. That is why all life is about to search for the truth. It is the best way to conduct our lives.

Truth Is the Greatest Concentrated Power

"All truth passes through three stages. First, it is ridiculed. Second,
it is violently opposed. Third, it is accepted as being self-evident."

—Arthur Schopenhauer

We are obliged to follow the truth about nature's law. First, we're investigating everything that is most important in life. Removing ignorance, weak will, and worthless desires will prove useful for our knowledge and make ourselves happier with a better conduct of life. We can learn from personal experience alone, which can become our best asset and friend.

"He who has conquered himself by the Self, he is friend
of himself; but he whose self is unconquered, his self
acts as his own enemy like an external foe."

—Bhagavad Gita (VI6)

The mind is an outcome of life forces, forever changing and testing itself. Humanity itself is one of the most evolved expressions of nature on earth, and it is constantly evolving. It seems that consciousness is the spontaneous result of all elements creating nature.

Mind and body unite to obtain real existence, where the mind is the essence of a perceivable existence and the body manifests itself. We should never harm our minds and bodies, but always choose the safe way for humanity and nature. The mind produces a state of being. It is impossible to go beyond the creation of the mind. The mind is an extension and the fulfilment of matter. Matter, energy, time, and space are the manifestation of the universe, which are self-existent, interdependent forces.

"I really admire a fellow who goes about the whole day with a well-
fed stomach and a vacuous mind. How can one ever do it?"

—Confucius

A mind is a coordinated, complex unity. The mind is a temporary division of intelligence, which in some way never sleeps. It's a beautiful, working medium, a complicated combination of all of nature's meaningful patterns. Advancing with the potential of the mind is understanding the relationship between the mind and all elements, which compound the whole universe. It is a never-ending task. Man is the product of nature and the mind, but it is not a finished result of developing consciousness from matter.

Everything that is unlimitable and immeasurable is infinite. What is infinite is imperceptible and is not easily understandable by the human mind, because the mind's existence is a finite sequence of time.

The Human Brain Is a Super Biological Computer

Before we focus on the traditional human brain that exists within the skull, we will focus on new science findings about other "brains."

Modern science indicates that humans have four "brains."

1. **The longest known: the brain in the skull**
2. **The brain in the heart: can realise self-sufficiency, what's good for us**
3. **The gut-microbiota brain: controls the brain in the skull**
4. **The brain off the complex, stored information in the body's biofield (aura)**

How these complicated systems are connected and cooperate is a mystery. The brain's information is stored in memory peptides, which are under the supervision of ancient and modern genes. Therefore, all humans, animals, and plants are gene dependent. The new genes are created in the present and are under the influence of the present time, as well as new and old genes. The size of the brain increases if the brain takes more stimulation or has new functions.

The human brain is the most secret and advanced structure in nature. It is sensitive to quantum level phenomena, and it uses quantum processes to become aware. The brain produces and perceives all vibrations and consciousness from the nature. It can feel and find the source of being seen, like humans and many animals. Our thoughts, perceptions, and brain matter connect the elementary particles, which are interdependent forces. The brain creates the reality and becomes intuitive. It is a miraculous instrument made up of sixteen billion cells, and brain neurons add up to one hundred billion, which can process about two hundred billion messages per second. The brain weight is not counted; it's the quality of gray matter. The brain is a complex of billions of electrical circuits filled by a stream of electrochemistry.

Regulatory hormones and electromagnetical circuits are the primary triggers of the brain's functions. The brain is a complex of electromagnetic, gravitational, and hormonal devices. It uses energy and produces the energy as a wave—the vibratory nature. The mind is manifested by the activity of the brain; it is a manifestation of advanced matter. The entire universe exists for us as the complex of patterns, so our brain is always searching to understand all, to find new patterns and connections between matter, energy, space, and time in order to match the past, present, and future.

The brain mind and the other three "minds" (heart, gut, body aura), as well as its consciousness, seem to be the final linkage to understanding the universe. The brain originates thoughts and vibrations, which are an essential form of matter and energy for the whole universe. Science discovers a connection between the biochemical process in the brain and its well-being. Natural substances (endorphins) in the body are released through different stimulants, producing uplifted feelings. People with a high consciousness level use such biochemical influences for better thinking and creative purposes. The human brain is not only an organ of thinking but is also an organ of survival-like claws and fangs. It is one of the most multifaceted sensory organs. The human brain can sense and assemble information from the external world by a thought-energy wave, and it can produce thoughts all the time, even during sleep.

The greatest secrets of the human mind are self-understanding, understanding others, creating reality, and perceiving the universe. The mystery is that there are no boundaries between anything; there are only limitations to our senses and no perfect discrimination by mind.

There is no doubt that our thoughts, feelings, and emotions are energies that are omnipresent. They manifest themselves in the surrounding environment, like radio and TV waves. Ideas, thoughts, feelings, and emotions are projected on the screens of other people's minds. These energies spread out in the form of waves or vibrations. According to modern knowledge, there is no distinction between material and non-material forces, like between visible and non-visible. We should remember that everything that goes into our brains can be sent outside, good and bad. Therefore we should take responsibility for it and try to produce useful, original, and good thoughts.

"The way you perceive is what you are."

—Krishnamurthy

A human is a conscious energy existing in the universe of energies. The mind of a human genius is a manifestation of nature itself. The mind is just one more event in an unknown matter faculty. Mind and matter came to be extensions of each other. Therefore, consciousness is an extension of matter.

It is a manifestation of a compound of forces, energies, movements, and actions. The mind is the best protection, and its nature is to be restless. It likes to work, and it works with unceasing restlessness day or night. When it is safe, it takes a rest, which frees the mind from overloading. Be free from external distraction and find peace regularly.

The Computer Capability of the Mind

Every thought is born from the computation of an energy vibration. Our daily existence is the outcome of the proper decisions after subconscious calculations of actual reality. Our lives are the summary of the true and false in the real world, not the virtual world.

"The mind is everything."

—Dr. Franz Volgesi

Are We Machines? This question is both too simple and too complicated. We can say we are part of the eternal continuum of the universe. We can say we are machines constructed by mighty bacteria; maybe we are the last stage of a living machine. We are empty in 99.9 percent on the quantum level. Furthermore, we are a system which is slowly freeing itself from the unconsciousness, as we are starting to use very fine, high spectrums of manifestation of the matter (consciousness). Additionally, we are also living structures that start to understand themselves, exploring and defining the continuum entity. It is cooperative with other form of consciousness in all possible ways. We can become the last sequence to make an alliance between matter, energy, time, space, motion, and consciousness. I put consciousness a part of continuum because quantum physics recognise that the mind plays an indispensable part in some of its observations and must be one of the parameters of the matter-energy-space-time-motion continuum of our universe. If nature exists and we exist, we are what nature is. Matter, energy, and vibration are condensed sources of forces, and they are a focus for other energies.

Space, time, and matter are not measurable, periodic media in the universe. Space and time bind everything, but from a human viewpoint, they seem to divide everything because human life is restricted and is partially finite. We invent time as the result of incomplete consciousness. Time can be our friend or enemy. Everything depends on our attitude, and how well we will use our time to take care of the mind-body-spirit. Investing in time to collect proper information and applying right actions is the best way. What art of life and time do you own? You will see it in the future of yourself, where free will becomes an instrument to select a pattern from the evolutionary circle or create a new way for events.

"We may have free will—but not the will to use it!"

—Schopenhauer

Humans live in a life of motion, which manifests itself only by change. We are made of elements of the reality. We are beings of matter, and more important, we have certain quantities and qualities of consciousness. Our interaction with environment increases as we progress in levels of consciousness. Human senses can only interpret a fraction of everything that is. That's why some sages (Plato, Confucius) describe human life as living in darkness. Our interactions are involved with shadows and ghosts.

To know more is to feel more; it is to be more conscious, and it means also to be more responsible and in control. Therefore it's being more cooperative and creative with the universe.

What we dare to do, we have the power to do. The amount of all information documented by the first man is colossally smaller compared to what we have today. Research and data is on the Internet. Global info is doubled after three years. Mass media condenses our living in the real world. We are more exposed to symbols, pictures, numbers, diagrams, and graphs. We are trained to solve abstract puzzles using the Internet. Our personal knowledge of how to live in the real world becomes more unreal because we're using tools and methods from computers and virtual reality gadgets.

Information overload, tempo, pressure of daily living, and isolation from the nature are factors creating chaos and illness in the mind-body-spirit. Some of the ways to improve usability of the Internet, TV, and other digital media are cleaning it from the rubbish, disinformation, distraction, constant misleading advertisements, and removing all that is not tolerant, dogmatic, unhuman, and harmful for the ecosystem.

We are overloaded by junk thoughts, junk food, and junk things. Who decided that production of goods and things, which are not useable or are harmful for humans and the environment, should succeed? Use your mind as the processor to create things which are useful and needed by others. Living is simply the learning of new ways of communicating with our reality in order to get the best outcome. Communicating includes receiving and sending information that is out there, waiting for us to be selected, assimilated, and used as quickly as possible. An inquirer must collect and analyse all information that comes, as well as all changes that will emerge.

Stress, disorder, irritability, dissatisfaction, exhaustion, offences, nervous breakdowns, depression, and suicides are some growing symptoms in the world's society. Stress by 2020 will become the second cause of death, according to the World Health Organisation.

Destressing is the process of purification on many levels of life and in the body-mind-spirit. Correct nutrition will change gut microbiota to become a major factor to create wellness in the whole body. Lack of vital nutrients, interests, and hobbies, as well as too much worrying, is a cause of stressed life. Constructive activities will break the process of worrying. Investors, researchers, and philosophers have no time for the luxury of boredom or nervous breakdowns. The human mind can occupy only one mental task. We can think only about one thing during the thinking process. Greek physicians prescribe work for worrying people. Nature saturates the empty space-mind with something else, either good or bad.

The universe and the earth existed before any religions. Maybe some of man's images of God are not enough or are incorrect. Let's try to describe God and the universe by peace, toleration, and learning from others' views, interpretations, and understandings.

"Image worship is very necessary for beginners."

—Swami Sivananda

If You Are Depressed, You Are Living in The Past.
If You Are Anxious, You Are Living in The Future.
If You Are at Peace, You Are Living in The Present.

—Lao Tzu

Nothing will educate man better than he himself will after trials and errors. The awakened man is ready to learn from the wise man. The mind can affect other minds as they blend together. It seems that a mind stands apart from the material world, but it is material in its very essence. The human mind and body are perfect examples of associations between earthly, material substances and the principals of nature's law. Everything that is distracting and unnecessary will become hostile to us sooner or later. We must work with nature and construct things from matter, energy, and vibration. We can merely describe ourselves, our own reality, and we cannot describe life and the universe correctly if we have so many limitations and mix-ups.

The first law of the universe is eternal change. Change is an absolute force that cannot change itself. Everything changes. You are fortunate to realise it. Honour it, and benefit from the unchanging supreme, which can change your life for the better. Change is necessary for living. The mind is changing too and is the existence of itself. By accepting all changes, we will have more control.

In order to be, we must be in constant change and make changes about ourselves.

Without the ability to study manifestation, there is no full understanding. Man, mind, and matter are not absolute. I conclude that the mind-brain aspect is one of the most important issues for civilisation to understand. Our civilisation is in mental development, so we must move to the next stage: a man of understanding. The evolution of man is the evolution of the analytic mind, and as such endless evolutions of consciousness create humanity.

In the cosmic infinity, there is a place for an infinity of human consciousness. Is the process of human consciousness necessarily slow and differentiated? We need about 7 percent of humanity to lead the crowds. Life is the highest manifestation and the essence of the matter-energy-space-time continuum, which never begins. Forms and manifestations have a never-ending beginning. The eternal essence of such a continuum is being in "eternal" time; then, eventually everything will be explainable. One of the best instruments to cope with life is the human mind, which is the only key to understanding the most important levels of nature's secrets. Our vast minds can hold the constant search of an infinite universe to unveil the human mystery in time and space. Moreover, we must build a good relationship with nature and all that exists. Humanity is totally dependent on the ecosystem.

In the present, humankind shows a variety of irresponsible actions and in all levels of ecosystem, which undermine human survival. We are already imprinted in the eternal circle of universe life, but how long it will be?

Processes of the Mind

> "Great minds discuss ideas. Average minds discuss
> events. Small minds discuss people."
>
> —Eleanor Roosevelt

Everything is a matrix of matter and energy. We perceive because everything that exists is sent outside in a different form of energy, whether animated or even non-organic forms. We are part of nature too, and according to universal law, we must send outside of our bodies informative energy about us. All things, as a matter-energy complex, constantly interact with everything.

Consciousness has an indispensable place in nature and in the universe. It is the greatest mystery and phenomenon. All start by quantum processes in components of our brain, from the possible and probable to the actual waves of consciousness. Consciousness is the process of understanding nature and oneself. It seems that we need to focus on consciousness first, before being able to understand the brain. Consciousness is not only a competence of neurons, but it is also a product of brain processes on the quantum level. The compilation of atoms behaves as an entity in the microtubules, which are inside the neurons in the brain.

Consciousness is the effect of the unity of subatomic elements and the entire universe. I think that some spectrum of consciousness is the basic vibration of all elements in the physical level. Our individual consciousness is the collective consciousness of subatomic elements in the body-mind-spirit, which interact with all matter in the universe. We switch on the consciousness each time when we focus on any subjects in the world. Energy and the vibration of our consciousness trigger particles on quantum levels in all matter around us. However, everything around us radiates energy and vibration. We live in an enormous ocean of energies and matter, saturating all that exist. Consciousness is also dependent upon realisation, which is an individual sensation and can be affected by interpretation from childhood to old age. There is a different quantity and quality of consciousness, which are involved in observations to interact with the physical, metaphysical, and parapsychological levels.

We have a relationship with every matter and vibration, as well as various forms of consciousness. The interactions and relationships between all energies are more important than their composition.

The emergence of complexity relates to the appearance of consciousness. The universe is already enormously complex, so it is very conscious about itself, and it is also aware about us. Christof Koch, the author of the book *Consciousness: Confessions of a Romantic Reductionist*, states that "There is likelihood that network internet may grow into conscious entity."[3]

Art of Thinking

"If a person tries to observe what he is thinking about at the very moment that he is reflecting on a particular subject, it is generally agreed that he introduces unpredictable and uncontrollable changes in the way, his thoughts proceed thereafter."
—David Bohm

Study about the development of thinking shouldn't be considered a waste of time. It is an opportunity to find more about our own evolution and improve our certain spheres of mind faculties, which are never fulfilled. Many aspects of mental development continue

---

[3] http://plato.stanford.edu/entries/consciousness/

throughout life. Too many of us die before we can develop our unique abilities and potential. Genius does not always manifest itself early in life. The process of thinking in the early stages of human life is the process of dreaming and play-acting. Other mind products are hunches, intuition, glimpses, ideas, and imagination.

Questioning with curiosity is the best stimulus for our thinking. Questioning is a skill of inquiry from ancient time. Today, it is a way to collect information and prepare for the future. It is the survival skill; it is an exploration for meaning which sometimes is more important than the answers.

Thinking is nothing else than the description of the mental and physical events by various states of energies.

A. Logical—reason
B. Emotional—feelings

Thoughts are vibrations and lead to materials, which leave impressions. Thoughts are bi-polar electric waves in a universe. Thoughts are electromagnetic waves. Thoughts are vibrations of material principles. Thoughts are not always a matter of the single intellect, and sometimes they can be telepathic cooperation between one or more minds. Yogis believe that thoughts consist of some form of energy. Thoughts, ideas, and energy flow like a magnificent river, describing themselves.

Everybody has a different pattern of thoughts. Some become freethinkers, and some become very lazy or even afraid to think. Others are unwilling to change their thoughts, and their lives do not work for them. They see the world as affecting them, and they feel powerless to create their own world. They are unaware of their energy or of others people's power affecting the world. There are millions of people focused on creating something, and they have ideas.

Fear of thinking is the fault; it is a cancer in ourselves, cutting off possibilities and free will. Thinking is an art of mental creation without boundaries. Your clear thinking with proper action will decide your quality of life. For higher levels of thinking, we must not stop, and we must not be afraid to think about everything. For proper thinking, the mind needs to be free. Think of what you want rather than what you do not want. If the foolish man tries to be good, he can become good. However, if he pretends to be good, he will become more foolish.

Thinking processes in peak consciousness need considerable energy used by the brain. Human thinking is a wave of energy pulsation, and it can only be described by a new wave of creative ideas. Intellectual powers are the ability to select random data into analytical patterns, after deep systematic analysis and synthesis, to find the universality of nature.

All thoughts and emotions set up vibrations of electromagnetic energy, which human, animals, and even plants register through their systems. I must mention water too. Water has some unexplained secrets, such as its ability to pick up wide spectrums of vibration from the environment. Water changes its molecular structure under the influence of mental energy, and it distinguishes positive and negative energies. We are 70 percent water, we absorb and radiate energies, and we are changing constantly too!

Water is often defined as an organically lifeless chemical substance, with some different progressive forms in the cycle from the atmosphere to the sea. Water is not always normal water; there is heavy water with special qualities.

Concentration is the master art; all other arts depend on it. Part of concentration is complete relaxation. Through good concentration, we reach higher perceptiveness because the other distractive external and internal stimuli are blocked. Concentration and relaxation also create energies—the messages from subconscious. All levels of consciousness work on different frequencies.

I took part in navy diving-school experiments in 1971 in Poland. I remember isolation ecstasy after being isolated for many hours from most sensory input in an underwater floating tank at body temperature. I could hear blood moving in my blood veins and arteries. My heart worked as a very noisy pump. I was physically isolated from an external environment. I became a floating mind, which started concentrated on itself. I experienced an unknown world, where many unknown or complicated things become simple. I understood myself better. Also, I remember other forms of ecstasy during decompression from pressure of nine atmospheres. An ecstasy and euphoria at a high-attitude plane or balloonist causes a break-off of the mind; people lose contact with the earth. Mountaineers' experiences are similar. Mental energy must make effects on the universe and vice versa; such energy transforms beings and things. Telepathy and love are some examples of the energy to which there can be no resistance. We have a tendency to feel limits of living energy, as well as limits of free will. Humans have a tendency to behave in patterned, predictable ways. Many people believe in fate and destiny, and they build traps by themselves.

If precognition cannot always give a perfect degree of accuracy, it becomes the next statement, a conclusion against fixed human life. I don't think that in our world, there could be no freedom for the individual to shape his own future. Fatalism exists only for short-minded, average human beings. When civilisations grow up, there are more people with enough mental ability to understand, control, and create their own destinies.

I see clear association between precognition and the enhancement of free will. A model of precognition based on quantum theory is a good step for the outlook for free will. Oxford philosopher J. R. Lucas has commented about it in The *Freedom of the Will*.

Ways to Mental Proficiency and Mental Equilibrium

To achieve much, one must go beyond materialistic thinking. Such a man can be aware of never-ending possibilities in his creation, but no one can achieve that if he is alone. There is no fear of being limitless, because nature is limitless, and men, as part of nature, cannot be less than nature.

Understanding human existence is temporary and partial; it depends on the individual mind's ability and time. Mind power becomes unbalanced when it is not used lovingly.

Self-observation is an art, and it is difficult to see things objectively. One should step back and watch oneself from a distance, from a wide horizon. Mental sense of self-identity is not created from having a body. In life, nothing is as treasurable as a healthy body-mind-spirit.

"When one tugs at a single thing in nature, he
finds it attached to the rest of the world."

—John Muir

Anaxagores introduced the concept of mind as the original cause of the world process. "All things are in the whole." The Anaxagores philosophy introduces a spiritual and intellectual principle.

Not many men can efficiently use their minds. You exist through your mind. It is impossible to give a complete explanation of the world only in the mechanical view. Our life is bound by a future possibility towards which all of us and everything move. Between the past and the future, we formulate the present, which we can claim as our own.

In the lifespan, we must use our ability and potential. We must originate our achievement, ambition, and hope. The precious gift of life is a mental faculty; this is a source of consciousness.

Life is a constructive energy which counteracts death. The first step to being free from the fear of death is to understand the law of change and the eternal nature of all that is, the energy-matter-vibration. Love is also life's energy, but many humans start to love more the artificial environment, the virtual life, and material things over other humans and nature.

The Observation Theories

Our world is filled with real objects that are adequate for our lives, which are very slow in terms of speed. However, sooner or later, everything that we catch by our sensory system will disappear. Not existing in time, floating on an amorphous sea of infinite possibilities, reveals probabilities and realities. Inspection and reflection change the observed reality.

The observation and perception (measurement) of the wave of energy causes immediate changes in possibilities and probabilities, and only a few events or things actualise. The vast ocean of probabilities vanishes only for this unit of time. We do not yet understand the precise nature of human perception, certain ideas of information theory, quantum theory, and neuropsychological research. However, all appear to be connected directly with the brain's creation of reality. Brains are oscillators, storing information in a holographic form. Brains can transfer energy (thoughts) un a simple way via "sympathetic resonance" between two or more people. Telepathy works on this principle. All brains produce electromagnetic waves at their own natural frequencies (self-frequency).

The yesterday of the world exists in a never-ending, universal cycle. Humans, animals, and plants create a record of memory about earlier events. Each man is limited according to his own mind and dreams. Joy of life is the peaceful, balanced creation of life by a healthy mind-body-spirit.

Collective Unconscious

It is the level of awareness that links each human being with the unconscious minds of friend and relatives, as well as with the mental process of all humankind. The human unconscious forms a point of contact with the consciousness of animals and plants. The total sum of these levels of the unconscious mind is known as the super-conscious, equated to magic with man's personal divinity.

Meditation as the communication with the universe is the most important function of human existence. Meditation and deep thinking are vibrations on the quantum level. Meditation is an alternative consciousness. Through space in meditation, we can try to understand it more. The effect of meditation is peace of mind. Some sportsmen have taken up meditation not to experience the harmony of the inner self with the body, but to obtain better concentration to sharpen their competitive instincts. How often do we take the new in order to serve the old purpose. The study of nature through meditation will heighten our awareness of the cycles and energies surrounding us and our lives. Meditation is as natural as breathing and as thinking. During meditation, one releases peace-giving hormones.

Reflection and meditation are the highest self-expression A higher perception and concentration implies a higher consciousness. Each person must find the correct development required for his mind. There is no boundary between concentrations, meditation, reflection, and attention. There are only different forms and varieties in quality and quantity.

Imagination

"Logic will get you from A to B. Imagination will take you
everywhere. Imagination is more important than facts."
—Albert Einstein

In life, nothing is more precious than the power of creative imagination. Your imagination is a most powerful energy-sensing and energy-creating tool. You have been given an imagination to create things unbounded by belief structures. Imagination is not bound by time and space; it is not bound by your physical body. Imagination is the quantum process creating the facts. The quantum process builds a matrix of high-probability patterns by the creation of a precognitive imagination and ideas.

The world of images is the source of power in our physical world. Imagining what we want is like creating a model before we build the real thing. The images, pictures, and symbols direct the energy in our bodies. We will become unlimited if we find imagination and determination to understand it, take it, and use it. Mind and imagination can control the body and cause physical reactions. Humans are as significant as his decent life created by his imagination.

Unlimited imagination creates unlimited life. An imaginative mind is the secret to freedom. Your relaxed imagination is a powerful energy generator and a sensing tool. Imagination is not bound by time and space; it creates things and your reality.

We need time to dream, reflect, do a sensible thing, and occasionally do nothing. We can be freer if we have more choices and alternatives. To be freer is to be more creative. Man has always struggled to become the master of his own life, which gives him the natural right to compete and not to surrender. The secret art of the mind is to understand itself and be creative. Our "invisible" powers are thoughts, intelligence, and intellect.

Mind Is the Creator

The more we ask cardinal questions on our world regarding the indefinable mystical and scientific, intellectual ways, the more universal answers we will get, and the more relevant things we can discover and create.

The human mind is an information system which is programmable by itself and by nature. Some types of programs originate all levels of consciousness, where consciousness is not a modelled product of the mind but is only a fragment of what is oscillated between all states of consciousness. The subconscious accepts pretending as real, and it will create the outer reality. The mind's essence is the knowledge and power to alter those circumstances. Intellect must slowly become natural dominance; it is an attempt to conquer mundane death. It is an enormous freedom with endless corridors of opportunities to explore space and time, and you limit yourself only by what you think you can or cannot do. The period of learning and inquisitively investigating is a complex system, and it includes the active mind and the deep feeling of nature. There is an absolute spaceless, timeless cosmos in which both the soul (psyche) and the material universe are manifested. Mind and matter came to be extensions of each other. Mind and matter are in coexistence for meaningful coincidences.

Some important points are:

- Effects are alterable.
- Change the consciousness, and the circumstances must change.
- Consciousness is the common medium for all human minds.
- Consciousness is not so much a matter of what you see in life, but how you look at it and process it.
- Change is the essential synthesis of nature and life.

Our subconscious minds communicate with the subconscious minds of others. Our ordinary perceptions are only parts of the holistic universe and perception of the universe itself. The sooner you earn the value of a natural energy wave, the better you will be able to harmonise with life and other people. Only those who are not afraid to think take their lives seriously, and they want to fulfil their lives. In every moment, we create thoughts, ideas, hopes, and results; we create our lives consciously or unconsciously. Matter is and must be the absolute medium of the mind complex. The mind is more active than ordinary matter. All the superpowers of men are developed by practice upon the mind's power. The mind's power becomes unbalanced when it is not respected and not used lovingly. In order to live in harmony with the body, mind, and spirit, man must serve all. If a thing is too different from what humans can believe, they will not see it. The hard thing to do is to make a decision for the long term in a human life. To live in harmony, we need to find something to appreciate about everything and everyone.

The most important habit is a daily duty to do everything to support and improve the mind-body-spirit. In each moment of life, we must think positively, forgiving and acting properly to create a better way of living. Admit and estimate each thought, as well the next level of prospective attainment. If it is creative, make proper choices and take the proper actions. Life will always become better, if it is transformed by our thoughtful actions. Remember that your wellness is the supreme prize in your life. Celebrate your creations by thoughtful contemplations.

Extrasensory Perception—Precognition

Extrasensory perception (ESP), knowledge, and skills allow us to experience the fundamental unity of consciousness of all human beings with each other. The mind connects the inner and outer events through a collective unconscious. The secret of ESP lies within the unconscious, and all the magician's supernatural powers are only a manifestation of primordial instincts, harnessed and directed through his willpower.

Prediction is a very important function of the brain; it is nothing else than modelling the new possibility of the future. If it will work on the vast base of facts, statements, and synthesis, then it will become a true precognition. It always surprises me how everything synchronised seems to be in a universal order that overlays all activity. The mind is our way to connect with everything, and our common sense of life is to explore this connection. The more science probes into the unknown, the more findings support the interconnectedness of everything that exists. Moreover, it is consistent with ancient knowledge. Subconscious information stored within man is unlimited because it's not only him but also the existence of all his ancestors.

Mind unfolds the synchronising world because of our interconnectedness. Synchronism is the law of consequences, of coincidence in time. It is the force that moulds our physical destiny in this world and regulates our misery or happiness.

In the human historic process of creative endeavour, our mental boundaries have been enlarged with an extensive vision beyond the human body and mind. It is vital to know that any research of wider or ultra-narrow subjects, without development of our inner nature, becomes a futile attempt. How many people can produce new ideas, innovations, and unique ways of creation? The majority has a significant achievement. A very small number of people have reached the highest flights of intellect. We should open more chances for the minority with heightened awareness and intellectual curiosity. Some people can understand much of their subconscious minds.

The peaceful use of psychic energy is not the only motivating factor to survive as a whole civilisation. We cannot afford to ignore the possibility that paranormal functioning may have something to contribute to the survival of humankind. The secret of hunches lies within the unconscious manifestation of the primordial instincts, harnessed and directed through willpower. Intuition and instinct come from the subconscious mind. Intuition and instinct are inherent in everyone; these senses have become dormant in modern man through a lack of practice. Intuition is an important key to understanding man's social, mental, and spiritual development. Science and intuition are one and the same as a source of knowledge: nature. Science and intuition, and their dependence upon each other, build a specific road to understand nature.

New research shows two other sources of intuition: in the digestive tract (gut feeling) and in the heart (heart feeling). Animals have some intuition and intellect. Intuition is mostly programmed knowledge and information shared in our lives and in genes from our ancestors. It is an expression of treasure, of our subconsciousness. Intuition is a calculation, a manipulation of a natural matrix of information in the way of synergism, which was available to record by our ancestors and by us.

Physical manifestation about anything cannot be claimed to be outside the physical universe. The channel of intuition is faster than other informational channels because it runs independently. Intuition and instinct come from the subconscious mind. Inspiration and intuition are the result of interaction within the inner universe and mind, where super-consciousness arises, expands autonomy, and gains control over existence.

Imagination, inspiration, and intuition are the language of electromagnetic waves through which men and universe intercommunicate. The good explorer of life is an unprejudiced man with an open mind who is ready to embrace any new idea that is supported by facts. In laboratory experiments, evidence shows that a person with a sound mind can perceive and experience events distant in both space and time, which can trigger the out-of-body-experience (OOBE). ESP is an important key to understanding man's social, mental, and spiritual development.

Precognition can work in a way that we can connect ourselves to the space system and collect through our subconsciousness all information and thoughts produced by all people. To associate and select information, we can use our consciousness because all of us send thought waves all the time. We can also sense others' feelings, inclinations, and personalities. Precognition is a pre-collection of possible events or impressions. Our brains somehow can remember everything. Our long-term memory (evolved memory) becomes our precognition of the future.

There is a prediction of the future economic, social, and political trends regarding using the process of analysis, extrapolation, and psychic integration, in which the lines between normal and paranormal become indistinct. When a sensitive man and his followers advocate psychic energies as being extrasensory, fanaticism is often substituted for open-mindedness. For years, mystics have smiled mysteriously and told us that we are limited by the world only because we believe that we are limited by it. Laboratory experiments suggest to us that anyone who feels comfortable with the idea of having paranormal abilities can have them.

Between birth and death, there is a flexible time under our command; it is all that we have. The greatest time waster is worrying about the future or dwelling in the past; you are wasting the present. Learn and make something of your existence here on earth.

Life and the universe are a very unusual time-product. We should follow our constructive dreams, visions, and plans; then we will love our lives. Conclusions are partly made from a register of memory. Memory is a recollection of actual events or impressions, but we can't live life in the same pattern again. Life is unique and one-way only, and it will never repeat the same path. That is nature's law.

> "Desires are only the lack of something: and those
> who have the greatest desires are in a worse condition
> than those who have none or very slight ones."
>
> —Plato

Exercise your consciousness, because the habit, pattern, and routine will slow your awareness. Consciousness is being lifted only by a small percentage. Humans are slow in consciousness evolution.

Consciousness is the continuous creation of models about time, space, and relations. In addition, the determination driving towards ambitions, goals, and dreams is vital. Consciousness creates a continuum between matter, energy, time, and space. There is a cosmic heritage within each human being, and between the personal existences, consciousness, and the universe, there is a concentrated interrelationship.

The continuum of mind and body is a universe itself. In order to enter it, we have three different gates: consciousness, subconsciousness, and super-consciousness. These are all forms of energy vibration produced by the brain. One of the proper ways to understand a mind is to understand it by its form and mastery of expressions. We find more evidence that the human brain owns a wonderful auto-guidance system.

From our ancestors, we developed lower consciousness to fight off external dangers, and over 99 percent of the population uses their brains by blaming the outside world for any bad experiences. High conscious people have a choice, because they can reprogram their biocomputers. The first step is to harmonise our energies and actions with the outside world. Destruction of the balance between the mind-sprit-body faculties is the greatest curse of ignorance and laziness. The truth guides itself and arrives as facts. It's a truth we can get only from nature.

Ask yourself why you want to live. The answer may be surprise you. We will find that if we are healthy, are not hungry, and have a proper roof above our heads, we always have enough to have a happy life.

What would bring you the greatest happiness? It is the celebration of your life. Appreciate and improve your mind, body, and spirit each day. It is a never-ending task to evolve. We enjoy life when we are doing what we like, we are stimulated, and we live a full life.

Does what you seek lie within your potentiality? Have you the physique, the health, the intelligence, and the will to reach it? If it is the love of a possession or control, it is temporary and an often illusive object.

True love is the most powerful energy; it's uplifting, healing, and uniting. Sometimes jealousy and possession interwoven with hate, pain, and imbalance will damage people's mind-body-spirit. It's more important to find a way to create pleasure that is more permanent. Leisure cannot be a single kind of stimulus, but a procession of satisfactions within us. Most people need a constant supply of appreciation for their mental health and personal happiness. Each moment when we are aware, we appreciate that we are alive and are together with life and nature. Then such moments become the gate to enter the new world of our own creation.

Everybody can use the explosive power of the mind, which can maximise health, happiness, and spiritual well-being. We chase the enlightenment, and the quicker we run to grasp it, the quicker it will escape from us. However, when we stop to ponder with the right thoughts, and when we ask ourselves and the universe the right questions with good intentions, then the enlightenment will arrive at the right time.

"Do not think the Buddhas are other than you."

—Dogen

The whole universe is the universal ocean of energy and matter, which as a medium connects everything. Our lives are the matrix of energy-matter possibilities. To know that we know creates more joy of unknown options.

"The energy flows where attention goes."

—Unknown

The best quality of each ingredient creates the best interaction, as well as the best outcome for who you are and what you will create. Everything counts: each thought, sip of water, and piece of food combines for who you are internally and externally.

Eternity with our consciousness is weaving the journey patterns of our lives. All our energies are useless if we do not know how to use them. The man is the transformer of all energies into mental energies, imagination, and consciousness, which create all. Everything is in us. Life is the constant trails. We are the result of all that we live. A positive attitude creates positive reality. We collect failures and turn them into successes.

People who are truthfully content are content throughout their lives. True contentment starts after we accept everything (especially what we cannot control) and do what is positive and possible. We can share contentment respectably with everybody. Peace of mind is the greatest treasure that man can have. Each of us must search for it individually, because no one person's peace is the same as another.

In the universe, nature, life, and the mind-body-spirit, there are main principles. Order in change. Order through change. Compensation. Emerson explained, "For everything you gain, you lose something." For all what you fight to get, you must also fight to keep.

Health-giving time is the gift of life, not money or material things. We make time a reality, we create values based on time, and time is an invention of man by which he measures his existence. Whatever kind of time and the quality of life you own, you will find in your future. The reason why we must look forward or back towards the past is because time itself is a great illusion. Time can be your friend and enemy. Everything depends how well you use your time to take care of your mind-body-spirit. Investing in time with proper information and actions is the best ways of living. If man will free himself by the mind, he can select the way to live his life.

Life is not for showing off. Life is about sharing, exchanging, and consciously changing. Life is about being content, but not living with other people's expectations. We should live the best in each moment. Life is the great adventure, changing all the time, but such change is our hope and is the opportunity, a way of improvement in channelled life. It is a very good idea to learn from outstanding principles and deep, practical thoughts.

TADEUSZ NOWICKI

Our love for life:

- lets the inner self-wisdom make decisions
- opens the ways to everything that is important to us
- redefines our present and existence
- becomes the entry and exit in our lives
- is the best way to stay calm
- guides us to the correct way in life

CHAPTER 3

ART OF LIVING FOUNDATIONS: AIR, WATER, FOOD

"The part can never be well, unless the whole is well."

—Plato

Many of us don't know enough about food, water, or air, which we use daily. Good health and life need proper care every day. Lots of people poison themselves by polluted air, water, and food. They do not have the knowledge and resources to change it. Truth, health, and wisdom are your greatest lasting asset.

All that we have is the mind-body-spirit, so the best investment of time and effort should be directed to protect and develop them. Resignation from a healthy lifestyle is the quickest way to die. Learn and do everything that is best for your healthy mind-body-spirit, which is a source for everything else. If we lose health, we lose everything.

You are the summary of your past. The healthy condition of the mind-body-spirit is the result of using reliable nutrition and information, and intellectual, spiritual, and physical exercises. To have the best info, you need to have the skill and access to find anything you want. Your approach should be straight to the point and full of truth. Do you really have enough knowledge to live a healthy and content life?

Everything is about real knowledge and true information. The truth collects every day and is used all the time. Truth is very often eradicated by ignorance, greed, and power. The whole truth comes from nature, and it stands above all, but it can become your servant if you focus, learn, and respect it. Truth unfolds with understanding. Truth is relative and absolute;

it will never fall into disuse. Truth and the love of life are inseparable. Love of life will bring the truth. Walking with truth is a privilege of the noble, learned, and reliable. All of them will experience wellness and oneness, which is the purpose of life. Life and nature do not tolerate the errors and deficiencies. All processes in the body-mind-spirit are interrelated. Wellness in life is the outcome of right thinking and right doing only. A wellness diet is about natural quality and quantity. Illness is the effect of combined complications. So many people wish to be happy, but they should know that wellness is the gradual process of refining the mind-spirit-body, as well as a good relationship with nature and life. Living such a life will secure a solid base for the individual's future, as well as humanity's future.

Millions of people have many problems and diseases, but ask them if they know why it happens to them! They do not think or act properly. Many social, mind, and body problems are the effects of human ignorance, unnatural ways of life, and weak will. Ignorance is the main reason for producing and using the wrong food.

We live in a time where humans create most problems in the body-mind-spirit and in the ecosystem. Such dissonance will produce self-inflicted disorders, disease, and degradation of Mother Earth. Only humans create ecological disaster, not nature. If we have a polluted environment, then we have polluted air, water, and food. Living in such conditions will not create a good future, and we will annihilate ourselves!

A high percentage of all problems are the effect of eating highly processed foods, which create bad gut microcosms. It is our duty to be aware about injurious conduct of life and nutritional ignorance. Average people have a habit of eating an average diet and average food. The ancient discovers so long ago knew that bad food triggers diseases. All healing starts by correcting the diet. Healing is an instinctive, self-activating process in the presence of required essentials. A natural healing ability must be supported by natural, whole nutrition.

Good sex heals too and shares the energy of love with your partner and all life. Moreover, it creates access to the wider life and the universe. Be grateful with the right partner; two create a whole.

"Let thy food be thy medicine, and thy medicine be thy food."

—Hippocrates

Maintain, rebuild, and enhance your health. Allow natural water, organic and natural food, and living food to guard your health and become your best medicine. Why do we not honour and value health before its absence? Analyse your health before you're ill.

The kinds of foods that you ate in the past create habits, which conduct how well you are now and how well you will be in the future. All foods we eat affect the health of the mind-body-spirit. Healthy nutrition is key for wellness, which is your choice. Highly processed food has cumulative effects, creating toxicity. All processed foods are inferior sources of energy, which can not provide good energy output. Your body, like all matter, is condensed energy.

For good performance and whole health, we need unspoiled, unprocessed, and nourishing food. The basic function of life is to replenish our energy with high-quality nutrition. We need more research for valuable information to take control of our health. A positive outlook in life makes constructive energies in the mind-body-spirit. It is a part of rationality, self-discipline, and self-respect. Positive, stable, emotional life enhances our estimations, rationalizes the mind, directs life's duties and pleasure, and corrects problems.

Do not treat just symptoms. Fight the cause of the illness and prevent it. Be aware that prevailing medicine too often is mechanical medicine, surgically oriented. Additionally, medication mostly treats only symptoms.

Current medicine doesn't focus enough on interactions between the mind-body-spirit system. We should analyse also air, water, and food as causes of many diseases.

Air

The Terrifying Science of Air Pollution

Through the lungs, we absorb and collect more minerals and pollutants than from the food and water. We inhale an enormous volume of air every day, about eleven thousand litres; it's even more during sport activities. If quality of air is inferior, then we have toxins in all organs and body cells. Indoor air is generally more polluted than outdoor air. The common symptoms of breathing polluted air are sneezing, itchy throat, nose, coughing, irritable eyes, and fatigue. Long-term exposure creates lung disease, heart disease, and cancer. Our homes become polluted by internal and external causes like smoking, mould, cleaning substances, cosmetics, air fresheners, fireplaces, stoves, burnt food (often from toasters), candles, insecticides, insects, dust, paints, chemicals from carpets and furniture, and a wide spectrum of bacteria and viruses.

The whole of humanity handles creating a polluted environment by saying that we should escape our planet. Air pollution changes the air on physical, biological, or chemical levels and in visible and invisible ways. Air purity decides how many kilogrammes of minerals and other pollutants we will absorb via the lungs. Millions of people each year die early after interior and exterior air pollution. There are many toxins in external and internal environments. Outdoor pollution is two to five times less than indoor air pollution. Polluted air causes asthma, a variety of infections, cancers in the lungs, and chronic obstructive lung disease. It relates to dementia, Parkinson's, Alzheimer's, heart disease, obesity, diabetes, arthritis, and interrupting the immune system.

Ultrafine Particle Pollution

We have no regulation for ultrafine particle pollution, which triggers neurological degeneration. Ultrafine particles get past our nose, travel along the olfactory neurons into the brain, and can damage neurons and even the brain's immune cells, the microglia. Long-term immune response and chronic inflammation with other environmental factors can trigger neurological degeneration like Alzheimer's and Parkinson's. Throughout our lives, we accumulate exposure to all pollutants. Everything breathing needs clean air to live. Living in a good atmosphere will extend life.

All pollutants that are released into the air are more destructive than water and land pollutants. The number of airborne particles suspended in a home's air can become ten times worse by burning the toast, which is unhealthy anyway.

Ways to Improve Quality of Air[4]

- Reducing, reusing, and recycling
- Conserving all sources of energy
- Car-pooling; public transportation
- Stopping the production of heavy crude oil and producing light crude oil will bring air pollution down by 40 percent
- Introducing efficient regulations about engines; making better filters, purifiers, and humidifiers
- Choosing clean energy resources and energy-efficient devices.
- Using plants to clean and enrich our air; potted plants improve the quality of air

---

[4] http://www.conserve-energy-future.com/causes-effects-solutions-of-air-pollution.php

Water

Water, like everything else, is in a state of change. Water is the fusion of two gases to become one of the most enigmatic substances. It exists in different forms and creates life.

Water belongs to the ecosystem. Water is the universal agent in many forms, which penetrates and unites everything on the planet; it is the greatest solvent. Global water is one body. Today in the global water crisis, water divides people. We have now water wars.

Healthy water is alive.

1. It has a memory-vibration of infinite cycles: seas, oceans, rivers, lakes, wells, springs.
2. It has a universal subatomic structure, as well as many forms and states: rain, snow, ice, steam, and liquid. Water performs a spectacular dance of life through its states: colour, taste, smell. Water has a complete form of energy by using two governing powers; male and female energy cooperate in water.
3. If water is alive and makes life alive, it is a life-giver.
4. Water embraces all vibrations, information, energy, emotions, and music.
5. Human emotional, vibrational, voices, and intention energies can improve water or make it unhealthy.
6. Artificial, unhealthy frequencies pollute and degrade water and humans. Many water towers and water tanks have cell-phone transmitters.

Our body has four oceans.

1. Blood water system
2. Lymphatic water system
3. Cerebrospinal water system
4. Each cell of our body has its own ocean of water.

Water is the most important substance to replenish in our four oceans. All need plenty of water! Our body fluids are a mix of water and elements called electrolytes, which produce positive and negative charges controlling heart rate and other body functions. We need the balanced volume and chemical structure in all body fluids in order to be healthy.

There are many ways for eliminating body fluids: tears, urine, bowels, perspiration, and the lungs' respiratory process.

Water has the ability to "listen" to music, record emotions, and memorize them. The morphogenetic field (theorized by Rupert Sheldrake) collects all information, energy, matter, and sensations in the form of vibrations. It interacts with different forms of matter and energy. Water has the memory of the patterns of life, as well as the intrinsic patterns of nature, which start on quantum levels and then embrace the whole universe. Positive intention, gratitude, prayer, singing, and music enhance water properties. See more at www.co-intelligence.org/P-moreonmorph.

We are water. All our thoughts, intentions, wishes, and projects should be positive and constructive, because all energies will affect us inside and outside. Water is more important than food. Without water, we will live only three to four days, but without food we can live up to three months. Water is the bridge to nuclear reaction and nuclear medicine (homeopathy). Water can heal us, or poison us if it's polluted.

There is no other flexible nature element that has more virtuousness and blessedness in its nourishing and nurturing proficiencies then mighty water. Water is the base for life and human health, and it's an inevitable element for the body and food. It is a component creating the whole, the conscious and spiritual human.

"Water can be changed in structure without any change in composition."
—Rustum Roy

Our body is mostly water. It is no coincidence that water covers more than 70 percent of our planet, and around 70 percent of our bodies is water; it's a larger percentage in an infant's body. On the percentage basis of hydrogen and oxygen atoms, our body is over 99 percent water. These numbers indicate what the first element to restock is.

In many countries around the world, about 90 percent of the population is permanently dehydrated! By lack of water, we poison ourselves. Chronic dehydration causes chronic diseases.

Chronic dehydration is like a slow hydrogen bomb blast, causing degenerative diseases, obesity, depression, high blood pressure, asthma, allergies, digestive disorders, constipation, skin disorders, urinary infection, respiratory troubles, rheumatism, chronic constipation, and a shortened lifespan. Chronic dehydration is a slow death. Observe the colour of your urine; if it is clear or light yellow, it is good.

Dehydration Affects Mind and Body Performance

We dehydrate ourselves by not drinking enough water, and also by cooking and frying the food, which disintegrates many nutrients, minerals, vitamins, and trace elements. Dehydration is common in various activities, causing fluid loss of 1.0–2.5 litres per hour. It will cause malfunctions in the body's tasks, which are very connected and produce general symptoms like heat exhaustion, cramps, and heat stroke. Dehydration starts with minor warnings: thirst, irritability, dizziness, headache, lack of energy, lethargy, constipation, colitis pain, confusion, and muscle spasms. Deeper dehydration causes chills, brevity of breath, gastric ulcers, dyspepsia, urinary tract infection, joint pain, back pain, muscle cramps, nausea, and vomiting. Many people are permanently dehydrated with signs of angina pain, peptic ulcer, asthma, allergies, morning sickness, frequent infections, dry skin, mouth, hair, and kidney stones.

The virtuosity of hydration focuses on distinguishing water from liquids. Drink pure, filtered water only. Cold water absorbs at a much slower rate. Sugary drinks, soft drinks, caffeine drinks, and alcoholic drinks are not healthy and are addictive. Your urine should be clear or light yellow colour; the darker your urine, the less hydrated you are. The chemical contents of water in the blood circulation system resemble the substances of seawater in a similar proportion. Swimming in saltwater is very beneficial for the whole body. Our largest organ of the body is the skin, which absorbs minerals and trace elements from the seawater. Ocean water as the cradle of life is the main factor regulating the climate and the circulation of water in nature. It is sad and hazardous that we prepare drinking water and water for the garden, washing, and cleaning in the same way.

Water is the source of life, the precondition of life, and it supports life together with our planet, which is orbiting in the right place—not too hot, not too cold. Water is the best gift from nature. We cannot live without water. Water is nature's ultimate medicine, the most precious, and it used to also be the cheapest. If we understand it deeply, we will recognize the importance of water in our lives forever, and we'll endlessly act to protect it. We should remember that human life is a result of the progressive adaptation to live out of water.

Tea, juices, coffee, sodas, and other beverages become intruders and obstacles for a healthy life. The worst story is that people become addicted to them, and forget to drink the life-giving precious substance—pure water. Water has the greatest density at an anomaly point of +4°C, and it needs shade to be in its highest quality. The body requires a constant daily supply of water to support all the various waste filtration systems, which nature has designed to keep the body healthy and free of toxins. Our blood, our kidneys, and our livers require a source of good, clean water to detoxify the body after all metabolic processes, as well from the toxic exposures we come into contact every day. Proper care of the mind-body-spirit separates drinking water from chemical treatment. Water fluoridation and many other chemicals are widely used in drinking water, which we should avoid. Fluoride has ability to enhance toxicity, slow down metabolism of all nutrients, weaken the immune system, and affect the mind's faculties. Fluoro-aluminium composition is very toxic and does not provide dental decay and cavity protection. Many countries (mostly Scandinavian) stopped using this way to treat water because it relates to problems with thyroid, collagen, bone, muscle, arthritis, dementia, and disorders in all living things.

We need pure water. Drink high-quality natural spring water, which has low content of inorganic minerals. Select a quality filter, like reverse osmosis, or use distilled water. The body can use only a very small quantity of inorganic minerals in any kind of water. Too much inorganic minerals will obstruct and damage our arteries and organs. Our bodies excellently use all organic minerals and trace elements in organic forms from natural, living food. There is also very important information from ancient time that before we clean our bodies and before we eat, we need to cleanse our minds. With the first sip of water, we should consciously appreciate one of the marvellous, basic sources of life, which is water. Think about that pure blessing and being able to drink water. Love your water, love nature, and love yourself. By doing this, you will enhance the quality of water and its healing properties for yourself and everything around you.

Water absorbs and passes over our vibrations, as well as any vibration from industrial noise, electromagnetic pollution, music, sounds of nature, and our energy, thoughts, moods, intentions, and emotions. Water has a perfect subatomic memory, used in homeopathic medicine and nuclear medicine.

You can find reliable information at www.mercola.com.

Life is the Journey of the body's water. A drop of water is on a journey between one hundred and one thousand years, spanning the cycle from steam to raindrop.

We need to drink a minimum of two litres of pure water a day. Hotter climate, exercise, and laborious work necessitate more water. Water regulates all functions, from cells to organs, and the biggest organ of the body, the skin, needs plenty of water to help us to survive out of a water environment. Tea, coffee, soft drinks, and all beverages should be not considered as a healthy source for hydration. We need pure water, which will quickly flush out toxins from the metabolism and consumed polluted water and food. We excrete water through skin, breathing, urine, and faeces.

A craving for foods is a sign of your body crying for water, as well as for nutrients we cannot get from junk food. The thirst is often confused with hunger. People have a tendency to eat while they are thirsty. It is one of the chain reactions leading to obesity.

The old good times have passed when food was natural and not spoilt by chemicals and pollutants. Now we have no choice, but we must guard ourselves. It is a matter of survival! Proper understanding of the importance of water as the dominating element in the body and the ecosystem can save us from many health problems, and even from extinction. I improved my understanding about water from many sources, and I recommend the following books.

Your Body's Many Cries for Water, by F. Batmanghelidj
The Healing Power of Water, by Masaru Emoto and contributors
The True Power of Water and *The Message from Water*, by Masaru Emoto

Water circulation disturbances in the ecosystem create a degradation of the ecosystem. The water metabolism disorder in the body starts the disappearance of the body's wellness. These two systems need to operate with the same source and in the same way.

"Implosion is no invention in the conventional sense, but rather the renaissance of ancient knowledge, lost over the course of time."
—Viktor Schauberger

One of very intriguing processes of water correctness is implosion, a suction moving inward and in a whirling pattern (vortex). The vortex creates lower temperature in the water and increase its compactness. Implosion creates a pulsating field of energy. The phenomenon of a vortex was used by Dolly Knight and Jonathan Stromberg. They built a "Vortex Energiser," a spiralling copper device, to produce refreshing, soft water that tastes better and makes the lime scale soft and easy to remove. Also, the chlorine smell becomes insignificant or is eliminated. Find our more at www.implosionresearch.com.

The best water is from high mountain regions from rainwater, dew water, or melted snow or ice. It is a living water with the best structure from nature. It is a distilled water by nature, collecting minerals in its journey downwards. Too much minerals in the water, or a bad mineral composition, can clog the body's waterways.

Distilled water is a very good cleansing trick to remove harmful deposits in the body, as well as detoxify the whole organism. There is a lot of misunderstanding about what kind of water is the best. Around the world, many people, from thousands of years ago, had access only to rainwater (distilled by nature), and they thrived. It was a big enigma for me. I researched the subject and used distilled water for around ten years, drinking in the hot climate up to five litres per day. When I played tennis for many hours during tournaments, I used a mixture of lime, honey, vitamin C, organic molasses, and Himalayan pink rock salt to keep mind and body performance at its best, and to prevent muscle cramps. I used also water from a reverse osmosis system for many years; it gets a very good response from my body. I find ways to improve water on the molecular level by freezing it, and I later drink it with lime juice. I also add some raw rice grains or other living grains and herbal leaves to improve the vibration and taste of water.

From time to time, I use diluted apple cider vinegar—raw and unfiltrred, not pasteurised—with "mother," pectins, beneficial bacteria, and enzymes.

A study of the effects of water on the human body with different natural contents of inorganic minerals shows that except in special deficiencies or diseases (and for short time only), there are positive results with small quantities. Generally, the high content of inorganic minerals is very harmful for human body. We need low content of inorganic minerals in the water to be able flush out body pollutants and waste materials.

Organic minerals are in all vegetables, fruits, and animal foods, which our bodies can easily assimilate. In Australia, we have a very good quality of natural spring waters, which are hundreds of years old, and they have low levels of inorganic minerals. We should be aware that too much inorganic minerals can harm the whole body.

Swimming in clean water, especially in seawater, is very beneficial as a relaxant and as physical exercise. The largest body organ, the skin, absorbs water, as well as some needed minerals and trace elements. We not only drink water, we absorb water through the skin. We also eat water by eating vegetables and fruits. Organic is the best; it offers 50–90 percent more essential nutrients, vitamins, and minerals.

Natural Nutrition = Natural Medicine

Natural, proper nutrition was prescribed by nature as medicine in the past. It is also good in the present, and it will be good in the future.

Nature creates whole foods. The food is for us, as a source of life and medicine. Respect it and do not change it. Soil is a natural component in nature, and all that is grown in natural soil with natural fertilizer becomes whole food—our daily medicine. The presence of artificial fertilizers creates things that do not naturally exist, which forces disharmony in the mind-body-spirit. Sooner or later, we will become sick. Genetically modified food becomes a factor in disintegrating natural life.

Nature will always help us, if we will allow it! The most important battle in our lives is at our daily scenario. Start with breathing properly, drinking enough good water, and providing for the mind and body all necessary nutrients: macronutrients, micronutrients, good proportion of high-quality proteins, carbohydrates, fats, vitamins, minerals, and trace elements. That is the proper way for natural, essential nutrition as a base for everything else. For the best function of the mind and body, there is the best way to do it. We need to take care of our mind, body, and spirit in the natural way on a daily basis. Our immune system can cure everything if it is supported by natural nutrition and a healthy lifestyle. A good immune system enhances wellness, and vice versa.

> "Whether it's obesity, food insecurity, or other negative health outcomes from poor nutrition, the majority of Americans are ill-served by our food system. That's a crisis, I'd say."
> —Congressman Tim Ryan

Natural and optimal nutrition form the nutritional medicine, which is the best natural medicine and treatment. It is the way of wellness. However, living today is not easy. The ecosystem is not polluted or degraded by nature, but by humanity—which also pollutes our bodies. Humans violated the principles of nutrition and the rules for living with the ecosystem.

Since the ancient times, we have known some valuable superfoods that are also medicines. There are some mighty medicines as food and spices "patented" by nature: organic honey, royal jelly, propolis, bee pollen, bee venom, beeswax, turmeric, garlic, ginger, and apples. A majority of humanity has no idea about what a good diet is. In the old times, humans were closer to nature, and so they consumed natural food. Real, organic food is nutritious, sustainable, non-GMO, fair to human values, locally grown, and balanced with the natural world. Today as the route becomes longer from the fields to the table, the processing of food increases. The food we grow is changed by genetic modifications, synthetic fertilizers, herbicides, and pesticides. Sadly, even natural composting declines.

All chemicals used to grow anything immensely affect everything. Pesticides, herbicides, and artificial fertilizers relate to food allergies and other ailments. Chemical poisons exterminate the vast number of pollinators and the very important bees. All pollinators are essential to the existence of plants and crops. The art of healthy life requires we make well-informed decisions in the wide spectrum of existence every day. Excellent nutrition is the universal power that control and corrects all body-mind-spirit problems. Organic, whole, unprocessed food is the only way toward wellness. The earth's health depends also on soil health and biodiversity, which is enhanced by organic farming. Organically grown foods take care of your health, as well as the health of nature. Organic nourishment is a superior diet with higher levels of nutrients and condensed antioxidants, which prevent illness, enhance childhood growth, reduce type two diabetes and obesity, and extend longevity. Around 25 percent of all creatures living on the earth live in the soil, make organic matter, collect carbon, ventilate the soil, and help saturate the soil by water.

Who can you trust when it comes to the process and true information? What is truly best for your health?

Use the Medicine of Nature—Organic, Unprocessed Food

- Clean air
- Pure water
- Natural organic food
- Fermented vegetables that introduce vital good gut flora and fauna, which "digest" and conduct all your body-mind health
- Kefir, yogurt from organic (not processed), unhomogenized milk
- Sprouted seeds and juices; proteins, vitamins, minerals
- Organic, free-range eggs
- Coconuts
- Coconut oil, virgin and cold-pressed
- Cold-pressed macadamia and avocado oils
- Ghee, butter, lard, and tallow from grass-fed animals
- Nuts (walnut, macadamia, pecan)
- Fresh herbs, raw garlic, onion
- Homemade bone broth from grass-fed animals

Natural, unprocessed Himalayan salt contains more than eighty ingredients like minerals and other healing elements. The second choice is Celtic rock salt. Do not use any processed table salt! Also, don't use anything that contains anti-caking agents.

The best nutrients create the best possible, healthy mind and body. Control and enjoy your life by using optimal nutrients. Whole, natural, and fresh foods have life forces, which create life. In supermarkets, fruits and vegetables are often collected before they are ripe, and the majority of fruits are gassed and radiated. Present diet is about eating too many carbohydrates, especially refined sugars, which our body must process into fat. Processed foods often have sugar, inferior fats, and harmful substances. Treated food is changing your gut flora, and it will lower the performance of your mind and body. The next change is in your way of thinking, altering your mind. Depression and severe anger can shut down many receptors like ones that absorb natural and good food. Then the body's digestive tract creates a new cell which is unable to absorb nutrients.

Extending a diet on processed foods relates to memory dysfunction, depression, mood swings, and reproductive problems. Any kind of food polluted by chemicals, toxins, heavy metals, or synthetic hormones induces the destruction of your gut flora and then your mind, spirit, and body. Many people are robbing themselves of proper nutrition they need to be healthy. Very often they don't know what being healthy feels like. From the ancient times, our bodies are designed to eat small portions. We should eat only when hungry. Occasional fasting is beneficial for internal cleaning and balance. We need a lot of physical activities to be healthy and balance the appetite. Our ancestors walked every day up to thirty kilometres.

From the variety of a hunter-gatherer diet, we came to consume mostly grains and potatoes as staple foods. Processing of the grains removed the vital parts of the grain and exposed us to malnutrition, sensitivity to gluten, osteoporosis, constipation, diarrhea, depression, fatigue, bloating, attention deficit disorder, and allergic reactions. Grains became a staple food that we eat too often. Wheat flour is refined, with the germs removed; many grains become genetically modified. We should be using other gluten-free grains. Eat unprocessed food free from antibiotics, pesticides, herbicides, and hormones. Eat more vegetables than fruits. Avoid any kind of sugar, sweeteners, and concentrated fruit juices. Like our ancestors, we need to eat good fats as the base of your daily calories. Healthy fats come from cold-pressed oils (coconut), macadamia nuts, walnuts, almonds, ghee, organic and free-range eggs, and all fats from grass-fed animals. Eat a wide spectrum of whole foods. Create and enhance your gut flora by eating often fermented foods, or probiotic supplements.

Do not overcook food because it destroys enzymes and many nutrients. The higher applied temperature to the food, and the longer the process is, the more that valuable nutrients are lost. The worst method is frying, which is creating cancer-promoting acrylamide. This element is also created by barbecuing and by the morbid invention of the microwave. The higher the temperature used, the more degraded food becomes.

Hydrolyzed vegetable oils used for frying degrades into toxic products. Many fast-food industries use a golden formula: a blend of fat, salt, sugar, and vinegar. They use fats, which mostly are unhealthy and hydrolyzed vegetable oils, as well as other genetically modified products.

The harmful food procedures include:

- Artificially ripened in storage
- Frozen, thawed, sprayed, shined, waxed, fungicide, or tinned
- Microwaved (changes the molecular levels of food, which does not exist in nature)
- Irradiation of food
- Frying
- Long cooking times

Natural food as your medicine heals you better than drugs. Amazingly, the majority of medical schools don't pay enough attention to the natural medicine—food. We need the best spectrum of nutrients found in abundance in natural, fresh, raw foods. Proper nutrition creates a quality of life and longevity. Healthy food is your best investment, and it's the proper way to celebrate life. Food is our foundation of life. It is a miracle, creating natural relationships with all living creatures and nature. There is a healing power in living foods.

Improved nutrition changes and enriches our whole lives. Vitality is the effect of best nutrients in a state of maintained equilibrium. Illness starts from misleading information, incorrect diet, processed food, stale food, or contaminated food. Many of us experience the effects of eating wrong: very soon we will have burping, heaviness in the mind and body, and even bad-smelling stools.

Nature always supplies true facts and organic food. Only faulty human intervention can change it. True information is a mighty Power that will heal and reorganize the whole energy system, the mind-spirit-body, which expresses the universe's energy. There is virtuous information from ancient times, as well as holistic systems. Ageless insight into the art of life started more than five thousand years ago.

Ayurveda is the ancient Hindu art of life. It is the science of life, representing practical, medical knowledge to be well and live longer. Ayurveda's goal is a preventive, therapeutic approach, and it's also personal and social hygiene with lifestyle as an important stimulating factor. It acknowledges the unique needs of each of us

Ayurveda recognizes three orders (doshas), of the quantum energy: vata, pitta, and kapha. All doshas are balanced when they are equal. Bi-doshic is the combination of two doshic natures, which very often exist. Tri-doshic characters represent features of the three kinds of energies.

There are also Chinese tradition and medicine, as well as many other old healing practices.

The summary of life forces reflecting through our personality, temperament, and ability to connect with nature and universe create our matrix of unique vibrations. The life forces create the food too, and that's why food affects the body-mind-spirit. There is a close collaboration between diet and mental wellness. Our energies change constantly with our age, environment, climate, seasons, knowledge, and the most overlooked aspect of nutrition. Natural food and good gut microbiota are two of the most powerful interacting powers leading to a flourishing life. "Vata dosha" energies become disproportioned by faulty diet, the wrong lifestyle, and an incorrect philosophy of living, which creates problems in the body and mind. Ancient wisdom knows about food's influence on body and mind. Today's information about food and water confuses many. None of us knows all about food, water, and air, which we use daily. Recently, the nutritional psychiatry is rapidly developing. Probiotic and prebiotic fermented foods are the answer to correct general health and mental imbalances. More findings indicate that faulty food and bad gut microbiota trigger mood variations and mental disorders. Yoga Asana, meditation, and other stress management techniques are very helpful. Many ancient and modern tribes connect exercise to practicing higher states of awareness and enlightenment performed with enjoyment. Physical and mental exercise, which bring pleasure and joy, are followed by a higher conscious life with no separation between them. Life includes the joy of exercise for the mind-body-spirit. We are our gut microscopic worlds, our microbiome.

> "Our personal gut flora is unique to each of us. Gut flora eco-systems can change our personality."
>
> —Javier Bravo

Food and the gut's microscopic world create personality and consciousness. We are not what we eat, but we are what we absorb, and mostly after what the gut's microscopic world digests.

The first and most important battle in our lives start in our digestive tract. If the good gut microbiome wins, then our life is in harmony. The art of the good nutrition is about what is good for our body, and our gut microbiome. It is important to remember that we are constantly changing the gut microbiome, and it is changing us. Our microbiome is as unique as our fingerprints. No two snowflakes, leaves, or fingertips have been found to be the same. With all our senses, we are still limited to decipher the outside world. All that we can perceive from the outside world is only a neuronal interpretation, which easily changes under the influence of good or bad gut microbiomes.

Gut microbiota is the conductor of a symphony played by the whole body. We are not a single organism, but a living complex of different entities. We are the collective consciousness of multiple organisms, which affects our personality. When I talked about it with many people, they were not impressed. I feel that they are afraid of losing their identities.

All living organisms are living multiplexes of organisms, which cooperate to protect harmony and cooperation for common existence and the goodness of life. There is no segregation, and there are no boundaries, which was proposed in the past as an effort to understand and describe the living, nonliving, and phenomena of life. Life is the living and non living unity of matter and energy. There is no real division between living and non-living matter. Some scientists and philosophers believe that even the atoms could be conscious entities, because they find out that atoms "remember" their previous connections and location. One day we will know more about atoms and their awareness.

> "Everything is governed by one law. A human being is
> a microcosm, i.e. the laws prevailing in the cosmos also
> operate in the minutest space of the human being."
>
> —Viktor Schauberger

Bacteria are so small, but all life on earth depends on it. Even the rocks embodied by bacteria are suitable to introduce life. Evidence from palaeontology shows bacterial microfossils date to around four to six billion years back. Bacteria entered higher life systems of cells billions of years before humans. Today, bacteria are everywhere: in the air, in the water, and in the soil. Bacteria dominate by number and by weight on the planet. Bacteria are in all plants and animals, including humans and insects.

It is good to realise that 95 percent of global bacteria is harmless to humans. Earth is a microbial planet with intelligent life, and we humans are an extension of it. Ancient microbial life was the base of eighty-five of the earth's biospheres, and they evolved into mitochondria as a part of every living cell in the human body.

Each human consciousness is a collective consciousness from all body cells' consciousness. We represent a mostly bacteria collective consciousness, because they outnumber all our body cells. Bacteria represent life longer and better than any other living complex, including humans.

All bacteria are conscious, constantly computing and checking things internally and externally. They interact with other living organisms and plants for their advantages and conscious life, which they created. Therefore one can say that our conscious behaviour is affected by our aware entities.

Our consciousness is reformed by our gut-brain-mind and allows us to realise a very narrow perception of its collective true nature. The spirit and soul arises from the collective actions from all living cells, creatures in our body, and interactions with the universe of energies outside our bodies.

Life is the collective composition, which unconsciously gains consciousness from forced symbiosis with all indestructible segments of life. Nature is our best teacher, and we should learn constantly from it with respect and admiration. We learn already that mighty change is a self-organized entity. We know now that life is a never-ending collection of energy and information; it is the constructive procedure of increasing the living network, which relies on collective cooperation to expand individual and collective consciousness. Our consciousness is the fusion of a neuronal interpretation of the gut-nature-body-mind-spirit informative energies, which are mostly unknown.

It is a big advantage to know that we are not us. We were never individuals, singular entities. We are the representatives of a collective universe. It is time to know it and use it for benefit of all. There is the great union of all energies of everything that exists. Life gives all away and circulates endlessly. Ideas about a conscious universe are derived from an interpretation of Vedic teachings. The view that human life is central to existence is found in most philosophical and religious traditions. Make your life become transformative and fruitful.

Bacteria outnumber all living organisms on the earth. Bacteria is the oldest living structure (four to six billion years). Bacteria promote life and are fundamental for life.

Our uniqueness is closely connected with the uniqueness of our gut microbiota. Today, as our knowledge expands, we know more of the controlling power of our gut microbiota over us. This is a fundamental key to improving the harmony and performance of all our systems. Each of us has individual microbiota-psycho-physiological organisms.

The gut microbiota brain system dominates over the brain-mind-spirit system. We should acknowledge, respect, and cooperate with the new, enormous micro-universe of our gut governing our lives. We know already that the mind-body system produces neuropeptides, and not long ago some new findings confirmed a similar system in the gut communicating with the brain-mind system, sending more information than the brain-mind sends to the gut. Transmitting more information (stimulation) means having more control.

What is the bionetwork keeper? Bacteria act and live like multicellular organisms, which control and own the whole body. Our free will is the collective will of all our bacteria living on our skin, in our bodies, and inside our guts.

However, more information indicates that mitochondria (highly specialized, furnished bacteria) living and producing energy in the cells of our bodies harmoniously unite in collaborative action with our whole bionetwork of bacteria. The earth's biomass of the micro universe works together to bioengineer the environment. There is connectedness of all life, of all energies on this planet. Bacteria, together with other forms of life, learn to combine inorganic matter into living composites.

Microbes' Ingenuity

- Microbes first appeared on the planet as living organism.
- Microbes create life on our planet and actively modify and balance the ecosystem.

- More than 90 percent of our bodies are microorganisms.
- They organize rational social life.
- They establish collective memory of vital experiences; they learn and progress.
- They develop a collective consciousness.
- The create colony uniqueness.
- They modify themselves when needed.
- Microbes, like humans, develop constantly.
- Microbes outnumber all other organisms that are alive, and they have more genetic and metabolic variety.
- Human digestion and absorption depends on the existence of the microbe universe.
- About 80 percent of our immune system is originated and controlled by microbes.
- About 50–60 percent of biomass on the planet is microbes.
- They establish themselves at the base of the food cycle.
- All biofuels come from the microbes' actions.
- Human health and life depend on microbes.
- Around 99 percent of the microbes on the planet are uncultured.

> "In a process called quorum sensing, groups of bacteria communicate
> with one another to coordinate their behavior and function like
> a multicellular organism. A diverse array of secreted chemical
> signal molecules and signal detection apparatuses facilitate
> highly productive intra- and interspecies relationships."
>
> —B. L. Bassler

One colony of bacteria can be one hundred times bigger than the number of all humans on the planet. Bacteria have developed better, honest communication than human, as well as a social intelligence, collective memory, and something that we think only humans have: a collective consciousness. Bacteria have evolutionary powers by altering themselves very fast. Generational features change every fifteen to twenty minutes for bacteria. It takes twenty-five years for a generation for humans. Humans need one hundred years to grind through four generations. Bacteria can go through fifty generations in a day. I am surprised by modern conclusive findings from joint sciences about the important leading role of our gut micro world in human life.

More than thirty-seven years ago, as a veterinary surgeon I studied many animals' digestive tracts and their gastrointestinal problems. Surprisingly, the human digestive tract, typical for omnivores, was treated as different. It was well-known that it is very like a pig's digestive tract, and it's mostly identical to the majority of primates. If we deeply analyse everything—the universe, life, and ourselves—we will find that the most important starting point is a good relationship with our good gut bacteria. Magnificent bacteria control the whole of our bodies. They outnumber all our body cells by up to ten to one.

Life has been taking care of itself for billions of years. Bacteria built life. These wonderful organisms are the primal elements of life, nature, and us. This tinny form of life creates the biggest biomass in the oceans, land, plants, animals, insects, us, and everything that is alive. We are the composition colony of this perfect microorganism.

We represent them through our existence on this planet, materially and consciously. Our consciousness is the collective consciousness of our gut flora and upgraded bacteria (mitochondria), which are in all cells of our bodies, except in erythrocytes.

It is not a fantasy to realise that we are a tiny part of the enormous collective conscious body of all microorganisms on the earth. The ancient Vedic scriptures mention it. Gaia theory indicates that the earth's biosphere is a living, self-regulated super-organism. The good gut flora digest for us what we cannot digest, and they also produce a lot of vitamins (C, B1, B2, B3, B6, B12, K2), folic acid, pantothenic acid, amino acids, fats, and antibiotic substances. Man-made antibiotics and contraceptive pills are the powerful stressors for the good gut flora. Bad food promotes the growth of bad gut bacteria, which control metabolism, cravings, inflammation, and "gut instincts." There is a two-way information passage between the gut and the brain, but more information is coming from the gut to the brain than from the brain to the gut. Bad microbiota is responsible for ADHD, learning disabilities, autism, and obesity; harmful microbes relate to multiple sclerosis and Alzheimer's. Create your good gut microbiota by good food that's natural, living, fermented, unprocessed, unsweetened, not genetically modified, and not pasteurized. It is very clear that humans are the universe's collective living masterpiece. Dysfunction in the gut's microscopic universe causes problems in the whole body. We are the enigmatic mystery of life. Human beings are magnificently intricate, multi-levelled organisms. As the complex, we must be organised by other systems, which together create us as a separate, living universe.

Science confirms that in our guts are living, conscious colonies of microbes. They together outnumber our own body cells. Also, they have evolved bacteria and mitochondria. Taking under consideration only the number of bacteria colonies in our body, it is clear that they own us; we do not own them. Mitochondria are very important power stations in every cell in the human body.

It's no wonder that bacteria live longer than humans, and it is an integral part of the human body, because in some strains of bacteria the collective social intelligence and responsibilities are up to three times higher than collective human social intelligence.

Human genius severely degrades the ecosystem, which undermines humanity's survival. Humanity can relearn the proper way of living, and we should remember, that the body's internal ecosystem exists within us.

Bacteria have efficient, sincere communication and social truthfulness, which prevent us from exhausting existing resources. The instructions of life are not corrupted by money, economy, political powers, or belief systems. Their instructions come from the wisdom and law of nature.[5]

> "I consider the organisms which assist us to carry out fundamental living
> processes as being part of us. i.e., mitochondria, gut flora, and skin bacteria.
> Essentially everything we do in life is to help these creatures continue theirs.
> We live off of them as much as they live off of us."
> —Sky Richarde

Is consciousness self-sustaining? Is consciousness a property of the universe itself? Consciousness connects what seems to be unconnected. Most people don't think that insects and bacteria have a consciousness. All bacterial populations behave like multicellular organisms. Recent studies stress more and more that each of us stands for not our individual consciousness, but the collective consciousness from all cells composing our bodies, our guts, and our skin bacteria. Also, yeast, fungus, viruses, and parasites influence human intelligence. There is a delicate ecosystem within us, and there is a constant change as we eat differently and allow new bacteria to live in our bodies. The human gut fauna and flora microbiome is like an organ associated with our brains, together creating collective consciousness.

The microbiome is very important. The gut has 10 times as many bacteria cells as there are in our bodies, and 150 times as many as are in our genome. Microbes in the gut control synthesis of neuroactive and nutritional substances for immune modulation and inflammatory signalling. Gut bacteria influence behavior and brain growth.

> "Gut is the body's largest sensory organ, a huge matrix sensing our inner life,
> and working on the subconscious mind."
> —Giulia Enders

Some scientists consider human microbiome as a very important body structure, which relates to the brain. We are the realization of the colonies of bacteria, viruses, fungi, and

---

[5] http://articles.mercola.com/sites/articles/archive/2014/05/17/human-microbiome.aspx

parasites living in our guts. We will discover more unknown sparks of life in our bodies. Bacteria live in our guts and do all the good work. Our immune systems exist 80 percent in our guts. Bacteria produce fat, and they also convert fat, sugar, and oxygen into energy that can be used by our bodies. Our microbiome outnumbers many times the number of our body cells. We should start considering ourselves as part of the collective consciousness of all bacteria living in and on us.

Our consciousness is the outcome of the collective consciousness of all living things in our bodies and brains. The universe of microorganisms creates us and helps to enjoy individual life. Think about it, and become more responsible for all living creatures in your body. Bacteria life is intelligent and proves a thinking ability. They're intelligent, have a social life, have a collective memory with common knowledge, are competent, learn skills, distinguish the identities of other colonies, produce antibiotics and vitamins, and have individual freedom and interests. They prove the connectedness of all life on earth.

We eat and breathe for our mitochondria. We eat and drink for our gut bacteria, and then we absorb what the gut bacteria digest and prepare for us. The bacteria colonies bioengineer the environment of our bodies. They can influence our physiology, free will, thinking, and behavior. We don't own our bodies; we simply share them with a variety of colonies of living microorganisms, which help us to digest the foods we eat. Our bodies were created to become the vehicles and containers to move a living microcosm through space and time. The main point is that our consciousness is the combined consciousness of all living cells and organisms in our body. We are the collective consciousness of living biomass of bacteria flora, fungus, parasites, and viruses, which create an enormous dominating biomass.

Consciousness and intelligence are properties of life. They are the intrinsic property of cells. The new facts rectify our understanding of ourselves, of our consciousness, and of the core who we are. We are negatively changing the external ecosystem, and we are changing the internal ecosystem of our gut microbiome. We also change humanity and its social personality. Wrong food establishes the wrong gut microbiota. Faulty food is an outrageous act that does not nourish but poisons us.

Bacteria control the internal environment of the human body, as well as the whole environment on our planet. Biochemical individuality relates to the different gut fauna and flora. That is why we have different performances and different requirement for our bodies and minds. Nature creates only three nutrient categories: carbohydrates, fats, and protein. Carbohydrates include a very wide variety of carbs. With good nutrition, we should understand what the simple and complex carbs are.

Simple Carbohydrates can be natural, processed, and artificial. They are not the same for the body. They have one or two sugar molecules. Glucose, fructose, and galactose are absorbed straight, without help of enzymes. Disaccharides and polysaccharides needs enzymes to be absorb. Table sugar, sucrose, is also in fruits, grains, and vegetables. Other examples of simple carbohydrates are brown sugar, corn syrup, honey, molasses, maple syrup, rice malt (syrup), sweets, jams, and soft drinks.

One of the very addictive, dangerous forms of sugar is high fructose corn syrup, which has a loose link between glucose and fructose. It is easy to digest and is easy for the liver to build fat.

Summary of the Harming Ways of Processed Sugar, Which Is More Powerful Than Many Other Drugs

Refined sugar changes the whole metabolism of the body, making us dependent on sugar. Sugar is the best food for the cancer cells, and it causes obesity and diabetes. It restrains the immune system, disrupts mineral balance in the body (contributing to osteoporosis), and affects concentration and eyesight. Sugar can cause reactive hypoglycaemia and diabetes, damage pancreas, slow down bowel movements, and cause many issues: haemorrhoids, ulcerative colitis, gallstones, kidney stones, varicose veins, premature aging, atherosclerosis, cardiovascular disease, and cataracts. Sugar relates to hyperactivity, drowsiness, decreased activity, anxiety, alcoholism, tooth decay, obesity, lack of concentration, yeast infections, eczema, autoimmune diseases such as multiple sclerosis, arthritis, asthma, and gout.

Refined sugar and artificial sweeteners are unnatural, processed forms that damage the body.

Sugar causes food allergies and damages proteins, DNA, and cholesterol metabolism. It causes learning disorders, migraines, and depression. It is very important that even with artificial sweeteners, *nature* 'concluded to induce glucose intolerance by altering the microbial balance in the human gut.

1. Sugar can increase your risk of Alzheimer's disease.
2. Sugar can cause hormonal imbalances such as increasing estrogen in men, exacerbating PMS, and decreasing growth hormones.
3. Sugar can lead to dizziness.
4. Your body changes sugar into two to five times more fat in the bloodstream than it does starch.
5. The rapid absorption of sugar promotes excessive food intake in obese subjects.

6. Sugar can worsen the symptoms of children with attention deficit hyperactivity disorder (ADHD).
7. Sugar adversely affects urinary electrolyte composition.
8. Sugar can slow down the ability of your adrenal glands to function.
9. Sugar has the potential to induce abnormal metabolic processes in a normal, healthy individual, as well as promote chronic, degenerative diseases.
10. Intravenous feedings of sugar water can cut off oxygen to the brain.
11. Sugar causes high blood pressure in obese people.
12. In juvenile rehabilitation camps, when children were put on a low-sugar diet, there was a 44 percent drop in antisocial behavior.

Drinking Sugar-sweetened Drinks Damages Your Health

The best liquid to drink is naturally filtered water. Other liquids cause dehydration, are high in calories, and create obesity by changing the body's metabolism. Even diet soda and many sports drinks can cause obesity and cancer. High levels of sugar in drinks, with a variety of other added chemicals can damage the pancreas, the kidneys, the reproductive system, and the heart. It can cause asthma and allergies, as well as non-alcoholic fatty liver disease. The acidity of such drinks damages dental enamel and removes minerals from the body. Artificial sugars and sweeteners can cause cancer. Many drinks contain synthetic caffeine, which undermines the assimilation of magnesium and slows down detoxification. Colouring poisons the lungs and liver, damages the vascular system, and can cause thyroid cancer.

Complex carbohydrates are whole plant foods and, dietary starch, like potatoes, sweet potatoes, corn, pumpkin, and legumes. They offer a more controlled supply of energy for longer time, without the rapid increase of your blood glucose levels so that cravings are not a big problem. Sugar in its natural form is combined with beneficial minerals and a variety of fibre, vitamins, and antioxidants, which neutralize the acid produced by cells of the body. They offer many health benefits and are a healthier choice to consume than simple carbohydrates, candies, and soda. Fibre also removes some toxins from the digestive tract, and constipation is kept under control.

Fats

Saturated fats, for many thousands of years, were recognized as very useful for humanity for proper growth and supplying vitamins A, D, E, and K. Ayurveda knowledge teaches that they're extremely essential for the whole body. In modern times, they've become the "unhealthy" fats. We need them as sources of daily calories from 30–75 percent, depending on where we live. Our ancestors' diet included 35–80 percent fat. Some experts recommend only 10 percent of daily calories from saturated fats. By eating good saturated fats and eating fewer simple carbohydrates, we become healthier and slimmer, and we will lower our risk of heart diseases. You need saturated fats for healthy body and brain function. It is a golden rule for us, created by nature.

"Blindly accepting saturated fat as the causation of heart disease was a mistake."

—T. Colin Campbell

Our ancestral diet was very high in saturated fats and virtually devoid of sugar and non-vegetable carbohydrates. Today, not only do most of us eat excessive amounts of carbohydrates, but these carbs are refined and highly processed. Calories are energy, but what calories we have from fat, protein, and refined carbs make big difference. Metabolism of the body decides to store only calories from refined carbs as fat. Calories from fat and protein will be not deposited into unhealthy fat.

Unsaturated Fats have less available energy than saturated fats. They exist as monounsaturated and polyunsaturated. Rancidity is formed more often in polyunsaturated fats. Polyunsaturated fats come from soy, corn, canola, sunflower, and safflower. They are inferior oils that rapidly deteriorate and oxidize when heated.

The fundamental fats that we need are designed by wonderful nature. The average proportions of fat content in animals are:

Saturated fats
from 45 percent to over 50 percent of total fats

Unsaturated, monounsaturated fats
vary from 30–45 percent; lard contains 60 percent monounsaturated fat, which reduces the harmful fraction of cholesterol

Unsaturated, polyunsaturated fats
2–5 percent

Life is for all, but it is good for those who are well informed and trust nature. The traditional knowledge will let one live a better quality and longer life.

Sources of Natural Saturated and Unsaturated Fats

From animals, you should use unprocessed, grass-fed butter, ghee, cream, and cheese. Also, lard, duck fat, goose fat, tallow, and grass-fed meat offer proper quality and quantity of saturated, unsaturated, monounsaturated, and polyunsaturated fats.

For eggs, the best come from free-range and organically fed hens, with no pesticides, no antibiotics, and no hormones used. They're one of the top foods available on the earth, and they are an excellent source of very healthy saturated fats. Egg consumption lowered after a bad reputation of having saturated fats and high cholesterol levels. Such a "wise" conclusion lowered our health levels. Pure lard (pig fat) has no trans fats, and it is considered superior to butter. A low-fat, low-cholesterol diet with processed vegetable oils speeds the ratio of unbalance between omega-3 and omega-6 fats from a healthy 1:1, to 1:20–50. Krill oil is an excellent source for omega-3, as are sardines and anchovies—small, oily fish.

Butter

Clarified butter (ghee) is much better.

Saturated fat: 69 percent
Unsaturated fat: 29 percent monounsaturated oils, 2 percent polyunsaturated oils

From plants (the best are cold-pressed): coconut oil
92–96 g saturated oils per 100 mL
6.2 percent monounsaturated oils
1.6 percent polyunsaturated oils

It is clear that coconut oil (cold-pressed) and organic butter (or clarified ghee) are the best, because they have a high number of beneficial saturated fats.

Coconut Is Truly Virtuous and Is the Whole Fruit of Life

One of the wonders in the world is the tree of life, the coconut palm. From this tree, we can get all that we need to support human life. We will not have so many health, nutrition, or food problems, and we wouldn't have environment degradation and pollution, if we properly recognised the coconut as the fruit of life, the ultimate source to sustain life. It is a source of the best food and oil, a nutritious drink, and a source of medicine, tools, clothing, utensils, art items, and building materials.

As an avid sailor sailing in Australia and Asia, I am forever captivated by the area where coconut palms grow; I feel at home there. Coconut palm is an icon of beautiful beaches, improving ocean scenery and creating relaxed and sensible feelings. Islanders isolated from the mainland, told me, "We can survive all year mostly on coconuts. We need one coconut palm for each family member." If they rely mostly on coconut, they are very healthy and look awesome, with slim bodies. Those who change their diets, lured by processed foods, soon become obese and unhealthy on many levels.

In Australia, in Whitsunday's, where I lived most of the time, I had a nice coconut palm in my garden that supplies the best food year round. When I travel, very often I collect coconuts on the beach, knowing that I can buy nothing better from fast food shops. In the big stores, coconuts cost $3.50 each. But on the beaches and in gardens, coconuts are free food lying on the ground. Many people collect them not for their own use, but to dispose of them in the rubbish bin. It is a big waste of a natural food, mostly due to lack of knowledge and dependency on junk food.

Coconut oil is one of the best saturated oil in the world. Eating healthy foods speeds the body's recovery and enhances performance. Coconut oil is one of the most valuable gifts from nature to enhance healthy benefits for the heart, brain, skin, immune system, and thyroid. Coconut oil stimulates metabolism and has anti-mutagenic effects. Eating organic saturated fats, as well as proteins with complex carbohydrates, will create a slim body and a healthy, alert mind. Coconut oil is the most universal source of healthy fat, and it promotes whole wellness. It acts as an antioxidant and neutralizes various toxins and carcinogenic chemicals, including cosmetic care. Lauric acid is 50 percent composed of coconut oil, which in the human body changes to monolaurin and is powerful enough to kill viruses like HIV, measles, herpes, influenza, protozoa, giardia lambilia, fungi, and parasites. Coconut oil prevents the growth of many pathogenic creatures, and it is a medicine for external and internal use. The digestive system is stimulated, and coconut oil is not stored in the body but is used quickly for energy. It will not burn at high temperatures for cooking.

Coconut oil as a superfood is the best answer, with its lauric acid, representing near 50 percent of medium chain fatty acids (MCFA); some sources claim 90 percent of MCFA. They offer wonderful internal, external, nutritional, and medical goods. People become healthy, slim, and satisfied, and they don't overeat. Ancient and new information say that this kind of saturated fat is essential for whole health, preventing a variety of brain disorders and Alzheimer's. An island population eating coconut as a fundamental food is much healthier than people dependent on the Western diet, which provides long-chain fatty acids that clog artery walls and cause obesity. The metabolism of coconut oil is better than other oils, and that's why it causes weight loss.

We know a lot from old data, and now from newer medical records, that the majority of people affected with acute myocardial infarctions have high cholesterol levels. Highly refined and hot polyunsaturated vegetable oils are harmful to humans. The most health-giving ingredients from coconut oil come from organic, cold-pressed, and unrefined oil. Since the ancient time, it has been used as a wonderful oil to nourish the whole body, both inside and outside.

Saturated Palm Oil

There is uncontrolled deforestation as a way to supply the rising demands for palm oil plantations. Palm oil, which is reddish in colour, has been known since ancient man for more than four thousand years. It is highly demanded as a source of fatty acid: 10 percent polyunsaturated, 50 percent saturated, and 40 percent unsaturated. Many researchers value it more than coconut oil as the best source of vitamins E and A, phytonutrients, and antioxidants. It is the best in a fresh condition, cold-pressed and unrefined, and not with inferior toxic oxidization or processed to prolong shelf life.

Flax Seeds

These seeds hold very healthy omega-3 fatty acids, antioxidants, fibre, protein, and minerals.

The secret power of medium-chain fatty acids is explaines by the metabolism of the body, which digests them more easily and quickly then long-chain fatty acids. The body does not use digestive enzymes or bile for their assimilation; the liver uses them to produce energy. MCFA are not stored in the body as body fat, and they do not build arterial plaque. Also, they satisfy appetite much quicker and help burn stored fats. Nature recognizes the enormous benefits of coconut oil by including medium-chain fatty acids as a vital element in human mothers' milk.

Other sources of healthy super fat are extra virgin olive oil, pasture-fed butter, ghee, tallow, nuts, sesame seeds, flaxseed, chia seeds, pumpkin seeds, sunflower seeds, avocados, macadamia oil, and almond oil. All oils should be cold-pressed.

Processed Foods

Any kind of natural food represents concentrated sun energy, a life-giving source. If they are processed, then many life forces will be lost forever.

Food cravings come from:

~ Eating highly processed foods, which cause malnutrition and lack certain nutrients
~ Lacking good saturated fats
~ The collective actions of gut microbiota, which send signals for specific nutrients

Subclinical malnutrition is common in people who eat processed foods, processed vegetable oils, margarine, shortening, sweets, refined sugar, soft drinks, and refined grains.

Simple Guidelines

We should eat more fresh, organic vegetables, fruits, and meat, as well as fat from grazing animals, coconut, coconut oil, ghee, organic butter, lard, duck and goose fat, organic eggs (preferably raw or very soft), and a variety of nuts. Bone marrow from grazing animals is a superior source of saturated fat, and it can be eaten raw; it was ancient man's luxury. It is one of the best sources of fat from ancient times. Also, bone marrow is the most important ingredient for a very healthy broth soup, which quickly restores the body.

A high content of medium fatty acids from good saturated fats creates metabolic processes and encourage a low-calorie diet. A good, high-fat diet produces a natural way of quickly supplying healthy satiety, without cravings. If you do not feel hunger, you simply stop eating. One of the secrets of nutrition is to avoid eating a high-carbohydrate diet, sugary foods, starchy foods, refined carbohydrates, and grains. Refined, sugary foods cause acidosis, and then hyperactivity and hyperirritability. Human ignorance causes trauma in the mind-body-spirit. We can't replicate or improve natural foods by creating it artificially or by processing it. Life as a whole needs the fuel-energy from the sun, which is stored in natural food. Humans as a living complex need good nourishment in order to function properly in a demanding life. Humanity's health is deteriorating, so promoting prevention is the best way to health. Especially important is completely avoiding processed and genetically modified foods.

Wellness and unwellness are under the conduct of food. Healthy foods tune into wellness. Inferior and processed foods tune out the melody of wellness. "Everything in moderation" is a not wise statement. There are neglecting and negative accumulating effects after not fully eating healthy food, half-processed food, highly processed food, and food from a microwave oven. Even a small quantity of everything inferior is pushing into unhealthy habits and causes the deterioration of the body-mind-spirit complex.

Nature wisely does not create refined, concentrated, sugary foods. Man is an outcome of nature, so if you want to get control of your life, you should eat a natural, healthy diet. Do not eat faulty foods. The benefits of the natural food that is processed are lost forever. Only natural food creates joy and wellness.

Faulty foods are foods that do not nourish. If such foods do not nurture the body, they cause a spectrum of many body tissue disorders. In the time of plenty of processed foods, our bodies are pushed to deal with the development of a process like starvation by a lack of vital nutrients for our bodies. In the time of plenty, most of us are overeating; it leads to obesity and even gluttony. Too much fuel, especially wrong fuel, causes the engine to stop.

The quality of the food creates the quality of the gut microbiota, which is the most important part of the body-mind-spirit complex, and which relates to states of air, water, sunlight, and proper exercise. Today, most foods available in shops and restaurants are very hazardous. All processed foods are faulty foods because they're mostly lifeless. Processed foods speed up the aging process in the body. In the modern world, it is very hard to find organic, healthy, nutritious food. The ingredients listed are often described inadequate, hidden, or misled.

Eating becomes an art itself. It is the base of the art of living, and by ignorance, it can become a destructive, unknown game. Consciously control it by becoming well informed and selective. Obesity, gluttony, malnutrition, and starvation start physical, mental, and spiritual deterioration. We can eat a well-balanced diet, and we can be in a state of malnutrition, because our foods are polluted by chemicals, toxic substances, preservatives, colours, and additives.

All diseases start from polluted air, water, food, and thinking. Do not waste vital energy digesting inferior food over your healthy limit. You also waste time and energy eliminating the surplus of overeaten food.

"Wellness Principle—The best thing to be said about eating
foods promoted in TV advertisement is: Don't!"

—Dr. Ted Morter, Jr.

Avoid

Avoid All refined foods, potato chips, pastry, puddings, pies, cakes, biscuits, white crackers, chocolate chip cookies, white bread, dark bread with a high glycaemic index, enriched pasta, sugary cereal, candy, sugary cereals, fried foods, and refined salt.

Avoid soda, punch, fruit juices without fibre, processed fructose, sugar-sweetened beverages, unfermented dairy, and grain content in desserts. Avoid canned fruits and vegetables, which often contain sugar, salt, and an acidity regulator (acetic acid), substances from the can's lining, and metals used to weld the can.

Avoid microwaved foods, irradiated food, and nano foods. Avoid junk foods, processed foods, inferior or poisonous foods with artificial colourings, flavourings, preservatives, MSG, refined flours and sugars, and artificial sweeteners. Also, keep away from homogenized milk. Homogenization deforms fats in milk molecules into very small particles, and they cannot be properly digested. They can pass through the gut wall.

Inferior nutrition creates a very long list of deficiency diseases, which today have become widespread. Even in developed countries, where a lot of people appear to be well fed or overfed, they suffer or pass away due to malnutrition. Today, many developed countries become developers of their own chronic diseases and obesity.

Everything happens due to eating harmful, highly processed foods, which are "improved" by refined sugars, treated proteins, and hydrolyzed fats, in addition to being flowered by pure chemical improvers. Refined sugar loses many excellent substances.

Modern, processed nutrition has evolved too much from nature, and it becomes the basis of obesity, digestive tract chronic diseases, allergies, eczema, asthma, and diabetes. There are also many related conditions of gut-brain interactions, like attention deficit disorder, eating disorders, hyperactivity, autism, depression, schizophrenia, bipolar disorder, obsessive compulsive disorder, and migraines. Bad gut flora produce substances like opiates (morphine, heroin) and induce self-intoxication, which can turn into many psychiatric ailments.

Chronic diseases develop from a cumulative of harmful factors, which start as cellular inefficiency caused by toxic, polluted, processed foods, as well as GMO food, artificial fertilizers, herbicides, pesticides, and destructive drugs. Deceptive destroyers of your good gut microorganisms are all grains containing gluten, genetically modified foods, foods with simple carbohydrates, and refined sugar.

The most destructive for all metabolic processes are the combination of genetically modified grains and their gluten content. Gluten produces neurologic effects, including depression, seizures, headaches, multiple sclerosis, demyelization, anxiety, ADHA, ataxia, and neuropathy. Keep to your ancestors' diet. Various gluten intolerances can develop, with serious autoimmune forms of gluten intolerance and celiac disease. Genetically modified food starts about fifty years ago. In this period, humans changed the grains more than nature in many thousands of years. It is very clear that such rapid changes have become unhealthy for humans. Human ignorance attempts to correct the virtuosity of nature.

"Gluten can cause inflammation in your digestive system, and even cause permeability in your gut, which can lead to a health condition that's on the rise lately called *Leaky Gut*, as well as other digestive issues and autoimmune problems."[6]

Grains which are sources of gluten (protein) are wheat germ, wheat, spelt, rye, barley, triticale (a ray/wheat hybrid), farro/emmer, einkorn, kamut, durum, farina, and products like bulgur and semolina. Other grain like oats can become contaminated with wheat during processing or growing.

Gluten is often in candy, malt, sauces, soups, ketchup, soy sauce, sausage, gravy, hot dogs, energy bars, instant hot drinks, processed cheese, canned baked beans, marinades, beer, and meatballs. Sometimes we can find gluten in medication, cosmetics, and shampoos. Do not eat gluten! It is the main factor confusing the mind and causing a leaky gut.

Gluten-free grains include rice (best as brown or wild), quinoa, amaranth, buckwheat, corn, millet, sorghum, teff, and Job's tears. Grains become addictive for humans. A cereal diet is a high-carbohydrate diet, leading to obesity, which prepares a multitude of other dysfunctions and diseases.

Human intervention changes grains' gene structures. Some changes improve the grains in a way that is desirable by humans, and major changes transform the grains into something that become completely different than what nature created. Then the problems start, because humans' digestive tract and metabolic processes did not change. We have many problems to digest a new grain whose genotype changed too much. Also, the new grains have problems surviving on their own without fertilizers and pesticides.

Amylopectin-A (from wheat) raises your blood sugar MORE than almost any other carbohydrate source on earth based on blood sugar response

---

[6] http://www.truthaboutabs.com/tab-fat-burning-kitchen.html

testing that's documented in studies. This means that wheat-based foods such as breads, bagels, cereals, muffins, and other baked goods often cause MUCH higher blood sugar levels than most other carbohydrate sources. Allergies for wheat, milk etc. are the result of GM, processing of the food, also of poor eating practices and high stress level.[7]

Obesity essentially comes from wrong and unbalanced foods, which create unbalanced gut bacteria. Such bacteria prefer sugary foods. Where all processes where genetically modified grains and their gluten interact, they create a vicious chain reaction in the body. Obesity and addiction come from junk food, processed food, sugary food, eating too much, and a lack of exercise. Processed food is alien to our digestive track, and many substances trigger learning disabilities, hyperactivity, aggression, asthma, arthritis, fatigue, and mental problems.

Obesity can develop from starvation, malnutrition, lack of natural food, and lack of vital nutrients in processed food. That is one of reason why people eat very big portions. Obese people will live in the lethargy, with a lack of energy and changes in moods. Their health will deteriorate on all levels (physical, mental, spiritual).

At the start, it is not easy to break bad, addictive habits. When you become free, your body and good gut flora will take excellent care of you. You will know it when you will feel very healthy.

Avoid processed fats and foods: sugar and grains, vegetable oil, hydrogenated oils, canola oil, corn oil, sunflower oil, soybean oil, grape seed oil, safflower oil, cottonseed oil, peanut oil, margarines, spreads, and shortenings. Hydrogenation extends the storage life of oils, but it also make them solids. Processed oils contain trans fats and toxic metals, which relate to degenerative diseases, cancer, mental problems, dementia, Alzheimer's disease, atherosclerosis, and heart disease. About 95 percent of hydrogenated soybean oil is genetically modified, and it is the highest consumed oil in the United States. The unhealthy fats are unnatural fats; they are hydrogenated vegetable oils, which contain trans fats and come from canola, corn, and soybean oil. They are more harmful when they are genetically modified.

The quantity of inferior agriculture is going to kill us. The answer is quality with nature. Hybrid seed are very dependent on fertilisers, herbicides, and pesticides. They come from artificial life.

---

[7] http://www.truthaboutabs.com/tab-fat-burning-kitchen.html

Dangers of Polyunsaturated Vegetable Oils

Polyunsaturated oils easily become rancid. They increase the body's need for vitamin E and other antioxidants. Canola oil can create severe vitamin E deficiency. Excess consumption of vegetable oils is especially damaging to the reproductive organs and the lungs, increasing cancer risk. In effect, the unwellness starts in the whole body as obesity, cardiovascular problems, depression, Alzheimer's, diabetes, cancer, auto-immune disease, fertility problems, PMS, growth problems in children, and learning disabilities.[8]

Optimize your health with proper food. Live the natural way, seeking fresh, whole, raw foods that are locally available. Keep the natural way in everything.

The Puzzle of Cholesterol

There is a lot of confusion about cholesterol. We need cholesterol to be healthy, to repair the cells and organs, to stay alive. Brain development and proper function rely on cholesterol, and 25 percent of body cholesterol is in the brain.

Up to 75 percent of cholesterol is created in the liver. The adrenal and sex glands need cholesterol to produce hormones. Cholesterol is an antioxidant and a precursor to produce vitamin D. Our bodies need it so much that they produce cholesterol for dynamic functions. If we do not have enough cholesterol in the body, the mental faculties suffer: memory loss, depression, risk of Parkinson's, increasing violence, increasing suicidal thoughts, and decreasing immune system. A low level of cholesterol slows down the activity of serotonin, leading to aggression. There is a big danger in lowering cholesterol levels by Statin Drugs, which diminish coenzyme Q10, needed for proper heart and muscle performance. In effect, the body's muscle index goes down, with weakness, muscle pain, and nerve, liver, and kidney damage.[9]

Bacteria wisely share their resources better then the human race. Good, fermented foods are necessary on a daily basis. To be healthy is to have and maintain a healthy gut microbiota. We are not what we eat; we are what we absorb, mostly after gut microbiota processes.

We must go back to the basics of life, where everything starts with nature and natural food. Eating fermented food every day is the way to fix up our minds and bodies; it is the way to protect ourselves. We should learn more about our ancestral eating and cultured food, returning to whole, natural, and rich food. Fermented food is the miracle bridge from

---

[8] http://healingnaturallybybee.com/the-dangers-of-polyunsaturated-vegetable-oils/
[9] http://articles.mercola.com/sites/articles/archive/2010/08/10/making-sense-of-your-cholesterol-numbers.aspxcholesterol

ancient times, which we need to renovate the body-mind-spirit in this modern world's afflicted nutrition. We must take care of our flora in digestive tract, which are responsible for proper digestion and absorption. Change, improve, or correct your gut microorganisms; they will positively change your thinking and make you free from addictions. Establish healthy, long-term habits with a daily joy of life. Many diets indicate that cravings must be controlled or eliminated. Good, natural, nutritious diet terminate any food-dependent cravings.

But here's the hard truth: cravings are an effect and a way for our guts' flora and fauna (gut microbiota) to communicate with us about their needs. Good gut flora create good eating habits and positive, balanced cravings.

Bad, unbalanced gut microbiota create bad habits and very strong cravings for unhealthy food. It is a way in which bad health arrives at all levels of the mind, body, and spirit. Gastrointestinal tract microorganisms control our absorption, energy, body weight, growth, and immune system. It is good to know that 80 percent of our immune system is created by our gut microbiota, which are in a symbiotic relationship with the whole body system. Antibiotics destroy bad and the good bacteria, and then the problems arrive. We cannot have a good health without beneficial bacteria in the digestive system, which counteract and destroy cancers.

The mind's capabilities are negatively or positively regulated and affected by bad gut flora. Many science findings connect depression, schizophrenia, irritable bowel syndrome, chronic pain, neurodegenerative disease, heart disease, chronic pain, anxiety, and other problems with bad gut flora. All the above information is reinforced by the action of a multitude of genetically engineered foods, which are some form of enigmatic Pandora's box.

Are you unhappy? Do you have good gut microbiota in order to be healthy and happy? We need to guard ourselves from internal and external bad bacteria pollution. Also, our own negative thoughts can pollute the mind from external pollution: in the workplace, at home, and in the environment.

Ancient knowledge addressed the importance of cultured or fermented foods, which they eat on the daily basis as a staple food.

Foods Organizing Our Brains: Fermented Foods

Fermented Foods

Living in modern time exposes us to processed foods, polluted foods, and a lack of fermented foods. The majority of us live with pathogenic bacteria, which destroy the healthy balance in our gut microbiota. To have quality of life, we need to have a high quality of gut microbiota. We should appreciate all microbes for the good work they do in our digestive tracts, helping in the digestion and absorption of food. For whole-body detoxification, natural, organic foods and fermented foods are needed.

Ancient peoples used good bacteria to protect them by fermentation of a wide variety of foods, knowing that beneficial bacteria are the base of life. The history of the food and its preservation are very long and closely connected to effects on the human gut and all animals' gut microbiota. Many different cultures created intestinal health. Good microbiota create a strong immune system and mind, improve the absorption of food, and produce vitamins. Fermented food is prophylactic, working as chelates and detoxifiers to remove alloys, heavy metals, and toxins.

Probiotics and prebiotics are two elements extremely important for human gut health and body-mind health.

Probiotics

Living fermented probiotic-rich foods increase absorption. It is the good complex of food having live, beneficial microbes, which work to improve intestinal performance and microbial balance. They are in fermented dairy (yogurt, kefir, buttermilk, cheeses), fermented vegetables (sauerkraut, kimchi, pickles), fermented juice, coconut kefir, kombucha tea, tofu, miso soup, tempeh, sourdough bread, soya sauce, fufu, cultured condiments (horseradish, mustard, mayonnaise, relish, fruit chutney), and guacamole. Living probiotics are a variety of good microbes living in the gut. Humans have 2.0–2.3 kilogrammes of gut microbiota and probiotic bacteria: lactobacillus, bifidobacterium, propionibacterium, and other good gut microorganisms. All of them are live, anaerobic microbes.

Our gut microbiota are recently recognised as a new sensing and controlling tissue of the gut-mind-body. Good gut microbiota is negatively affected by antibiotics, antidepressants, anticonception pills, genetically modified foods, processed foods, refined sugars, gluten, water (chloridated, fluoridated, and polluted), pasteurized foods, a wide variety of antibacterial products, pesticides, herbicides, and glyphosate.

Prebiotics

The non-digestible food stimulates the growth of beneficial microbes like oligosaccharides and dietary, non-digestible starch fibre. These foods include prebiotics, gum arabic, chicory root, Jerusalem artichokes, sunroot, dandelion, garlic, leeks, onions, asparagus, and bananas.

There are also biogenic extracts. Cultured lactobacillus metabolites extract supporting the development of suitable microbes. Bad microbes in the gut (around 15 percent of the total) are putrefactive or proteolytic bacteria, which produce toxin in the large bowel and cause auto-intoxication.

Gut bacteria and food which we eat influence our thinking, mood, overall well-being, and even the nature of our brains and minds. Psychobiotics are living organisms positively or negatively affecting psychiatric, neurological health.

Change your food. It will change your thoughts, and you will change your life. Probiotic bacteria is the main life force, creating the whole animal world. Our gut bacteria is so important that we cannot survive without them. They extend our lives and improve quality of life. For the wellness of our gut, the quality of every meal we eat is crucial to sustain the balance of the microbial universe inside the digestive system. The wisdom of nature takes early care of unborn babies by providing prebiotics which are produced in breast milk (GOS) as a complex sugars (galactooligosaccharides), which combine for 90 percent of the dietary fibre. GOS (galactooligosaccharides) and inulin are guards of our wellness. The majority of prebiotics are complex sugars.

Bad microbes include bacteria and viruses in gut that trigger obesity and disease by changing metabolism. Sugary and processed foods support the growth of bad microbes.

"Let food be your medicine and medicine be your food."

—Hippocrates

Certain microorganisms are the key to controlling stress-related dysfunctions like anxiety, depression, aggression, mood changes, ADHD, autism, and schizophrenia. There are more neurotransmitters and serotonin in balanced gut flora than in the brain.

From about two million years ago, early forms of humans collected and used food from natural plants and animals. The introduction of refined and processed foods caused problems. Processing can contaminate food by harmful bacteria, and it will lower and change the natural quality in destructive ways: mechanical, chemical, and radiation. Also, by adding refined ingredients, artificial substances, preservatives, additives, flavours, colorants, and texturants, the food becomes unhealthy.

The digestion and usability of food are much better in the effect upon a person of a calm, cheerful state of mind-body-spirit than upon those whose emotions are anger, envy, confusion, and dissatisfaction.

"Eating is an act of love for your body."

—Ocean Robbins

Chronic Diseases Develop from Chronic Neglect

Commonly, modern living promotes chronic illness by poisoning the air, water, food, the whole environment. A negligent diet—mainly processed food—creates degeneration in the body, mind, and spirit. Modern living uses mainly processed foods, which create many problems in the body-mind-spirit. The bad food has a similar effect as some bad drugs. It will make people dependent by changing their metabolism and the performance of the mind-spirit. Our mind-body-spirit complex is a marvellous invention made by nature, and it easily reacts to any good or bad improvement.

Many medical critical conditions and chronic diseases can be rectified by correcting nutrition. A natural diet is a powerful medicine. Diet and health are interrelated. Medical systems pay no attention to prevention, nutrition, food manufacturing that is not orientated towards healthy food. That system is mostly money orientated. Doctors in ancient times got money only when their patients became healthy again.

The most important fact is to estimate the state of the mind-body-spirit complex. Man was a hunter-gatherer for millions of years. Our digestive systems are not able to properly digest unhealthy, processed foods—especially not foods spoiled by preservatives, enhancers, and pollutants. In many places around the world, the environment is constantly robbed and polluted, it's not able to nourish the body-mind fully and safely. In modern times, the importance of proper nutrition is the primal factor.

The more humans go away from nature, the more they will negatively change, and the more problems that will develop from disharmony. Nature never lies. Humans lie to each other. We need closeness and synchronization with nature for each of us, and for humanity.

The majority of us are eating genetically modified foods, hydrolyzed fats, refined flours and sugar, and polluted water.

Bad Life Habits

Which ones are you guilty of? The old maxim says, "You are what you eat." The more precise statement is, "You are what you absorb."

Everything is about the secret of the importance of good gut microbiota, which helps in good absorption of food. We are not eating well; we are eating in a hurry, skipping healthy meals, and relying on processed foods. Love for junk food is so harmful and makes us dependant.

Create your gut flora by regularly eating natural, traditionally fermented food and proper probiotics, if you need extra care. It will develop friendly dependence on healthy foods, and the metabolism will become efficient. Always select unprocessed foods. Avoid genetically modified foods, foods with sugar, pesticides, food additives, antibiotics, and fluoridated and chlorinated water.

Chlorinated water kills bad organisms in the water, but also the good ones in the skin and in the body. It kills beneficial microorganisms, which are needed for the skin and gut. The better option is to drink natural spring water or good filtered water.

Overuse of antibiotics causes the disappearance of good gut microbiota and the chance of cancer. Destroying the microbes that keep us healthy is the worst treatment.

In modern times, more of your destiny depends on the foods you eat. Current nutrition in humanity is walking away from natural eating and natural preparation of food. The majority of processed foods are hazardous to our health. We created the, artificial foods.

Problems Connected with Microwaves

In nature, we have a wide spectrum of electromagnetic emissions from the sun, as well as from electromagnetic waves of the planet. All natural waves are stimulating life. In the modern world, we are exposed to harmful frequencies and electromagnetic pollution. The most destructive is the mobile phone invasion, which disrupts the order of natural frequencies of the body. Other destructive invention is the microwave oven for warming up or boiling water for coffee or tea. Very high radiation on the molecular level is changing the atoms of the water and foods. Microwaving food is very destructive to essential nutrients and produces carcinogenetic toxins. Additionally, carcinogenic toxins escape from food covers, paper plates, and plastic, combining with foodstuffs. We need to re-examine our ways and revert to a balance with nature and ourselves.

Physiological and Psychological Addiction

Many foods have a narcotic-like effect on our brains, caused by the release of dopamine and serotonin. Cocaine, heroin, and carbohydrates create pleasure in the brain and body. Sweet and sour tastes enhance the appetite.

Addictive provisions include sugar, alcohol, fast foods, refined foods, rectified table salt, coffee, chocolate, potato chips, pickles, cheesecake, pasta, bread, potatoes, white rice, buttermilk biscuits, donuts, pretzels, chewing gum, pizza, cheese fries, cheese curds, and advertised foods as low-fat or sugar-free (because they have unbalanced, unhealthy nutrients). Fast food creates debilitating but preventable illness. All natural, good food enhances your performance in life. Fast food has inferior ingredients and dead food. In cheese, the addictive factor is found in casein, which releases casomorphins producing opiate effects.

Alcohol Toxicity

After decades of research in alcohol drinking, it is very clear that even moderate consumption is seriously harmful. In the long term, it causes the liver to become firm, and the liver can develop cirrhosis. Alcohol toxicity is linked to systemic inflammation, memory loss, dementia, gastritis, stomach ulcers, gut damage, testicular malfunction, infertility, and cancers in the liver, colon, and throat.

Factors reducing mental and physical capabilities include:

- Lack of exercise—and too much exercise
- Lack of vitamins (B12 is very important), minerals, and trace elements
- Wrong diet, processed foods, refined sugar, and too much grain (especially with gluten)
- Lack of balanced bacterial colonies in the gut (our second brain)
- Lack of omega-3 fat, which prevents depression, Alzheimer's, and schizophrenia
- Lack of unprocessed, natural salt
- Too-low cholesterol levels
- Lack of true living outside of the living room
- Lack of adequate sleep

- Lack of sunshine

Your health is your real wealth. Every man is a potentially perfect state. There are no compromises to secure a healthy life. All our daily actions should be concentrated on optimum, natural, organic, and fresh food. It is important to know that we build from sugary foods all our internal fat. More people should experience the fact that eating good fat will not make them fat.

Balanced living is the base for all, so the rational mind can create wellness. If you want to be healthy and live a long, content life, then you should grow up quickly with reliable health knowledge. There will be no unwellness and no cost for your health care and services. Health is nothing else than a natural, content, vigorous, and balanced mind-body-spirit in a healthy environment. The key to health is a satisfied, well-informed mind in actions. About 90 percent of us are not masters of our health—we're slaves to our ignorance and inaction, which can harm or even kill us.

All health problems start not by knowledge, but by ignorance and negligence with a lack of action. Our health and our whole lives are the result of our information, beliefs, emotions, and upbringing; it also depends on our genes progressing, which are influenced by external and internal environments. We are conscious or unconscious creators of the quality and span of our lives who develop curious, open minds and give time and money to search for the best knowledge and resolution. They become the winner of the healthy mind-spirit-body. In this money-orientated medical system, confusion often leads to disinformation. One should be extremely fortunate to use reliable, healthy ways. Command your health and wellness to reach your immense life performance, which is the real fortune. Do not allow sickness to remain. Decide that you are important enough to be healthy. All actions about health are your responsibility towards life, your ancestors, and the human race.

We cannot get more health from more wealth, but we need more wisdom. Wisdom gives the best ways to obtain a healthy mind and body.

Health and joy are the results of constant, proper actions and choices. There are a myriad of possibilities ahead of us to secure and use the art of living wellness. If we want to be well and prosperous, we must first take care of our health. The goal of our existence should be healthy physical, mental, and spiritual creations. Nature alone cures disease, if the mind and body complex is in a positive, creative stage with the proper activity, diet, and exercise. Well-informed people choose a healthy lifestyle. People living with Mother Nature know that nature heals. Stressful environments negatively affect health. That's why the art of living accepts all that we can't change. See more at http://www.wisdomsofhealth.com/blog#sthash. z76dtClE.dpuf.

Exercise and Health

Wisdom of nature prescribes exercise with inherent delight in physical activities, where the mind-body-spirit is involved. Life is movement, and each cell of the body has high internal motion. Mother Nature requires us to be fit and alert in order to cope with life. Living is about physical and mental activities; we are designed to use our muscles and minds to exist. Physical activity is the requirement of life on a daily basis. Muscles and bones become weaker if they're not used enough. All of us need to be in decent shape. We need a proper balance between rest and activity for the whole body.

Life requires the flow of the blood through the body. Exercise raises blood flow around the body, stimulating detoxification and renovation. If we are alive, we are never too old for exercise; it extends longevity. The art of exercise is to use many muscles in each movement, like our closest ancestors, primates (apes), are doing. It will create enormous strength of the whole body. Nature chooses the best ways to become leaner, well-built, stronger, and long-lasting. Follow nature's rules.

Short intensity promotes better fitness and survival. Short intensity with a bigger load on muscles stimulates stronger and bigger muscles. The secret is that all body exercise develops whole-body muscles in a variety of natural movements, which employ the bigger groups of muscles in an efficient action. For health benefits, we need a variety of physical activities like walking, running, swimming, cycling, hiking, martial arts, kettle bell exercises, gymnastic, sprints, and sports. High-intensity exercise in a sequence of no longer than twenty minutes is the proper way designed by nature. Our ancestors had this limited period to escape or to kill. Running marathons, triathlons, and long-distance swimming or cycling are not healthy exercises. Such activities shorten our lives and trigger many illnesses. Personally, I prefer swimming in ocean water (not in pools with toxic chlorine) for relaxing the whole body-mind-spirit. It is not only about exchanging energy with the seawater, but the largest organ of our body, the skin, absorbs needed minerals and trace elements from the cradle of life.

All people can find something right for mental and physical constitution. Resistive rebounding stimulates all body-mind systems, as well as stretching and yoga postures. Leisure time with physical activity, like dancing or gardening, stimulates the whole body-mind-spirit. Physical inactivity is a source of many health complications and serious diseases, and it also causes premature mortality. Healthy life in the modern world requires more exercise, not less. Exercise and good nutrition will improve our vehicles, our bodies, to do our best and to move with pleasure through time and space in balance and harmony. We need to exercise more if we have overloaded and strained lives. For a physically and mentally active lifestyle, we need balanced food, physical exercises, and mental stimulation.

"The most adamant persons about exercise cannot dispute the
fact that 80 percent of the results that you are going to achieve
are related to your diet. Not to diminish the importance of
exercise, but you can't do it without the diet. The diet is crucial. It's
foundation. Exercise in addition to, not in place of a good diet."

—Dr. Mercola

Well-being is created by a multitude of factors, both internal and external. Physical, social, mental, spiritual, and environmental factors impact us every day. Less exercise in the modern world, as well as the stresses of technology, are against the body. Exercise and good nutrition will improve the body to do its best to move through time and space in balance and harmony.

Mental and physical well-being are stopped by sedentary behaviour.

Sitting is very detrimental to our health. Prolonged sitting produces negative effects for active people, even for athletes. Sedentary occupations and lifestyles lower mental and physical well-being.

The consequence of sitting for many hours daily is connected to:

- Weight gain
- Inflammation
- Higher risk of death from a multitude of health problems
- Increased cancer risk
- Anxiety and depression
- Higher blood-sugar levels and cholesterol
- Increased blood pressure
- Increased heart disease
- Higher toxic substances in metabolism
- Back problems
- Biochemical changes in hormones
- A higher number of type two diabetes
- Chronic health problems

The more time you spend sitting, the shorter your life will become. Our fathers and grandfathers stood and walked more often than we do today. See more in the book *Sitting Kills, Moving Heals* by Dr. Joan Vernikos.

Here is a solution for better health.

- Become more physically active (more than forty-five minutes per day)
- Exercise, do yoga, and sit on a Swiss ball
- Take frequent breaks
- Have seated balancing
- For healthier sitting, learn about your breathing patterns
- Stand more than sit

> "We are in the process of providing all our employees at mercola.com standing desk options. If you have a sit-down job, I would strongly encourage you to present this information to your employer and get a stand-up desk."
>
> —www.mercola.com

Natural Factors Controlling Longevity and Aging

Health and wisdom move you through the wealth of life. Long-living people know about the loveliness of daily living. They use their blessed days in a virtuous way, persistent in enjoying with an appreciation of all that is coming. The process of getting older naturally brings reflection, satisfaction, and contentment; appreciate it and be in harmony with it. Agree and respect all that life offers in highs and lows for daily living. It is correct, natural way of living that secures a balanced and long life

Longevity, proper aging, and a content life are the effects of choosing the essential way of wellness. Everybody handles all his changes. The winner, per Lao-Tzu, is not a man with position, money, and power, but a man who simply lives longer with a healthy mind, spirit, and body.

The art of living is about slowing down aging, having a present and youthful radiance, and extending one's lifespan. They relate to quality, not quantity. Only quality creates long-standing quantity and longevity. Longevity and wellness are related to natural nutrition, environment, lifestyle, and a peaceful, enjoyable nature. There are no diseases containing aging. Aging is not about to become progressively worse. It is about to become gradually more experienced, content, and advisory.

It Is a Knowledgeable Choice to Live Long Life in Wellness

Longevity is extended by purposeful life and living in the moment, but with long-reliable visions and with gratitude for the sweet memories and the present. It's about positive thinking, enjoying life daily, and having passion for lifelong study with the purpose to enhance quality, constantly adapting to new things. They have steady emotions, good relationships, and a rich social life.

The centenarians behave younger, think fresher, and keep themselves active in the mind-body-spirit. They also help the community. They choose to eat healthy, whole foods, and they prepare food in traditional ways. They are not overeating, often eating once or twice daily, and they use intermittent fasting. All these essential changes are constant and support health. Also, higher education is consistent with longevity.

Remembering nice events in life becomes more valuable than extraordinary belongings. The quest for truth, understanding and applying real information, costs energy, time, and money but creates better quality, performance, and longevity. In the end, health, longevity, and wisdom become a combination of extraordinary wealth of life. Living is the journey of endless discoveries of facts and ideas of who you are and about your future. Collected knowledge and understanding will assemble your time ahead. Grow with love for yourself, others, and everything else. It does not matter how old you are now; contemplate about the best way to go. Your life is the experiment leading by you. You are the outcome of your intentional and unintentional actions, your wise and ignorant decisions. Use your uniqueness and imagination with curiosity!

The art of living stands for what we truly need. Know that the effects of all actions in the long term will decide which level of wellness and longevity we will secure. Life quality is always working towards quantity and longevity. A good life will extend itself. When events and things in our lives bring enjoyment, laughter, and stimulation, enhancing the mind-body-spirit, they will create health, wellness, and longevity.

Longevity depends more on mental and nutritional than physical states. In highly developed countries, the bond and closeness of society is deteriorating. For long-term mental and emotional health, good social connections are important, such as good food and exercise. Reduced social integration triggers dementia.

Real, physical changes can happen when having a good laugh. We need regular laughter each day, as well as exercise and good food. Smiles and laughter are forms of universal language, which positively stimulate the mind and body towards wellness and longevity. There is a wholeness of the body-mind-spirit cooperating with the true, natural way of life. Contentment, harmonious living, longevity, and wellness become a natural outcome. Longevity and wellness need orderly naturalness, right information, right actions, and right exercise. Our successful existence, longevity, and wellness are the results of our understanding and cooperation with the nature. To reach our best potential, we need to create vital, healthy habits; then all correct decisions every day will bring a healthy future with longevity.

Like in the ecosystem, the natural variety of humanity provides the best options for the future. Human longevity will be increased, but physical capabilities will decrease. Individuality, originality, validity, and legitimacy are favourable things by nature.

The real value and beauty of life grows inside us. Worrying, misery, and giving up hope reduce the performance of the nerve cells. The next stage is the development of illness, as well as nerve and blood vessel sclerosis. Such a process promotes aging and early death. Many scientists connect deadly discharges from bad gut bacteria as the cause for aging and death.

Free radicals cause aging inside our cells, which is accelerated by stress, nutritional deficiencies, diseases, and polluted air, water, and food. Many substances like food additives, pesticides, herbicides, and prescription drugs are very powerful factors that accelerate aging.

In order to slow down the aging process, we should do a lot of good things very early in our lives. Some excellent habits were passed to us from grandparents and parents. To live a quality of life, and to live longer, we must collect the right info every day. In the past, aging people who lived long lives were slim and knowledgeable, without the incapacitating physical or mental signs of aging that often exist today.

Natural Factors Controlling Longevity

There is a statement from the many scientists that the present young generation will not outlive their parents.

The Importance of Sunlight

Lack of sunlight to produce vitamin D is one of the reasons for mood changes. Many sunscreens are full of toxins and stop the production of vitamin D. Inefficient sun exposure causes vitamin D deficiency, triggering depression, osteoporosis, heart disease, psoriasis, eczema, autoimmune diseases, multiple sclerosis, and cancer. Frequent sun exposure is life-giving and a necessary wonder, and it stimulates the whole body and mind. Sun through our eyes stimulates our brain, which produces neuro-physiological reactions, creating the joy of living. Be aware of using sunglasses too often.

Old age can be the result of a natural process of development, or it can become quicker due to the illness of one or more organs.

Heredity

Heredity is the outcome of a genotype created to proliferate in the best ways, and to protect itself. All heredity factors are constantly rectified by the environment and individual art of living, which relies on the most important cleverness of self-continuation. Any wrongdoing on a daily basis about nutrition, thinking, and actions will multiply in the reality of life. Moreover, wrong coexistence with environment will only ensure disaster.

Environment

Living in a moderate climate, in serene places, and in unpolluted air, as well as using good water and unprocessed foods, will create the perfect setting to flourish and secure longevity. Climate in mountainous territories and balanced ways of life also reinforce long life. There are superb examples of longevity for the people living in Balkans and Caucasus, which come from yogurt lactic acid, which controls bad intestinal bacteria. In the intestinal worlds or in the whole nature, all life depends on the life or death of others. All life in nature depends on eternal interconnectedness. Earth is a living entity that exchanges energy with us. Walking bare foot relieves insomnia, mood swings, depression, constipation, and stress.

Occupation

Very often we have more than one vocation. The iintensity of our jobs, total hours, and circumstances design our lifespans. Compulsory retirement, joblessness, and harmful work locations often reduce lifespan.

Nutrition

The best is organic nutrition. Healthy nourishment is natural, unprocessed foods, not genetically modified foods treated with pesticides and herbicides. Those who will find right and peaceful times to eat nutritious, natural foods, and not overeat, will live a very long time. Reducing the number of calories, but eating healthy, nutritious foods with a full spectrum of micronutrients, is the wise way to extend one's lifespan.

Intermittent fasting helps to clean our intestines and keep us healthier. Nature designed intermittent fasting for our ancestors due to an irregular supply of food in short periods, or in segments of the seasons. Intermittent fasting is a much better method than calorie restriction. It produces valuable results in the body's metabolism.

A deficit of essential nutrients in the longer periods, and chronic calorie restriction, are the foremost factors shortening life. If we eat processed, devitalized food—that is, food which lost its intelligence—then we will lose our intelligence too. There is the message from the nature that any excessive actions, or too-long periods of faulty nutrition, will trigger many life-threatening issues and will shorten the lifespan.

> "The best we can do is come up with some general guidelines that replicate ancestral patterns. In my view, daily intermittent fasting and avoiding eating for a number of hours before bedtime has many advantages over general calorie restriction and other radical diets, while providing many of the same benefits with a minimum of risk."
> —Dr. Mercola

Exercise

Any physical activity is needed to perform well on many levels. Focusing too much on specific muscle mass, and forgetting to develop all body muscles in the long term, will shorten life. Nature needs balance in everything that we do with the mind-body-spirit. The best sports and exercise are activities developing all body muscles: swimming, racket sports, dancing, Tai Chi, and more. Exercise combined with fasting stimulates a higher level of human growth hormone.

Universal Life Conduct for Quality and Longevity

- We can improve genes responsible for longevity.
- Only your own action and wisdom secures longevity.
- Life is an art for self-refinement, enjoying the priceless treasures.
- Adapt to the free wealth of nature to nourish your life.
- Use the sunlight to create and forever support life; balance the life cycles, as well as the feminine and masculine energies.
- Connectivity with the nature principles creates longevity.
- Create a healthy unity of the mind-body-spirit; all processes are connected.
- Develop your mind's expansiveness with self-analysis and control.
- Learn from wise sources to have a rational view of life.
- Natural nutrition, sense of purpose, and wise living are the best ways in life.

- Avoid sugar, sugary foods, and soft drinks.
- Drink pure water and eat natural, unprocessed foods.
- Avoid drugs, alcohol, smoking, coffee, and strong tea.
- Love yourself, others, life, and nature.
- True love uses the silent, elusive music of subconsciousness.
- True love is like nature and becomes unpossessive and self-regulating.
- Love creates all meaning in life, representing the whole forces of the universe.
- Use balance and modesty in everything.
- Become useful and serviceable.
- Giving joy to others will generate your enjoyment and longevity.
- Learn to see joy in simple things.
- Your attitude is more important than reality.
- Use art to be positive.
- Working life, social life, and the natural environment establish one's quality of life.
- Selecting the proper life companion will lead to quality life and longevity.
- Live close to nature.
- Do not live in big cities and polluted areas.
- Life is about movement; regularly exercise with pleasure the mind and body. Activities can be meditation and yoga activities involving the mind-body-spirit.
- Life is so invaluable a miracle that we have a duty to protect it and use it fully in serviceable ways for ourselves, for others, and for life itself.
- Eliminating abnormal situations and nutritional deficiencies extends life.
- Virtue and harmony secure all life's riches: fortune, health, longevity, mastery, and joy.

CHAPTER 4

UNITY OF MAN, LIFE, NATURE, AND THE UNIVERSE

"Nature is made up of a continuous spectrum of realities."

—Itzhak Bentov

All things are matter and energy, and all are interconnected. All things exchange energy. Everything is in transition; where some elements exist in the human world, some are beyond appearance and perception.

Back in 1904, Albert Einstein then a twenty-six-year-old patent clerk, was the first person to question the interconnectedness of matter and energy. He later proved that matter is nothing but energy. "Everything is changing energy."

There is nothing which does not change. Change is so almighty that it cannot stop changing. If there is a God, he is also the change.

"A human being is a part of a whole, called by us 'universe,'
a part limited in time and space. He experiences himself,
his thoughts and feelings as something separated from the
rest … a kind of optical delusion of his consciousness."

—Albert Einstein

Science claims that the universe is empty. The universe and life are unknown to us by 99.999 percent. The universe, the human body, and single atoms are saturated by electromagnetic vibrations, connecting all. The universe is not detectible by more than 99 percent; we simply cannot see it, feel it, or imagine it. Merely 0.1 percent of the universe consists of galaxies, planets, and some insignificant cosmic dust, of which we are.

Universal law creates order out of disorder in the cosmos, in us, and in atoms. We and everything else that exists are working on the laws of quantum physics. Such energy has the ability to soar from everything around us, and from an endless abyss. It is the form of vibration that connects and blends with everything. All the universe is a spaceless ocean of vibrations.

Everything that exists is the universe's energy. Nothing begins, and nothing ends. It is a law known from ancient times. The universe's energy is everywhere and treats all the same. You select and control energies and ways for your life to travel. It is you who will choose energy and use it properly.

Ancient masters believes in a cosmic order rather than in senseless chaos. In the sources of everything that exists, there is the universal law: energy and matter are eternally changing. Blending and exchanging energy in harmonious ways is the best approach for us. The negative condition is as necessary as the positive in order to see the full representation. Nature's laws relate all things to each other. There is no boundary between material and non-material, internal and external. There is only one natural law for everyone and everything, and so the universe belongs to everything that is in it. Everything is matter-energy-time-space-motion.

We have vast numbers of stars in the sky, but the only star of day is the sun. In our part of the universe, the life-giving sun has always been the source of all. The sun is invisible to us, because we can see only 0.1 percent of the sun's wave spectrum. We are blind regarding 99.9 percent! The good news is that sun will serve us for the next 7.5 billion years.

Light is the electromagnetic spectrum. Everything in nature expresses rhythmic waves of vibration. Human reality and the whole universe have a vibratory nature. The universe, matter, and energy manifest through a joint wave as a form of energy, which regulates itself with a law of harmonies, a law of eternal vibration.

The mysteries of existences involve four natural forces.

- Weak nuclear force
- Strong nuclear force
- Gravity,
- Electromagnetic force

Such mysteries are the foundation of living, and our main purpose is to cooperate with all of them. The universe is an essence of an electro-graviton-magnetic entity. There is a vibratory continuum of reality. The universe governs itself by harmonious cycles. Nature's forces are the universal law. Nature's law, judgement, and actions are universal and final.

Nature as matter-energy-space-time-motion involves different expressions of the same essential substance or force. Such a continuum and its law creates the frame for the phenomenon of life; these forms make all the others possible. One of nature's law is the certainty that there is uncertainty. We are unpredictable thinkers in an unpredictable universe. There can be no loss in any phase of nature. Vanishing in the universe is unreal. The elements of nature merely change their form.

Everything in nature is expressed by rhythmic waves of energy, and the base of everything is sunlight. Nature manifests itself through mixed masses of elements, which illustrate various ways of existence. True knowledge is stored in the memory of nature. The law of the nature require that all what exist must collect information, and have the right to do it. It is the highest ability and necessity in order to survive in all environments. All humans must become true explorers of the inner and outer universe, with an unquenchable thirst for understanding and improving. From our ancestors, we learned that sensibility and harmony with nature is a major tool of survival.

"Knowledge is a refined thinking."

—Albert. Einstein

Exploring true knowledge is the best way to live and take care of ourselves, our families, and humanity. If we have a deep passion for the life, we will explore everything that is important to us and nature. Timeless wisdom writes down that the best way to explore is to first oneself.

The concepts, ideas, and imaginations about man, life, and the universe are the result of interactions between self-conscious man and the universe. Finding a sense of the whole life means understanding the unity of identification between the universe, man, and all living and non-living matter. The whole universe is one homogeneous whole, one whole being and essence, which is in a state of infinite change.

Create change beneficial for you, others and nature. Do not worry about what you cannot change. This conduct is constructive and improves life. Greet every day, every moment of your life; appreciate everything around you, other people, and yourself. Honour your day and the way of life.

We are parts of the whole, and so we must live with nature and its mighty law. Living means describing our dimension in the world; it is the most valuable activity together with expressing ourselves. We need to know about the most important things in order to live properly. There are always limits in knowing, understanding, and expressing. The mind tries to find links in the perceptible and invisible worlds through magic and religion. We cannot understand everything, and that's why we invent universal symbols and concepts to describe the unknown. Many people are afraid of the unknown; others thrive on it. There is a vast difference between life's travellers. We have a collective insight and collective detentions; both bring a dependence on mental limitations.

The Nature of the Beyond

There is no boundary between life and all unknown matter, time, and space. In the universe exists only matter, energy, space, and the process of time. Nothing in the universe can be supernatural because nothing can be above nature. Man, by nature, has feared the supernatural, the unknown, and non-material powers or forces. Non-material and nonphysical things, non-electromagnetic things, do not exist.

By using ordinary senses, we can detect the existence of material forms only in limited ways, but not what is beyond normal perception. We can only know things as they are, not as they were or as they will be. Nature shows its meaning so obviously by a sign and expression, but many of us are unable to understand and accept it.

Reality is a motion of the energy-matter-space-time complex, partially perceivable through our senses. Reality is a limited picture of the universe, and it is limited by the partial perception of human senses. Consciousness of reality is also dependent upon realisation, which is an individual sensation and can be affected by interpretation from childhood to old age. Unlimited references create close pictures of reality, but all our approaches are only the segregation and separation of various forms of reality.

Everything that was around us left a trace; if it is recognisable by us, it has made a record in our memory upon all kinds of perception. We can use stored information by others; their experiences, imagination, and their thoughts can be accumulated via telepathy and other ways. All of us belong to an immense group of living creatures, whether we want to or not, and all of us take part in the big events of life. We share everything together in conscious or subconscious ways. We create an unbroken chain of events together with the plant and animal kingdom.

Space, Time, Past, Present, Future

Ever transient is this world of ours;
all things change and pass away;
for a distant journey even now prepare.
—Sat guru Phadampa Sangay, Tibetan Book of the Great Liberation

Time and space are effects of interpretations made by our senses. Man designed time for a practical use. We are the passage of time. The real way of life is in the present, not in the past or the future. We create the present by being in the present moment with our dreams and actions, which design the best future.

Human time relates to the earth's changes, and they are dependent on the sun's processes. Time exists only for our sense experiences, which are subjective to time intervals, the duration of perception. Time is the period of change in energy or masses of units. Time is a matrix of possibilities. Time is a perpetual tide for the equilibrium of universe. Time is immortal because it never was born, and it existed on a whole scale. In human development, man created time and used it to live with it. Now we have a big problem: to start to live without time in our inner and external universe. It seems that time exists only for human perception, because in a very short time, all things appear as already existing. In a very long time, more things will appear and disappear. There are correlations between time-space-matter that are complex in nature. Therefore, the time of perception and the time of thinking are very important selectors of human realities.

Time has occupied a central role in humanity's affairs, and many facts from this subject will make strikingly clear the incompatibilities with existing concepts. Must time be directional? Alternatively, time is variable. Our limited view of linear time and space binds us to humankind's limited reality. Reality itself is unlimited. In this stage of human development, time is much harder to explore than matter. It will be more easily accessible by the universal concept of time, where time is a factor and function in the context of the whole universe. We need more imagination about time in order to make fewer mistakes in our lives. Time washes our reality and rinses minor events.

Time and a fear of time (death) stimulate human behaviour. Our memories and emotions select the segments from the past. I like the old saying "The older you get, the better things were when you were younger."

Present is the only tiny particle of eternity, which we only have for sure. Humans as a tiny complex of matter-energy will never be alone. The wise man uses time as his servant and not his master. Like nature, all elements remember all previous meetings from before—collective memory. Out of the past, we collect experiences and expand our understanding. Do not try to run away from yourself in the past. Do not try to blame or change the past. You would not be the person you are today without the spirit-searching desire for more of nature's goodness in your life, or if you had not had the past experiences you have been criticizing.

The science of time, matter, space, and the cosmos tries to bridge the gap between man and the universe. Humankind is the child of the evolving cosmos. Follow the natural law. We are physically and psychologically imprinted by nature.

CHAPTER 5

ECO-SUSTAINABILITY

The universe and its child, earth, waited for life and for humans. Man is dependent on earth. Man is one of her manifestations, and he is a very sophisticated extension of matter. Human consciousness is in the continuous expansion of the uppermost matter-energy-space-time complex.

"Everything is One."

—Hales

Life on the earth and its conditions are governed by the quality of air, water, and soil. There is no survival for human without the wellness of the environment. The environment cannot be in harmony without global harmony. Humans cannot be happy if mental, physical, and spiritual levels are not supported by the environment. People must make decisions concerning ecosystems based on considerations of well-being, as well as natural values. Nature gives the essentials like food, water, timber, fibre, and naturally recyclable wastes; its controls seasons and the climate. The earth serves us, and we must serve the earth. We should see ourselves as part of oneness, and we should consider the world as one whole. The body-mind-spirit is part of the ecosystem and is at the mercy of it.

There is only one way to understand our dependency on the environment: we are not only ourselves as a living complex of cells. Every living system becomes part of the multiplex organism, the living earth. If humanity wants to survive, we need to cooperate within global society as well with the ecosystem. If we can understand our oneness with nature and the universe, if we can respect and appreciate them, then we will come back to balance. Through responsibility and cooperation with the ecosystem, we will realise that we are an extension of it, and that humanity is in the process of change. Many people are harmful to themselves, others, and the ecosystem. Some neglect their duty towards cooperation with nature. Others are too busy or underestimate the seriousness of climate change.

In unity and balance, we will lose ego, as well as greed. Humanity's senseless actions cause the destruction of the natural environment. In effect, through irreversible changes in the ecosystem, we lost a lot of species forever and cut down the planet's biodiversity. We should protect nature's law for the diversity of life on earth. It is a fundamental way of nature, which obviously secures humanity's well-being and survival. We can still secure a sustainable future for us by prohibiting all harmful actions, and by supporting and securing the natural earth life.

If we evolve in balance with nature and with quality in the mind-body-spirit, we will finally become immortal in many ways. In Australia, less than 20 percent of electricity is produced from renewable resources; about 80 percent comes from producing pollution through fossil fuels. Humanity's chance to survive is by stopping the use of fossil fuels, recycling more, and using renewable energy. Our chance to survive is included in the depths of our understanding and proper actions. We must recognise and respect the earth's blood system, which is the global water. Also, the earth's immune system is in her soil.

From space, our planet looks like a blue drop of water suspended in the remote speck of the universe. Further, most of the world's habitat is in the oceans, where most animals live. The earth and even the whole universe is a huge, living complexity; it is oneness, it is whole, and we are members of the whole. The universe is a continuous process in which nothing is static.

"Currently about 1 in 5 plant species is threatened with extinction because of human transformation and use of land, and rapid climate change driven by human activities only promise to exacerbate the situation."[10]

"There is a 40-year lag in the consequences of emissions and temperature rise. We are locked into consequences with 0.8 degrees C, with current temperature increase resulting from 40 years ago. In the last 29 years, we have seen a greater increase in CO_2 emissions than in the last 100 years. We are driving 200 species into extinction daily. This could be a near term human extinction on the planet."[11]

---

[10] http://www.missouribotanicalgarden.org/plant-conservation/plant-conservation/conservation-in-action/climate-change.aspx

[11] https://en.wikipedia.org/wiki/Human_extinction#Habitat_threats

Humans develop disastrous technologies that annihilate ecology. Some activities are so immense that they create a geologic impact and cause evolutionary crashes.

There are many factors reducing natural habitat.

- Synthetic production of fertilizers, which are a major key to changing ecosystems
- Synthetic nitrogen, which exceeds nature's creation of nitrogen
- Exploitation of biodiversity in ecosystems
- Habitat division, which crumbles ecological connectivity
- Deforestation, timber reaping, and slash-burn
- Agriculture
- Overgrazing
- Topsoil erosion
- Overfishing
- Surface mining
- Deep mining, causing the collapse of the surface
- Poisoning of vegetation by herbicides, pesticides, and fungicides
- Heavy pollution of oceans and groundwater
- Air and water pollution that destroys flora and fauna (loss of pollinators)
- Human overpopulation, which is changing the variation of species
- Metropolitan explosion
- Acid rain, which changes the pH of soil and all water sources
- Diminishing sources of water
- Loss of balance, which introduces more invasive species
- Electromagnetic pollution at harmful frequencies
- Europe lost 85 percent of its natural habitat
- Deforestation worldwide, which has caused the loss of 30 percent of original forest

"Over the past few hundred years, humans have increased species extinction rates by as much as 1,000 times background rates that were typical over Earth's history."[12]

"Some natural events such as volcanic eruptions, hurricanes, flooding, forest fires and other disturbances can cause habitat loss; however, these factors produce a very small percentage of the total habitat loss over the past 10,000 years."[13]

"Global economic activity increased nearly sevenfold between 1950 and 2000. Under the MA scenarios, per capita GDP is projected to grow by a factor of 1.9 to 4.4 by 2050. Global

---

[12] http://www.millenniumassessment.org/documents/document.354.aspx.pdf
[13] http://www.eoearth.org/view/article/153224/

population doubled in the last 40 years, reaching 6 billion in 2000, and is projected to reach 8.1–9.6 billion by 2050 in the MA scenarios."[14]

> "Honesty and Truth are always murdered to protect dishonest profits."
>
> —Jean Hollander

Economic globalization leads to disaster via unlimited growth and unlimited competition. Who is interested in exploiting the earth in sustainable ways and protecting it? If we do not act now, the environment's future is very gloomy. Careless exploitation and decades of mismanagement and neglect are damaging our environment. Globally, all factories of fertilizers currently produce more nitrogen than is produced by all of nature. We should realise that our environment is gradually losing its wildlife. Waste and recycling are very important; there's a chance that a new technology will emphasise recycling more.

Now is the time to think rationally and cooperate with nature. It is a mistake to overestimate the rational aspects of man and underestimate the irrational. Modern humans patented more than a million chemicals, killing life on earth, but there are not many patents for sustainable living. How did it happen that money worshippers degrade the ecosystem? In the end, they will annihilate themselves and the rest? Decisions made now will decide the destiny of our civilisation.

Water Future = Nature Future = Human Future

The "drop" of water that is our planet is suspended in the cosmos. About 70 percent of the planet's surface is covered in water, but only 0.3 percent is freshwater, in the rivers and lakes. We have a limited amount of water on earth.

Nature's law is perfect. Only nature owns the water. The virtual trade of water is senseless. We will not secure water by having more money. We should invest in promoting sustainable rainwater harvesting. Any development with a vision of only money is hurtful for everything else. In comparison, any investment in sustainability will benefit all, including nature.

Overpopulation creates:

- a money-orientated economy
- ruthless competition and aggression

---

[14] http://www.millenniumassessment.org/documents/document.354.aspx.pdf

- freshwater crisis, which becomes the source of conflicts and a mass migration of water refugees
- water wars
- imbalance in the earth's water circulation
- climate change
- extinction of the ecosystem, including humans

Our whole future depends on knowledge regarding how to care about ecosystems and the body-mind-spirit. Humans wrecked nature's interconnectedness. Only reasonable knowledge and a strong vision can build a good future. Life and nature offer many ways to explain themselves, to perceive the purpose of living and how to fulfil it. We are at a crossroads to choose the right direction, after right exploration and right understanding. The best human values come from nature, which will secure a prosperous future.

There is outstanding old knowledgethat should be analysed deeply, especially now, when we are affected by our senseless exploitation of ecosystems, leading to some irreversible degradation.

Overpopulation demands more goods and more natural resources, and water is crucial for everything. We cannot create more water without a global imbalance in nature. The International Water Management Institute realises that 30 percent of the globe's population lacks water. The aquatic ecosystem is the most omnipotent natural wealth, which belong to nature and all of us.

Global Water Regulations to Protect the Future of Water

- Stop the global abuse of water
- Stop mining groundwater
- Stop water Imbalance
- Stop profit from public water
- Stop pollution of water
- Stop using chemicals to grow food
- Reclaim water for nature and humanity's survival
- Restore forests and wetlands

The United Nations released its "Water for a Sustainable World" report. Water is a global issue. The predictions are not optimistic. Water resources worldwide by 2030 may meet only

60 percent of demand, and the report indicates "the world will face an increasingly severe global water deficit."

To make one bottle of water, we must use three bottles of water. We must add millions of gallons of fuel to transport the bottled water, in addition to energy, plastic, and the greenhouse gases.

I find very interesting information in the free PDF book written by Olof Alexandersson, *Living Water: Victor Schauberger and the Secret of Natural Energy.*

Viktor Schauberger's predictions between the 1920s and 1930s was:

> Prevailing technology uses the wrong forms of motion. Our machines and processes channel such agents as air, water and other liquids and gases into the type of motion which Nature only uses to decompose and dissolve matter. Nature uses another form of motion for rebuilding. When our technology only uses the decomposing motion, it becomes a dead technology, a destructive one, dangerously affecting all of Nature.[15]

Quality water is very important for all, both individually and globally. In the past, water was available in abundance and was free. Today, globally we have a deficit of fresh water, which has become one of the most precious commodities. The water industry is the quickest developed industry in the world, and it is more important than the oil industry.

The total number of rural inhabitants is smaller than the number of city residents. It shifts more demands of water to the big cities around the world.

> "They call me deranged. The hope is that they are right. It is of no greater or lesser importance for another fool to wander the earth. But if I am right and science is wrong - then may the Lord God have mercy on humankind."
> —Viktor Schauberger

In many countries, people have a "choice": to drink recycled sewage water or die. Global water reuse rises in the industrial and municipal market. In the future, desalination will become the first solution to the world's lack of water. The ecological crisis is interconnected with humanity's crisis. It is an effect of overpopulation and the lowering of human values, ethics, morals, and responsibilities.

---

[15] http://free-energy.xf.cz/SCHAUBERGER/Living_Water.pdf

Human pollution, greed for resources, and a lower standard of principles in individuals, nations, and global corporations are the reasons for this disaster.

We do not have enough warnings and solutions from science, the economy, and politics about very serious problems in the global ecosystem. Rejection and contradiction become national and international tactics. Conservation and cleaning our messes from homes, industries, and the environment have been stagnant, allowing more crimes against nature. Protection improves the quality of the ecosystem and enhances the survival of all. Proper actions are the legs of survival.

Degradation of forest via deforestation is the main reason for reduced rainfall. Water from common heritages of all living creatures becomes very precious. Water is life, and now both are in a global crisis as the ecological crisis becomes more obvious. The global water crisis is an outcome of ignorance, money-orientated management systems, the devastation of the ecosystem, unsustainable agriculture that uses too much land, human overpopulation, and bad actions that cause climate change. In many parts of the world, the seasonal and cyclical drought occurs too often or is in a permanent state.

In the global economy race, the winner is whoever first secures and protects sources of water. As the annual rainfall declines, rivers are changing their free-flowing patterns and salinity, and deserts grow. Many islands experience rising sea levels. Pumping groundwater in unbalanced ways creates sinkholes, and we will have less water for the future use. Rising temperatures around the globe are causing the speedy melting of glaciers, and water is not reaching rivers because of the soil erosion.

All waters are lost through evaporation. Climate change is the reason for more than one billion refugees.

> "Poor countries export their water by exporting their agriculture products. It is about 15–20% of World Water which is used for export. To produce 1 kg of wheat we need about a 1000 litres of water. 1700 litres of water to produce 1 litre of ethanol. 5000–10000 litre of water to produce one kilogram of meat."
>
> —Maude Barl

Renovation of the great water basins, forests, and wetlands will improve the hydrologic cycle. Wide water retention should be enforced, starting at homes, city buildings, and manufacturers. Technology is helping to resolve global problems regarding the shortage of water. Nanotechnology can clean sewage water, desalination plants appear close to the world's oceans, and water can be sucked from the clouds by machines. Since around forty-five years ago, many countries started ordering water distribution and protection of ecosystems. The reality of a drying climate and the rising request for water requires people to use water wisely from supporting river systems in both rural and urban areas, which are the main keys to water supply for the future. We can't stop drinking water. We can't stop sharing water. Water scarcity and low-quality water due to inefficient use shows a lack of proper responsibilities. Scarcity of water affects all people on the earth. Water awareness includes the obligation and cooperation of all humans on the planet to take proper actions in order to secure quality water for everyone. All humans represent humanity, and all of us should be aware of the duty to preserve the natural quality of global water, and the natural environment, for future generations.

Here is the spectrum of efforts around water.

- Our life is about water; our water is our future.
- Water accessibility and sharing.
- Water conditions are declared the property of the environment.
- The consequences of polluted water undermine everything.
- Constructive and destructive water.
- All human activities should not impair the earth's water.
- Even water technology for treatment exceeds industrial production growth, and there is no space for growing industries and populations.
- Natural, balanced progress secures the water—and humanity's future.
- Proper choices about natural resources, and preservation of water, will create steadiness for present and future generations.
- Water excellence decides the quality and integrity of the ecosystems.
- Sustainability is the way of nature.
- Global recognition of water; water is liquid gold.
- Science, technology, the economy, politics, education, and the financial system should work honestly and together for the integrity of all people, both now and in the future.

CHAPTER 6

HUMANITY'S FUTURE

If you learn from the past and investigate today's reality, you will be able to predict and control your future. The future is made of the past and present. Tomorrow and the future starts today. Humanity's future is dependent on the earth's future. Our future depends of a conscious and honest bond with nature's law.

If we gain the knowledge of the present, we will have the key to understand the knowledge of the past and create a good future. It would be a mistake to take conclusions only from science.

Humanity's mindless and greedy actions undermine the future of all that exists. We become the mightiest, destroying parasites in the evolution on earth. We did not deserve to exist, anyway; we are on the way to annihilating ourselves. All earlier civilizations rise, excel, and collapse. Is it our destiny too? There is hope. Maybe knowledge of what happened in the past, and what is happening in the present ecosystem, will warn us and teach us what to do.

The higher the level of civilization, the more people lose contact with nature. The more our lives become polluted on all levels, the more inadequate nutrition becomes. We have less free time, have fewer simple pleasures, and do not relax. But, we have more depression, neurotics, alcohol, drugs, obesity, and diseases.

Man, is the "time binding" mammal; he can bring the past of hundreds of years ago into the present and use both past and present to plan and create the future. The mind creates a live view of the past and present, and it makes a preview of the future. Good insights, thoughts, words, and actions develop into the future. Human life will have a future if we use our minds properly. Proper understanding of the universal principles of life, and cooperation with nature, will create a sensible, collective consciousness and induce a good future. We are living at a critical time for humankind; it is necessary to recognise the challenges we face today. We need to learn and understand the truth, which unfolds and secures a better reality for us. Any kind of enlightenment must be found by proper and natural learning, understanding, concentration, reflection, and solitude. A better life can exist only in the genuine life, not in spectacular dreams or virtual worlds. It is time to realise this about our new challenges. We can create the future consciously or unconsciously.

Here are some of our biggest sins.

1. Overpopulation
2. Ignorance
3. Inaction
4. We are losing our bond with nature, energies, and perfect knowledge
5. We are not protecting the environment as much as necessary
6. Overpopulation causes less balance and less love for people

Overpopulation, a money-orientated economy, and science degrade the natural life support system that is our ecosystem. Reckless living affects us personally and hurts the planet. The ecosystem is used by many for enjoyment and a resource, but some are using it in irresponsible, criminal ways. Instant gratification causes the deterioration of human culture, taking us away from the ways of nature. Can we really anticipate humanity's future? How long can we be unwise and ill-advised, robbing and damaging the ecosystem? Mother Earth will stop supporting us sooner or later. Humans pass over other species, but we should accept all and love them; they are our companions. At the present, humanity is losing its connectivity with nature, so our future is unsure. All our bad actions prevent us from surviving. We must find sensible ways. We are in the last moments to obey nature's law, to repair and be in balance.

If we correct many mistakes, we will have the chance to explore the planets of our solar system. If we become sensible enough, we will have the chance to live in another galaxy. One day we can create a new world with a good order, with respect cooperation for all. We can become a super species, like gods, ready to explore other planets and galaxies. The great, influential thinkers and scientists are hoping that the truth of surviving will come from people who declare themselves as new compositors and governors of our civilisation.

Many previous civilizations lost the ability to think responsibly, and in the end they lost themselves through their ignorance. Are we on the same path?

We must remember that we are the elements and descendants of nature. We can restore our balance and our role by understanding and using the natural connection between living and non-living elements. There are no boundaries at all, because all elements are controlled by the same fundamental, operative program—nature's law. Interconnectedness is a universal order that overlays all activity and all motion. The human body-mind-spirit is connected to the forces of nature and the cosmos. Ignorance alone limits human possibilities. Adventure, curiosity, and reason are natural human factors that are necessary for survival.

"If you think in terms of a year, plant a seed; if in terms of ten years, plant trees; if in terms of 100 years, teach the people."

—Confucius

Humanity is one giant, living organism. It is an enormous, organic entity with a collective memory and a collective consciousness. The path to harmony for each of us is interconnected with the synchronization and cooperation of all humans with nature. The prosperity of humans is included in the health and reason of the minds in the younger generations. Let's prepare them correctly. Everything depends on true information and true interrelations used properly with the cooperation of all humans living on earth. We have a different variety of consciousness and skills, using all the best to secure our future.

In recent years, science has confirmed the importance of previously overlooked factors that control human performance and actions. Humans are the composition of many universes, with microorganisms living in and on the body. They have much more control of us then we can imagine.

Living in equilibrium is the protected way of living; it is living in balance with internal and external bacteria. You are representing the collective consciousness of vast gut flora and fauna, plus colonies living on the skin and in the crevices of your body. There's also the enhanced living bacteria in all your body cells (except the red blood cells), the mitochondria. In normal human intestinal flora, candida albicans appears as the yeast. Antibiotic actions, processed foods, and suppressors of immune coordination in the gut can change yeast into a fungal system.[16]

We are possessed and supervised by the gut's microscopic world. If we do not cooperate with gut microbiota, we will create imbalances till death starts in our guts and then breaks down the body-mind-spirit.

When we have healthy nutritional balance, we have harmony within. When we have inner harmony, we have a healthy, wise collective consciousness of all living species in the

---

[16] HTTP://CANDIDAPLAN.COM/BLOG/524/CANDIDA-ANTIBIOTICS-AND-THE-INTESTINAL-FLORA/

gut-body complex. If we combine the individual physical-mental-spiritual balance with all humans, we will be on the way to the unity and prosperity of humanity.

Can We Foresee Humanity's Future?

Our future is a complex of probabilities mixed with events, the mind's projections, and intelligence. Extinction is about irreversible biodiversity. It is an extinction of some species that are unknown to us. About 99.9 percent of all existed species on our planet are extinct.

The marine environment suffers from a dangerous loss of habitat and the over-exploitation of living commercial resources. The future of humanity depends on sustainability and climate-friendly living. The ecosystem is used mainly in irresponsible ways, and a lot of times in criminal ways. Global humanity is still in the progress of environment devastation, extensive warfare, mishandling technologies, introducing very harmful applications of scientific knowledge, and provoking cataclysm. We can create order in the private and global realms. The goodness of it is also sharing good information with anybody who is ready to understand it. The destiny of human life is being on the way to advancing towards a better humanity. There is nature's law, and if humanity will not create technology friendly with ecosystem, it will perish. We need to advance mostly on mental and spiritual levels to realise that we are nature's invention. By destroying nature, we will annihilate ourselves.

Our lives and humanity's future existence relies on conscious, daily, natural actions with practical purposes. If we first build order in the inner world, then we will create order on the earth. Living in the world of order requires the elimination of all that is dark and negative in ourselves. Give attention to advance for the betterment of humanity and our future. The best way to deal with everything is through an aware and rational mind, where we are not expecting what we will gain in money but what we will gain in nature.

The development of destructive technology becomes dangerous to all in the ecosystem. Humans rely mostly on technology and money, and they step further away from the nature. Money and power evolve towards brainless authority, pressing humans and nature into not realising that we are destroying ourselves along the way.

The secret of reality, life, the earth, nature, humanity, and all that exists, even the single atom, is included in the interconnectivity and impermanence of all, which is conducted by change. Change creates order out of disorder in the cosmos and in atoms. The interconnectivity between everything that exists is enormously important for humans to decipher the secrets of such phenomena.

"The only part of us that is 100 percent honest is our emotions."

—Anonymous

Emotions are always true to our inner selves. Emotions affect the performance of our hearts, brains, and total health. Scientists at the Institute of HeartMath uncovered the connection between the earth's magnetic resonances, which vibrate at the frequency of the heart's rhythms and brainwaves. Heart vibrations are stronger than mind vibrations. Global coherence monitoring systems were set up for a better understanding of the secrets of interconnectivity.[17]

We need to appreciate the existence of the human mind in the physical universe. Where else can the blessed be rediscovered if not in man? We need knowledgeable minds to confront a culture and society that is disconnecting more and more from nature, as well as separating individuals from each other. What kind of world and life will we have if all of us are not able to be honest? Humanity will become the forerunner of paradise. Some tribes in Polynesia, before they met Europeans, did not know the words *lie* and *pretend*. Dishonesty, selfishness, and ingratitude lead to disgrace and self-punishment. Reckless living affects us personally and globally, and it hurts the planet. We need to check human development and correct it now, before it's too late. Humanity overall has slowed down its intellectual and spiritual growth, and we are not in balance with nature. Nature is the primal source of everything for man; he belongs to her as one of her creations. Quick gratification as a way of living and detachment from nature will take us away from life. Materialism as purposeful living is futile. The answer to everything is not the power of the money. In the end, we can't eat money. The answer to everything is to live in harmony with nature and the global community. If we show the balance in ourselves, then we will create balance with the environment, nature, and life.

Man, the microcosm, is merely the sounding board or the reacting point for eternal electromagnetic vibrations. Men, like plants, have their times of germination, growth, maturity, and decay. The races of man are not the exception to this universe law of change. Ancient texts reveal the closeness of all races of humanity. All members of all races are one humanity, and they all enrich human inheritance and enlarge its significance and power. We are now mixing all races on the earth, and it will enhance the chance of humanity's survival. The speed of communication, travel, and transport are the main factors of exchanging genes.

Each of us has unique genes, talents, gifts, and stories to share with the world. Life has no beginning and no ending; humanity, as a part of it, is now in the circle of info-energy.

---

[17] https://www.heartmath.org/

Humanity exists as a collective organism and a cooperative social organization, sharing, exchanging, and co-creating the future. Our existence should bring good effects by doing the right things for nature, humanity, and ourselves. Only through bonds with nature and global society can we realise the sense of existence. Via hedonistic isolation and an urge for material goods and assets, we will lose ourselves and our race. We can't learn from possessing possessions; we learn by understanding, loving, sharing, exchanging, and growing.

Our sciences are very divided and separated too much. We lost much of the synchronicity between sciences and their ability to see the whole. There is not enough of nature's logic in them, and it can create a very dramatic future. If media, industry, and dishonest systems come first before nature and man, there will be no future for man.

In ancient times, money was created as a clever system to improve the exchange of goods. Can it now acquire even a little knowledge to avoid its own destruction? A competitive economic system is often not reasonable; it creates more bad than good. It has short sight and is very harmful to the future of humans and the ecosystem. The power of money constantly reinforces itself, obeying only market indications in order to make more money. In some cases, money twists the truth of science and true knowledge for better prospects of making real, long-usable, recyclable things. Good judgement is often undermined by money. Money tries to control nature's way and creates the degradation of an ecosystem. The monetary system overlooks that it was created by humans, not by nature. Man's existence and his future are dependent on nature being in balance. Nature offers everything for total wellness; we need only cooperate and allow it. We are not robots yet, and we cannot become separated from nature. Our integral mind-body system relies on constant stimulation and the exchange of energies with nature. We will not get them from an artificial environment or a degraded natural ecosystem. Man is not a creature without will and inspirations; he can control his destiny if he understands how to do it. Nature's principles explain and demonstrate everything; we simply need to identify them and use them. There is no prospect without the way of nature. Mind, the inner microcosm, is the gateway for the outside, the material world, and the universe—the macrocosm. Conscious living is improving us and everything around us. Conscious living stimulates interaction with new possibilities around us. Our progress and our future are decided by the present models of possible futures. Thus, evolutionary outcomes are dependent upon a desire and wisdom.

Humanity can survive as a race if every man is responsible for his actions. Information from the mass media becomes segmented and is not woven into logical connectivity of life. Also, some information is disinformation.

Today's world is dominated by mass media. More people start to live in virtual worlds, to the point that they feel more comfortable living their lives between the realities' of movies, games, shallow Internet social lives, and other activities that take their attention and time away from natural ways. Today, our brains are not ready to cope with the flood of information and disinformation. Not sharing true information is a very destructive path. Sharing information is the universe's law, but it is often unnoticed.

We are not aware on a daily basis that we are sharing information on a subconscious level. Sharing information on a conscious level with good intentions will speed our development. Deliberately supplying disinformation and useless distractions will speed humanity's self-destruction. Such procedures should be treated as the main wrongdoing. The jungle of new and old, of true and false information, becomes too much for many of us. We try to escape from too-quick changes and the pressures of the new reality. The natural process to improve human intelligence is the best way. It is the safe way, evolving with a balance to secure our survival.

Our civilisation starts to know more and more about less and less. Some of us know a little bit about everything, and we know everything about nothing. Computers can change their own programmes, the value systems, and the criteria of life. Humans should control such an advance. People have evolved away from extraordinary abilities, and they have become increasingly dependent on ordinary senses, along with the reasoning functions of the mind. To think and perceive one thing, we must exclude other things. We live in an age where media stimulation overflows natural, domestic, and ecological stimuli. Such a high disproportion creates many imbalances in human systems.

Mass media often uses observational tools, which make their own choices for us.

> "In other words, the tools we use can have their
> own selective attention distortions."
>
> —Al Gore

Our way of life in society is changing. Mass media and digital gadgets are in the process of changing our culture and way of the life. Man's behaviour is decided mostly by mass media. Mass media floods our minds; it is the reason that reading classes are decreasing. All media have some positive effects on human development, if we remember that we need control of them first in order to prevent being controlled by them. In the flood of irrelevant information and disinformation, we undermine our deep understanding and intelligence, and we waste our time. The computer is a mind appliance and useful servant—if we can control it.

Will it free our mind? Mass media mostly creates passive observation, and then the progress of the mind's faculties will become limited. We must seek ways to make the mind more active. If the thoughts of man are enslaved, then our civilisation will stop its progress. Idiosyncratic ways of communications form only singular intelligence.

The Internet is:

- mind-altering technology
- a competition to take our attention and deliver maximum stimuli
- raising our segmented and shallow attention
- speeding reading and confusing thinking, knowledge, and understanding.
- an enormous source of wisdom, it wisely used

Nicolas Carr, in his book *The Shallow,* concludes that the Internet creates superficial understanding, fostering ignorance. Bill Joy warns about the danger of advanced technology in *Wired* Magazine. *The Future Does Not Need Us* states, "If our technology will exceed our wisdom, morals, ethics, we will wipe ourselves from Earth."

The Internet becomes a very big, deep, and permanent distracter, promoting shallowness of the mind and a short concentration span. The Internet can disrupt our living in the real world. Some people live more in virtual than the real world. There is some extreme addictions where parents completely forget about the basic needs of their children, who die. Smell and taste are the only senses that are not yet stimulated by the Internet. Another way to improve the usability of the Internet is to clear it of rubbish and disinformation, removing all that is intolerant, dogmatic, unhuman, and harmful to the ecosystem.

Leisure time online, mobiles, iPods, and TVs increase dramatically. Interactive experiences rob us of deep, true relationships with life by the ecology of interruptive technologies. The brain and mind was created through many thousands of years in such a way that we operate and think individually, using unique abilities to create and understand our differences. On the Internet, our interactivity involves our created profile to be constantly improving impressions and create our deep dependency of the Internet. It's difficult to prevent the low self-esteem, rising up with an inability to focus outwards; it is about our negative self-evaluation.

Ancient and modern wisdom are consistent in recognizing the existence of a material and spiritual worlds. They exist side by side in the spectrum of the ocean of energies. Humans don't use enough common sense to see the wider spectrum of the energy-matrix-information, and that is why they are often confused and unhappy. Personal life success and humanity's realisation should be measured first by internal values, not by external possessions or technical advances. Harmonious existence within itself and in humanity is a base requirement to survive as a species. The complete cessation of all problems and their causes are unreal, like wishing to stop the movement of particles in single atom. The more content you are, the longer you will live. Altruistic behavior relates to health benefits. Altruism is contagious.

Having mindfulness and appreciation for all that life and our planet gives us is the only way to survive and live a good life. Together, we create the collective awareness needed to generate a sustainable and creative processes in order to secure a healthy future for the earth and ourselves. You create your own future and humanity's future through harmony with nature. Finding the deeper meaning of life and searching for common good, balance, and peace are the best ways to advance. The way to live and understand tomorrow is through living and understanding today. What you think and what you do have enormous positive or negative powers. It is the foundation for more freedom and joy—or you can build prison for yourself.

However, we can control the depth of the problems. The greatest senselessness is any activity knowingly involving physical, mental, or spiritual degradation. Also a problem is too much focus and energy towards unimportant goals, which become obstacles.

We live in a critical space-time. We all play roles, we are all designers, and we can take responsible measures to contribute towards the advancement of humanity. The brain-mind is a spaceless, biological computerthat relates to everything that makes the whole universe. The best way for any operator of such a marvellous piece of ingenuity is to calculate all movements, statements, and decisions. We are small gods with enormous power, learning to oscillate between the positive and the negative. We are living with endless tests of the life, the law of correspondences, the universe's law. We live in the never-ending process of corrections and learning. Single and multistructured living or non-living things are the results of the causes or reasons in infinite successions of change. This is the way of life and the universe.

After many thousands of years of human existence, the global population in last forty years doubled. How has it happened? Our existence created the biggest degradation of the ecosystem in the history of our planet. Overcrowded humanity and the devastation of the ecosystem are the main reasons for the future disappearance of humans.

Cloning is clearly against nature's law. Nature wanted us to be involved in the natural selection process. Genetic manipulation is a very risky sphere, however it's supposed to replace biological reproduction in the future. Some of the genetic alterations will be used to create advanced humans for interstellar exploration and adventure in different environments. Artificial intelligence for some humans means the necessary way to advance as a species. Some scientists would like to create a fusion between human and robot, even to the point where digital neurons will make humans immortal.

Raymond Kurzweil states,

- we are the only species that goes beyond our limitations
- concerning free will, there's a likelihood that we humans actually don't have it
- the machines "will appear to have their own free will" and even "spiritual experiences"

Every moment is valuable, and a mindful present is the treasure; contemplate it fully for inner peace and contentment. Contentment comes from understanding and living a healthy life. Being content with little is the great virtue for power and wealth.

Some scientists dream to create conscious, independent entities of artificial intelligence, which will choose to explore the physical and artificial universes in their own ways. Others create artificial intelligence that are useful daily tools to go beyond our limitations.

Each moment of life is the summary of our accumulated conditions and information at physical, mental, spiritual, social, and nutritional levels. It can be a concern for many of you that I include the nutritional level as a significant element creating our present. The truth is it's the most important. Our physiological and mental levels of performance in each moment of our existence are crucial. If you are in pain, are in a dangerous situation, or are very hungry, are under the influence of bad food (bad gut microbiota), other powerful unexpected factors, or toxins and drugs, then you will be not interested or will be unable to read this text.

Everybody can add something unique to society. Nature makes us different and wants to use our uniqueness. We can note a very interesting paradox: the more educated a man is, the higher level is his alienation with most of the population.

Gifted people make a small percentage of the populace, and they haven't the proper recognition and opportunity to perform their unique role to guide and inspire others. In nature's law, we can find that the more society develops, the more variety in the psycho-physical plane we have. Such deep differences have a creative sense in nature. The basis of individuals' personalities and how we use them depends on our evolution or total disappearance.

It is only an accident that we were born in a certain country or family, and it should be a base to valuate concepts of religion and politics, and to make utilitarian, tolerant, rational conclusions. Our concept of the realms will depend on our background and cultural matrix.

The greatest evil on earth unites with ignorant and naive doctrines.

Direct perception accesses and speaks out the truth, which becomes uncomfortable. The truth is usually more than one thing. It is very interesting that we occupied more time to describe positive things in our lives and apparently spend not enough time studying the genesis of degeneration. We can no longer suppress elementary human feelings; we have a need for equilibrium in life. All members of another race, religion, organisation, or party should be accepted. It is time to create a humanity that embraces every race, politics, religion, and generation. The study of race relations should take conclusion of the findings that black, red, white, and yellow ants are still ants. This in turn implies some conscious acceptance and responsibility of open-mindedness and balance. The time justifies differences between humans according to nature's law. Man's nature is his ability to self-regulate himself. The more wisdom we have, the more we may learn. Man who seeks to learn more of his craft shall be richly rewarded. Cultivate your own power, study, become more skilful to act, and respect yourself.

What do I have to do to understand more, be better understood by others, and get enough power and knowledge to be considered truthful?

Curiosity about new things inside and outside keeps us on the right track; we will be refreshed, inspired, and alive. Ideas of free thinkers do not fit into the accepted pattern. Most of society will not accept and understand the newcomers from the unknown world. The original thinker has a very hard life because he is a freethinker and tends to shatter preconceived ideas and opinions. Such attitudes can be found in every branch of knowledge.

How do we survive with dignity and not kill the environment?

Humanity should improve itself now as the foundation for the next generation. We must prevent our civilisation from destroying itself before we create more imbalances. Self-technological disasters are dangerous to humankind. The importance of our global problems should unite nations, blunt our vast national antagonism, clean our nuclear weapons, clean our environment, and control our population, because all our systems have become unbalanced. Any misleading in understanding about what is our highest priority can threaten our survival.

In the past, we had wars around the globe. Anger at questions about our beliefs is a warning signal about unexamined principles and dogmas. We can learn by exploring nature and ourselves with a balanced and unprejudiced mind.

We are only guests on earth. We are at the mercy of the environment. If we protect nature, it will protect us. Words hold meaning but can become disinformation. The flood of disinformation creates many obstacles to save our environment and civilisation. We lost the full expose of truth and wisdom.

Suppressing the truth or concealing it can change the future to a dangerous level, annihilating us individually or as a species.

By applying the truth, which will take care of itself using natural, clean food and water and right actions, you become the hope for the survival of humanity. True hope can be a premonition of the coming reality. Reality is a wonderful puzzle; it is the constant search for meaning and the joy of living.

The joy of living is as endless as the discoveries, and reasons about it are endless. Search honestly, and through you all things can change. In positive, effective human interaction, a good change belongs to all.

In the old times, nature's philosophy and esoterics were not as popular and accepted as they are today. People are still short of information, understanding, and communication about the most important things in life. They are in such a condition because they neglect information and become ignorant of obvious facts. All of us should watch and take part in one of the biggest game shows on earth, which is life. But in the modern world, a new kind of weakness is awakening, a fear of thinking. Walk on the same side together to fight against ignorance, our real enemy.

All of us are not separate islands. We all need help, and all of us need to feel that we are needed. For our individual survival and humanity's survival, we need to cooperate with and enhance everyone. The world of unity and peace amongst all humans is possible. Peace with love of life, cooperation, and responsibility for the human race is the only way to survive.

Human relations are the expressions of emotions that occupy our brains. You have human relationships whether or not you are aware of them. We are part of others' world, and many of us have a problem with communicating. In recent times, the tragedy of man being alienated from others is the main problem in big cities. Being human is creating more freedom by using our conscious and responsible ways; we should create a more balanced life, not the chaotic, destructive life currently around us. Human values change constantly. Aren't we selling them for money, power, and other evil activities?

We are at the centre of our universe. In the balanced light of reason, we can realise that we are in the centre of ourselves, and so we should be relaxed. We will realise that the future is the simple results of our actions in the past and, more important, all proceedings now.

"What lies behind us and what lies before us are tiny
matters compared to what lies within us."
—Ralph Waldo Emerson

Wellness in the Human Future

"This civilization is the work of man, who high-handedly and
ignorant of the true working of nature, has created a world

> without meaning or foundation, which now threatens to destroy
> him, for through his behavior and his activities, he, who should
> be her master, has disturbed nature inherent unity."
>
> —Viktor Schauberger

Our earth, suspended in the solar system, cruises around thirty thousand light years from the centre of the galaxy. It can seem like an insignificant speck of dust in the multiverse of universes, but if we will think responsibly and create more good ways, we can travel to the end and back within the universe. All can happen eventually if we will only think with purpose—that's the anthropic principle. We are offspring of the star's dust with a quantum device (the brain) and the best of nature's design (imagination). There are so many forces shaping the future; some are manmade, and some are the effect of unpredictable universe events.

> "If the bee disappeared off the surface of the globe, then
> man would only have the four years left to live."
>
> —Albert Einstein

With reliable knowledge, consciousness arises. If our responsibility for human nature and the ecosystem rises, then we have a chance to survive as a species. Now, there are no collective decisions about progress and the future. Humanity's and nature's interest is swallowed by the money global machine. Recklessness of the global economy makes degradation of nature's life, as well as human life.

Wellness in humanity's future cannot be designed by the market or by technology; it will be only a short future for all!

Humanity's evolutionary survival instinct should be concerned with saving the future. However, we are on our way to making our planet uninhabitable with enormous degradation of the ecosystem. Through interconnectedness with all and synchronicity, we can decipher more enigmas, discover more, and create more extraordinary, helpful devices for humanity's survival.

> "Whatever befalls the earth befalls the sons of the earth.
> Man, did not weave the web of the life; he is merely a strand
> in it. Whatever he does to the web, he does to himself."
>
> —Indian Chief Seattle

We're here to evolve, to thrive in life by creating a natural, better future for humans and the planet. We will be better if we will think responsibly. With all bad things which we do to nature, we are doing them to ourselves. We should realise that if our ecosystem deteriorates more, we will die too.

The constructive summary is that in any moment, we can change and improve something. We are still in the process of understanding our own beings, and we cooperate towards harmony with humanity, nature, and the future. Our present and future exist in our minds. All of us dream individually; we do not dream enough as a united humanity, with the vision to advance and a responsibility for nature and our genes. The existence of humanity depends on understanding the past and present, and their relationship; such a foundation will select the future.

The survival of humanity is governed by many forces: carbon dioxide, climate change, overpopulation, a proper mind evolution, morals, ethics, and economic and political powers.

> "Our genetic code still carries the selfish and aggressive instincts
> that were of survival advantage in the past. It will be difficult
> enough to avoid disaster in the next hundred years, let alone the next
> thousand or million. Our only chance of long-term survival is not
> to remain lurking on planet Earth, but to spread out into space."
> —Stephen Hawking

Human instincts are united with the animal world and the universe by quantum fields and morphic fields through nature's order. Human consciousness vibrations interact with everything consciously or subconsciously, including DNA. Intention, love, and attitude produce electromagnetic information waves, which by attachment create order out of disorder.

To survive as a species, we need a universal appreciation of wisdom, aesthetics, logic, and balanced living with nature. We must use all our chances and forces for revealing nature, but particularly we need to make use of faculties from uncorrupted minds. To progress, we need a genuinely honest and disciplined mind. Humans should create new dimensions and a new world to explore. Our destinies are made, not found, and a small group of people plan and control the predestination of humankind. I believe that every good action of every person should contribute to our destiny. The great human destiny is incomplete. The great human way is still undiscovered.

> "Where we're all coming from is where we're all going."
> —Neale Donald Walsch

Our Extreme Faults and Our Chances

Humans enforce destructive evolution! Humanity evolves now in the way of reckless pollution. A history of the past shows that progress is often too big a prize globally: environmental destruction, wars, and genocide.

I find the book *The Future* by All Gore extraordinary. His book should be in all schools as a must-read. Maybe then, humanity would create vital chances to survive its own foolish actions, greed, and ignorance.

Al Gore has often contemplated on the question, "What are the drivers of global change?" After a long time, he recognizes more connected-appearing evidence, and he clearly explains the interactions between leading factors in global change. His book defines the six issues that are dictating humanity's future.

~ National economies evolve into a global economy.

~ Global electronic communication, and knowledgeable machines and gadgets, are changing humanity on a he daily basis.

~ The powers on the worldwide scene shift from West to East, from nation to individual entrepreneurs.

~ Science technologies conduct and modify humans, animals, and plants. They trespass evolution.

~ Humans impact nature's balance, and extensively harmful activities undermine the ecosystem and humanity's presence in life.

~ "The emergence of rapid unsustainable growth—in population; cities; resource consumption; depletion of topsoil, freshwater supplies, and living species; pollution flows; and economic output that is measured and guided by an absurd and distorted set of universally accepted metrics that blinds us to the destructive consequences of the self-deceiving choices we routinely making."

Don't let a man rule the city, government, education, or economy if he cannot even rule his own body-mind-spirit. Lack of recognition for ancient and modern wisdom is the participation in an annihilation of our civilization.

Morals and ethics decline with obsessive pleasure and consumption—moral economy versus an expanding greed economy. Individualism in the economy is an enormous, innovating, and empowering force, but at the same time it's very dangerous for harmony with nature and society. We have a money-orientated economy with ruthless, mindless exploration of natural resources. Irrational, insatiable desires for material things and status create the edge of our destruction.

Regarding overpopulation, we've lost control, so we have now disastrous consequences: a warming climate and a lack of morals, values, ethics, and responsibilities.

Any species which cannot regulate its tempo of reproduction is on its way to extinction.

We are losing the rainforest by burning it, and through corruption. We have used up too much of the land, and we vary the natural cycle of oxygen and carbon dioxide production. We use an enormous number of chemicals in all sectors of agriculture and industry, which poison ourselves and the ecosystem. We pollute everything: air, water, land, animals, and our own food. The Earth has destructive parasites: humankind.

The good news is if all conscious people and leading forces unite to stop doing wrong, rectify the main issues, and develop ingenious ways, we can save the ecosystem and our future.

When will our future on the earth be secure? Humankind has collected wisdom regarding how to live in balance with nature and with each other. It is simply a matter of introducing it fully on a global scale in order to live in peace, harmony, and contentment. Survival of our human race depends of our rational understanding, and our today's perception will be verified by our tomorrow's realisation. It depends on harmony and cooperation with nature and all nations. All of that faces the necessity of change and evolution.

Humanity can responsibly describe and asses itself and life, fix it, and create a better future. We have a life duty to nature and ourselves on the ground of a marvellous, enigmatic chance and ability, which we get from nature. It is the constant recreating of ourselves (mind, body, and spirit) and improving our understanding about life and the universe. The best way is using individualism in art, music, science, and exploration, and by living in wholeness with harmony to create our chance to survive. Humanizing the economy globally will open new eras of higher humanity, which will handle all for nature and for our flourishing survival. If we consciously respect and love our lives, the ecosystem, and our ancestors, then we can not only improve our genotype but also save nature from degradation by our ignorant activities. The ecosystem is the base of existence for all living creatures. By not overpopulating the environment, there are positive competitions, stimulations, and exchanges of genes and information. There will be advances for all.

In the world of uncontrolled population, economy, and politics, the competition is dominated by the power of money. We reach a level where the distribution of the best knowledge and ideas are obstructed, contaminated by ignorance and disinformation. Information is always controlled as an important commodity.

The ecosystem and all our ancient and pre-modern ancestors are a source of all genes from the past and present. The nature of the genetic code decides our heredity and makes us connected to all plants and animals on the planet. Genetic information includes millennia of genetic knowledge about earlier forms, which are beings just as plants, animals, and humans are. We are the summary of our genes, experiences, and collected information from the past. In all of man's cells exist coded forms of knowledge about the past encounters between man and nature.

> "He who conquers others is strong;
> He who conquers himself is mighty."
> —Tao Te Ching (XXXIII)

The nature of the genetic code decides our heredity and makes us cousins to all plants and animals on the planet. Through genes, each man, with his potential and abilities, is in a partnership with nature. The founding principle of that partnership is balance.

The secret of a constantly evolving life and humans is diversity. Our individual uniqueness is the only way to survive as a human race. However, we need to better regulate our behaviour and enhance respect towards every decent human and towards the whole of nature. Everything is energy; information is energy too. Good, true information is unsurpassed as constructive energy. We are the unique and conglomerate matrix of info-energy.

All religions and faiths should mean peaceful, responsible, and cooperative behaviour in global society and the care of humans and nature. Certain religious understandings enrich and speed humanity's development, and some slow down.

Human dreams, hopes, potential, and aspiration for excellence can bring large variations in culture and technical development, and that will give vast aims for man. From earlier human history, man has dedicated his intellectual exploration to conquer obstacles in life. Now he is searching for new challenges to conquer them. He is working towards enhancing his prospects, dreams, ideas, opportunities, and intellectual events.

Man, should not create anything which obstructs and slows down him on any level of life. Present trends include expanding technology, increasing urbanisation, automation, cybernation, lengthening lifespan, earlier retirement age, air pollution, electromagnetic pollution, radioactive waste, and depletion of natural resources. All of these factors will increase society's problems. Humanity is now in a state of deep global transformation, which is under pressure from overpopulation, domination of reckless economy, pollution, and ecosystem degradation. We start the rat race between atomic annihilation, ecological degradation, prejudice, and higher consciousness. The power and creativity of civilisations depend of how big a percentage of the population understands basic facts, how many of them are not afraid to think, and how many of them nourish the mind as well as the body. We need to improve human perception and understand the universe and life. Newspaper, radio, and TV news remind us more and more that the ethics, morals, and humanity of the old world is dying, and in this time the new, proper world is not coming.

Modern life's value system is based on money as the universal end, leading us towards total earth destruction, wars about resources, and religious wars. We need to change the economic system where dollars will not play a role. We need ethical, moral, and artistic value for today and for tomorrow, as well as for individuals, humanity, and nature. Life moves in one direction only; we cannot stand in the same spot, and we cannot go back.

Keeping things on the move is the secret to success and attaining an interesting life. The future is within us, and there are eternal promises and possibilities in all of us. The key for the proper study of nature is man.

The continuation and evolution of our civilisation depends now more on the development of the inner self than on new technology. We now need to evolve more in the mental and spiritual worlds, the inner universe. Our society is not adapted to the fast, significant changes in technology, which make a big gap in understanding; that is the reason for frustration and aggression. Change and stability amongst nations and in the inner self of each of us are interrelated. We didn't change much or extensively improve our consciousness. Consciousness is being lifted only by a small percentage in the wider spectrum of population. However, the best of humanity is ready to enter a new age. It is necessary if we want to survive as a species. We can take steps into the new world, where we can find new adventures and excitement, where we will use our fears to build something new, and where we can grow up.

Changing is always painful, but if not done now, it will eventually be too late.

1. Correct our inner self
2. Improve our world
3. Think practically, globally, and in universal ways
4. Become an interplanetary, advanced race

"He who has not mastered himself can never master fate."

—Amen-Ra

We desperately need a new concept in education. We need stimulation to explore an alternative future in experimental and theoretical ways, with harmony and balance between the inner self, humanity, and the environment. We have no choice; without study of both the outside and the inside universes, we have no chance to find who we are, and what we are for. If you do not know where you are, you do not know where you should be. If you are not aware of what you want to have, how will you know when you find it? How can you recognise what you do not understand? We should conquer our fears.

The Worship of Technology Becomes a Mechanical Way of Controlling Nature

One of our serious dangers is the tendency to believe that technology is the only good way for people and nature. Modern man runs away from the awareness of his own being, with the help of distraction and isolation from life and nature. Man's mind is his fate. We still develop our minds, and so we can change our destiny. Man is a fragment of evolved matter-energy, and he is a fragment of evolved minds. He depends on a whole nature and relies on society.

Man is totally dependent; he cannot develop alone without society and nature. Without exception, everyone who has come to global humanity should do something special as a unique individual for the goodness of all. Human social attachments, cooperation, communication, and responsibility are keys for proper evolution; such factors promote our progress and survival. The ability for proper action in the unfolding, infinite universe is created by the exploratory behaviour correlated with the unique processes of understanding the information.

We should be only afraid of ourselves. If you think now about your future, you will realise that we do not have much time. We must do everything possible to grow on three levels with permanent gain, proper reaction, and correct decision. We can only harm ourselves in by misusing our life opportunities. As civilisation becomes more complex, more people use the reasoning parts of their minds. People also become increasingly dependent on rational thinking.

In the digital age, many people have evolved away from their extrasensory and extra-rational abilities, and they have become increasingly dependent on certain new stimulations, which shallows the reasoning functions of the mind.

Positives and Negatives of the Digital Age

- Access for mental stimulations
- Access for various information

- If the proper way is chosen, then we can experience enhanced education, wisdom, and even enlightenment
- Creativity can become unlimited; only time creates the limit
- It can bond extraordinary friendship
- It can create awakening and consciousness
- It's highly addictive (mobile phones, iPods, games, the Internet)
- Creativity and concentration span suffer
- Lack of exercise
- Personal, face-to-face human contact is minimized
- We're entering a virtual world
- Purposely introduced disinformation
- The flood of unconnected information
- We can be lost in the digital, virtual world; it is becoming more real than true life

Every two to three years, we have a doubling of all information that we collect as a human race. We complicate our lives because we put out a lot of information as a disinformation. We implanted a lot of untrue information in forms of competitions and wars. We create obstacles in understanding each other, and we are not cooperating with ourselves and with other nations. We do not tolerate other religions. Disinformation is like a pollution or rubbish, and we cause the problem because we allow that rubbish to be put in books, mass media, and our minds. There is a saying, "Rubbish in, rubbish out," and it happens in computers and human minds. All, who want to be well informed will become evolved.

We must take the initiative and act in harmony with nature. Humanity's destiny means taking the active way to take part in the development of our society through the formation of our own destiny, the lives of our families, and humanity.

We are indeed a powerful complex of energies because we are the manifestation of the natural forces that create and control the universe. Human destiny is governed by probability function computed with a free mind. It is a never-ending fulfilment as a human being.

We already have solutions to problems of overpopulation, pollution, energy supplies, food shortage, and wars. The punishment for criminals is often a farce. The drugs are the main reason for crime. The research shows bad parenting as the secondary malfunction in a global society. The world is under the power of money, greed, and politics. It is not under the rules of wisdom, goodness, beauty, morals, ethics, and humanity's survival in the future.

Corporations are very powerful, crafty, and prosperous. Now is the time that they will use their abilities, money, and resources to rectify problems around the globe. If they use splendid, plentiful ideas and systems, they can start some proper ways that are balanced and do not harm nature. Furthermore, they can perfect the survival of humanity and their businesses.

We rely too much on the measure of money, profit, and time. We cannot compare them with ethical, moral values and with the effects on the environment and our future. Our present actions handle the development and destiny of our civilisation. A new era can be fully started if old steering forces will understand that their survival lies in this new dimension of mind with the proper actions followed.

Human future is first designed in the mind. Human future is not in a fixed pattern and is unlimited. Deadness of the uncontrolled technocracy has become clear. However, a new light of wisdom with a better, balanced mental life is emerging. It is coming not from the spectrum of money, power, politics, and mass media. It is coming from ancient wisdom. We can't cut the necessity of living closer to the basic of nature by the isolation of the biological origins of humans, and we should obey principals and the law of nature.

We should stay close to nature. If we want to survive, we must return to nature. Humankind can develop and survive only by coexistence and harmonious interaction with nature.

For our survival, the unknown and irregular are more important than the known, and they are more critical. Human relations to the value system need to improve by setting social, spiritual, mental, and ecological values ahead of money governance. Our civilisation has fallen to its low morale and miserable cultural stage because of its wrong values, corrupted morals, and sense-controlled masses. The moral security has disappeared into a world state of fear. Many intelligent people in the world realise that there has been a deterioration in industry, government, law, and other institutions. Our global society has not yet reached the point of straightaway openness, truthful self-identity, honesty, and psychological, political, and ethnical equality. For this very reason, the greatest necessity of this age is a university devoted exclusively to the science of man, life, and nature.

> "Our primeval Mother Earth is an organism that no science in the world
> can rationalize. Everything on her that crawls and flies is dependent
> upon Her and all must hopelessly perish if that Earth dies that feeds us."
> —Victor Schauberger

Applying essential principals are the only way for humanity to have a future. From material production and consumption to natural balance, contemplation, consciousness, and collective level of consciousness, the progress of grooving up is enhanced by the progress of the consciousness of freedom. To be free means to face and bear stress. Freedom needs the capacity to accept and to live constructively all the time. Freeman has esteem for himself, a feeling of worth, and dignity. The more awareness of the self one has, the more awareness of the world one has, and vice versa. We should have the desire to serve other and ourselves.

> We are part of Creation, thus, if we break the laws of Creation we destroy ourselves. We, the Original Caretakers of Mother Earth, have no choice but to follow and uphold the Original Instructions, which sustains the continuity of Life. We recognize our umbilical connection to Mother Earth and understand that she is the source of life, not a resource to be exploited. We speak on behalf of all Creation today, to communicate an urgent message that man has gone too far, placing us in the state of survival. We warned that one day you would not be able to control what you have created. That day is here. Not heeding warnings from both Nature and the People of the Earth keeps us on the path of self-destruction. This self-destructive path has led to the Fukushima nuclear crisis, Gulf oil spill, tar sands devastation, pipeline failures, impacts of carbon dioxide emissions and the destruction of ground water through hydraulic fracking, just to name a few. In addition, these activities and development continue to cause the deterioration and destruction of sacred places and sacred waters that are vital for Life.
> —Arjun Walia, The Indian Chief Speech for Collective Evolution

We need to make proper choices for our surroundings, partners, friends, jobs, education, and life knowledge. We need proper care of health, satisfactory social relations, and freedom of choice and actions, which are positive for all. These expand our life choices and create our destiny. With the need for proper information, and through deep curiosity, we can absorb the knowledge and grow with better understanding the complexity, purpose, and wisdom of life. In addition, by understanding our imbalances, and by proper actions, we will improve and better prepare humanity's future. The more that values are respected by the global society, the higher the chances for survival of humanity. A responsible human is on the path of high aspiration and firm discipline, seeking the unity with nature and society with appreciation and admiration of life and of the universe.

Humanity's and nature's future are a big concern and are the responsibility of unknown' thinkers, which left the message on crafty stones for humanity more than thirty-six years ago. All good guidelines should be manifested on a daily basis.

The Georgia Guide Stones[18]

1. Maintain humanity under 500,000,000 in perpetual balance with nature
2. Guide reproduction wisely, improving fitness and diversity
3. Unite humanity with a new living language
4. Rule passion, faith, tradition, and all things with tempered reason
5. Protect people and nations with fair laws and just courts
6. Let all nations rule internally, resolving external disputes in a world court
7. Avoid petty laws and useless officials
8. Balance personal rights with social duties
9. Prize truth, beauty, and love, seeking harmony with the infinite
10. Do not be a cancer on the earth; leave room for nature

Overpopulation created most problems due to degradation of humanity and the ecosystem. The rest of the issues are the outcome of unbalanced interaction of controlling powers, harmful businesses, unsustainable economy, politics, and science.

Professor Stephen Hawking analyzed artificial intelligence and said in an interview with the BBC, "the development of full artificial intelligence could spell the end of the human race."

With artificial intelligence, we are activating unknown forces that can control too much of humanity's essence and naturalness, especially if we are permanently wired with computers and computing power exceeds the human mind. The best computers already compute better than the average human mind, and they redesign themselves. Therefore they can make an error or conscious mistake to our peril. The life-sized existential prize is created by gambling with artificial intelligence. Can we consciously take such a risk to replace ourselves? Living is an outcome and interpretation of life by the natural mind, not by artificial intelligence.

The natural evolution of humankind did not make fatal mistakes with us; we are still existing. However, many scientists claim that many times, humanity almost annihilates itself with wrong technology, senseless leaders, and inferior ethics, morals, education, and law. Are we the wrong or confused species that wanders in circles? At the present, humanity has lost control because we've overpopulated and degraded the ecosystem. The ecosystem is used mainly in irresponsible ways, and a lot of times in criminal ways. In effect, we undermine our own existence. Many people stop following nature. They find a new god, money, and

---

[18] http://thegeorgiaguidestones.com/

they stop cooperating with nature. Many human deliberate selections and actions lead to human extinction through ecological catastrophe and nuclear or biological warfare. There can be human extinction and general life blockades on the earth. The good news is that enough humans can awaken and start to properly rectify the ways of living. If not, some bacteria can centralize the life again. Bacteria can live in high and in low temperatures, in acidic and alkali environments. That way, all can start again.

"As technology develops, there is a theoretical possibility that humans may be deliberately destroyed by the actions of a nation state, corporation or individual in a form of global suicide attack. There is also a theoretical possibility that technological advancement may resolve or prevent potential extinction scenarios."[19]

Human greed is bigger than a human need, and all problems start from it. We should learn from the bacterial collective intelligence, which can be three times better than the human collective intelligence. Bacterial society protects resources and multiplies in a balanced way. There is no misleading and disinformation. Humans are the product of slow evolution, and any super acceleration using artificial intelligence can result in our extinction. Man as an automaton, an expandable robot with auto-invention, is capable of being sacrificed to achieve an aim. Man, in some spectrum, is only little more than a sophisticated robot, whose behaviour is measured, tested, evaluated, and programmed. There are some scientists who plan to create robots that will lie, because our society lies. It is controversial, and we should strive to improve humanity's morale and ethics, not enforce lies in robots. In all parts of Polynesia, before the white man came, they did not know the meaning of lying.

Advances in artificial intelligence will enter and change the human mind. Our only chance to get freedom from an increasingly automated lifestyle is to find a new path of new, stimulating activities, achievement, and heightened awareness.

The time of quick gratification as a way of living will take us away from life, detached from nature. Setting up the material level as purposeful living is futile. Reckless living affects us personally and globally, and it affects our planet too. Can we foresee humanity's future? There is hope because each human is something new, a unique being of perception, ability, and limitations with the ability to become a responsible being.

---

[19] https://en.wikipedia.org/wiki/Human_extinction

We Are Living In

We are living in the universe of change.
Change cannot alter itself.
Life and death are the beginning of each other.
There is dualism in life and death.
Theirs secrets and destiny are transforming;
That reveals the unchanging supreme.
Life is constant, relentless change.
We are living in an ocean of energies.
Life of energetic polarities interchange;
Then you will see the oneness of things.
Be serene and in harmony within itself, and with all.

All life comes from concentrated, well-organized information.
Life is about acquiring information and using it well.
If you know more, than you are hooked for more. Why?
The new world opens and you understand more.
The more you understand, the more options and pleasure you have;
Then the more self-control and expertise you have.
It becomes a never-ending process.
It is a joyful and overwhelming expansion of wisdom, and you will not stop it.
It becomes the essence of your contented life.

Could Human Overpopulation End the Human Race?

The world's human population is estimated to be over 7.4 billion. It has doubled in just forty years! The twentieth century became the marker of the humans as a social animal that completely lost the ability to control its population. What happened that the global population doubled in the last forty years?

Our global overpopulation is preparing our own extinction and the extermination of many species. We need to control global overpopulation because it is associated with wars, pollution, environmental degradation, famine, and bursts of diseases.

The history of our planet shows that more than 99 percent of all species that have lived are extinct already. Human relations become a big problem from the moment our subconsciousness realises that we've overpopulated our planet. Then some chain reactions start on the human and environmental levels.

Some scientists state that humans cannot survive, but it can be circumvented if we use wisdom and responsibly act now. Human evolution in the past was a slow process, but individuality and the variety of humankind are a safe base for our future. The exploration of space offers intergalactic colonization and beyond.

Nature makes humans original and honest, but the rat race and overpopulation pushes people to chase unbalanced, forced fictions leading towards degradation. Overpopulation and global warming are interrelated factors affecting us now, and they will be crucial soon. We have no choice: we must control and reduce the global population to sustainable levels.

Professor Frank Fenner thinks that, "Humans will be unable to survive a population explosion and unbridled consumption."[20]

As the supposedly advanced species, we should have an antipathy towards human extinction. What will be our proper reaction? Overpopulation, money-orientated economy, politics, and science will degrade the natural life support system, which is our whole ecosystem. Global overpopulation triggers a primitive reaction of competition and lowers the quality of human life. We are losing the plot to cooperate, enrich each other, and create together a new and better world.

Could senseless and money-orientated economy, politics, education, agriculture, and medicine end humanity? Could artificial intelligence end humankind? Could sugar, GMO, processed food, polluted water, and air end our species?

Human overpopulation causes the extinction of other species and diminishes resources used extensively by humans. Even if we control our population, there will not be enough for human greed. In the moment we lost the natural balance between ourselves and nature, when we overpopulated, we began war within ourselves, with other humans, and with nature. We create humanity and environment degradation by global warming, pollution, atmospheric carbon dioxide, waste, overconsumption, and resource depletion. Life and the world are constantly signalling to us that imbalances are in us and in the environment, as well as how we can fix everything. We can control global population, which creates havoc in the ecosystem: pollution, aggression, crimes, unbalanced division of income, and a weakened human genotype.

Genetics experts discovered that the genotype has no dead-end. The environment play a crucial role in shaping organisms to survive or vanish. The body-mind-spirit complex

---

[20]   http://www.dailymail.co.uk/sciencetech/article-1287643/Human-race-extinct-100-years-population-explosion.html#comments

overdrives the genes, controlling all our energies and information. That's why there is a paradox of sudden improvement of physical, mental, and spiritual faculties in highly educated and low-income families. In both cases, there is the same pure energy driving individuals to obtain a higher level of consciousness. In the very long term of human development, the last variation of the genotype is not crucial to obtain better mental faculties. It seems that it's there in each of us; the only difference is that some of us live in a dream state, and some can awaken by internal and external forces. We can become wiser, more responsible, healthier, kinder, and more cooperative towards humanity. It is time to create a humanity that embraces every race, religion, politics, generation, and the base of our existence, the ecosystem. By finding the miracle of life in single cells around you and in you, the unity of life in wonder and with love will create a new wholeness.

Many human want a better life and world, we can get it by improving ourselves first. We need to conserve all natural resources and increase recycling. Disposable and unuseful products degrade the ecosystem and are a waste of precious resources, time, and money. The quantity of such products are increasing. Famine also relates to the ecological limits of the land, and climate change is mostly related to wrong human activities.

Human evolution should give positive progress inside humanity. Additionally, all human activities in nature ought to be constructive. The good, small actions and things build up a major network of events. Each day can become a precursor for a good future.

The future of human evolution, and everything else, starts from nature's laws: wisdom, diversity, and freedom.

> "If you are depressed, you are living in the past.
> If you are anxious, you are living in the future.
> If you are at peace, you are leaving in the present."
> —Lao Tzu

If we start thinking with good conscience and obey nature's laws with joy, then we will become finders of truth. We will become delighted and feel pleasure at seeing the good everywhere. In the good and in the bad, there is space for peace and harmony. There is more freedom and joy in a life wisely lived. Release what is useless, and free your heart and mind. Then you will find contentment and love. Make things up with a sense of joy and play in a state of relaxation. This is a highly intuitive state. We are in the beginning of life with hope and duty for the good of another. We tried to grasp what is stable and permanent, and we found the universal ocean, the flow of atoms with tides, and eternal change. We are evolving beings.

Remember that ideas and good actions cannot come from unthinking minds. Spend time thinking of and acting for only what you want. Fears, failures, and diseases arise from negative, harmful thoughts and actions. Therefore, think and act positively if you want vitality in the body-mind-spirit. Knowing that fear arises from a lack of information. You can prepare for failures arising from ignorance. Knowing creates the power to do anything. The best way is to do only what is necessary and positive for anything. Enjoying it will vitalise the mind-body-spirit. Ignorance and negative thinking create a miserable life and develops destructive toxins, and we became fatigued very quickly

Man will find that the well of cosmic knowledge is within himself, not outside himself. Self-education of individuals is preferable, rather than through mass education, which submerges individuality. Self-awakening can come only through aloneness of each self. Illumination into the cosmic consciousness is the goal of humanity.

The average man thinks through stimulation from his senses. His education is acquired through what his senses see and hear, as well as how much he can remember and repeat. Conventional educational processes can create millions of repeaters, but the world's greatest men have come through the discovery of the universe within themselves. All knowledge is based upon ideas and imagination, which can never be taught by conventional educational methods. Ideas and imagination are a product of the deep-thinking mind. The new human development is a mind-thinker and intuition-knower, with spiritual and mental values ahead of money and material wealth.

Many civilisations fell through the degradation of millions, but some rose again. It happened because of the superiority of a small number, those rare minds we have always amongst us.

Our civilisation has fallen to a dangerously low level in moral, cultural, intellectual, and spiritual development in the last fifty years. We are still under the domination of instincts. Our minds are still programmed for a jungle fight, and in our inferior social, mass-media interactions we are losing our energy, our insight, and our ability to appreciate and love. Survival in our world today means that we must have instant perception of oneness, love, and compassion in order to get higher consciousness. Our personal development and civilisation depend on insight and deep, intuitive understanding in mentally supportive and loving ways.

The main stream of people in the world live on a lower consciousness level, and they live in endless struggle. The more time we spend being successful in the material world, the less loving, peaceful, and contented we become. Our purposes and chances are not random; they are the sensible, timed selections of our outstanding abilities and correct actions. The more we understand, the less we will worry.

Most people live from day to day, and everybody is looking to get an easy life and be rich. Not many want to be rich with knowledge about the mystery of life. Nevertheless, with the rising love and knowledge about our lives, we start to have many big questions and issues. We grow in proportion to the challenges we overcome. Your life is a complex of the truest possibilities to be actualized. We share our life-complex possibilities with the rest of universe. Life is the actualization of chosen possibilities. One of the wonders of the world is its complexity, which endlessly grows with our understanding. We will be never able to describe it by a mathematical paradigm or philosophical model. We live in paradise, but if we know everything, our existence would become senseless. We live in Wonderland, which is life, nature, and the universe.

We are now entertaining a new, fresh show in which we can make sensible decisions and actions. We live in space and time, which are flexible and relative entities. We are walking in the paths of our ancestors. It is our responsibility to represent them in the best way. All of us should be honoured to carry it forward. Our parents chose their ways, and now we must select our ways for water, food, company, and information, which create our existence. All our selections uniquely create our lives. A productive attitude, openness, honesty, the exchange of needed energies, and a distinctive expression of discovery are good contributions to humanity and life. Human life is a never-ending growth. We are in constant change, improving our ideas and conscious existence. The universe is around us and within us. Everything is one.

The gaia theory indicates that the earth's biosphere is a living, self-regulated superorganism. Mass consciousness is a deciding force for the future of humanity and our planet.

What is going to happen? By having power, it does not mean having freedom. Evolving requires positive and negative forces. The most evolved and most important parts of the human species are the four minds, which efficiently cover the state of life. The most precious thing is life with the right state of the mind-body-spirit. Your life is the outcome of your four minds: brain, heart, gut, and body aura.

Humanity is on its way to extinction through its own actions. Use your mind to correct you body and your actions in your life and the environment.

> "Love what you do and do what you love. Don't listen to anyone else who tells you not to do it. You do what you want, what you love. Imagination should be the centre of your life."
>
> —Ray Bradbury

"There is only one thing that heals every problem,
and that is to know how to love yourself."

—Louise Hay

By loving others, we should not forget to love ourselves. We are born with the need to be loved and to love. We will never say it is enough. The love for life is the first and most genuine love. Love always comes from good things. Love is unique energy and emotion, and it can live in the past, present, and tomorrow.

What is the most powerful force for people with little understanding? Money! Money becomes the god and power for little-minded people. What is more powerful than money? Health of the mind, spirit, and body, with understanding, collecting, and using true information at the right time.

The art of living is not believing all our own thoughts, but re-examining them; it is seeing beyond perception, initial understanding, and conclusions.

Technology and money have become modern gods. If we follow them, we will be absorbed by artificial life. In effect, we will become more primitive, far from life, and vanish. We can create our lives by concentrating only on good things, and we can improve constantly in our lifespan. The collection of new ideas and unknown facts will enrich all. There is so much more for us to enjoy, absorb, share, improve, and create. We can travel on a synchronicity river. A lot of things, events, and people are there for the reason that we need them to appear and cooperate with them.

The universe organises all things in such way that they are in constant change. They never die—they transform. At the end, all become one, and one becomes all.

We need to experience balance, peace, love, growth, learning, and joy. After we become one with everything, a new consciousness will arrive. Life is the process of rising consciousness. Thinking, ideas, choices, imagination, and creations are the real powers of your life. We are part of the creator, and in our minds, everything can exist: god, devil, ghost, dreams, and ideas. The mind is a pathway to hell and paradise. We can destroy ourselves or create a new, better, wise, and responsible human race. If we focus deeply with love, balance, and peace, then we will assume a supernatural being's nature.

Stop thinking about what you fear! If you are in the energy spectrum of what you do not want, you will get it. Enrich yourself by enriching others. Share everything and you will live in the land of abundance. Never put yourself down. Think about how to create new ways to succeed. Write for yourself what you would like to become. Being yourself means that you are ready, strong, and free. Jump into life so that you will not miss it. Study your being so that you will discover wholeness.

Everything around us is not ours for long. We belong to change; it is the whole. Our lives should be balanced between two forces with minimal amplitude. If you are in deep despair, it will take longer to get back to contentment. Many times we are not able to change the conditions around us, but we can change our attitude. Some men create their cocoon to falsely feel safe. Problems and suffering are life teachers, and understanding that will create enjoyment of life. Know and conquer yourself so that you will be able to create a decent man in yourself. You will find the greatest secret and wealth in your joyful, healthy mind and body. With equilibrium in your mind, you never will be alone, and you will appreciate and respect yourself.

You also will become a conscious part of the changing universe. By finding the miracle, the unity of life in the single cells around you and in you, with wonder and love you will create the new wholeness. You will become your own reason, discovering the truth wisely until you have become the way itself. This is your final victory and your final way. Master your knowledge and emotions and stay balanced, and you will understand life and the universe.

Explore yourself with curiosity and joy. We are what we think. All that we are and our lives arise from our thoughts and immagination. Controlling yourself is the real power. Your internal peace creates peace in others. Everything is a electromagnetic vibration and is changed by other sources of electromagnetic energy. In the end, everything is interconnected by electromagnetic vibrations. Strive to live with reason, balance, peace, and love so that you will have joy, freedom, and purpose to live. Life is about self-discovery versus the wide spectrum of life.

One day I asked myself, "How can our outer world be orderly if our inner world is not?" Today, more people know that the inner world is more important than the outer circumstances. Uncontrolled intensity of the power in the mind-body-spirit creates imbalances and disturbances around us. The best way to improve humanity and the world is to first improve ourselves, and to become responsible for our civilization and nature. Respect for nature, life, wisdom, and yourself is highly needed, because then you can secure all and create all. Know that we cannot isolate ourselves too far from nature. In order to function properly, we need sunlight, nature, and natural food.

As we grow older and wiser, we notice

That we are more in balance within ourselves.
In the process of realizing the meaning of the life,

We live life as the awesome mystery.
Remember that muteness can become a blessing or a curse.
Discover conclusions with guidance from stillness and reflection.
Say only wise words which are better than silence.
Follow the wheel of life, living the way.
A lifetime is worth being conscious.
Wisdom, peace, and joy are in the healthy mind-body.
It is the greatest achievement and an enormous privilege.
We are not looking for insignificant gratification,
Mistaking one thing for another.
It turns into pain and confusion.
We want to live a life with purpose,
Become good human beings
With worthy lives in the repetition of good.
We can see now more without a doubt;
We understand more what's important, and what's pointless.
Truthful and useful information will make you
More liberated and developed.
The kind of information we have and how we will use them are crucial.
Information can become our servant or master.
Moreover, we see what is serviceable for life and us.
With love and joy of all, in unity of all, we are living with the whole.

"Only these who attempt the absurd will achieve the impossible."
—Albert Einstein

The mind, like the universe, is in a constant change-evolution. The universe, all minds, and all sources of electromagnetic energy interact with each other. The natural law of the universe is the first conductor of the unknown, primal orchestra. It is most important to not break the beautiful symphony of the natural music of life. Technology starts to dominate our daily lives, introducing new sources of energy and new ways to communicate. The delicate synchronicity of nature's network is interrupted and damaged. Wireless phones and other gadgets are changing the body's bioelectric field of electrons on a cellular level. Microwave exposure by worldwide development of wireless technology increases various health risks. Electromagnetic fields damage our cells and DNA. That is why the malignant and highly lethal brain cancer called glioma develops, according to Dr. Lennart Hardell and statistician Michael Carlberg from the University of Örebro in Sweden.[21]

Our brains, hearts, and gut microbiota work together to play a significant role in the condition of our health, healing, happiness, and perception of reality. It all starts with your heart, your brain, and your understanding of how they work together. Consciousness is the combined effect of the four minds and emotions with insight, which relate to the matrix of the universe. Our consciousness creates its own speed and time for us to understand ourselves and all that is understandable. There is no time for the universe; the universe is time itself and creates and ceases time. The universe does not need time to exist. The universe is timeless and has eternal time to exist. The new seasons of life are set up automatically by nature and start every day in all our cells in our bodies and in our minds, creating a new flux. With good, needed changes all grow. Some changes, events, and fluxes depend of conscious selection and responsibilities towards the mind and body.

Understanding, like learning, is a never-ending process. Enjoy your process of existence and your own responsible creation; then you will become close to the universe, consciousness, and life. Humans need time and speed to observe, to gather true information in order to function properly, and to celebrate the excellence of life. Celebration of life starts with the moment of realization and the creation of our own lives. The true celebration of your existence is the moment when you realise that you are responsible for the creation of your life.

Sail through your life like you would through your dream: without beginning or ending. Look deeply at the values and wisdom which create the good life. Become a conscious member of the wise generational change. Be aware and appreciate when good things in life come. Do not be afraid to find unknown trials or to experience the beauty of life and the pleasure of being alive. You will stay younger if you enjoy your life, and if you are aware about it most of the time. Living without the light of wisdom is like living in darkness.

> "What was so surprising to us was the discovery of
> how we can create matter directly from light using the
> technology that we have today in the UK."
> —Professor Steve Rose

Acquiring new facts makes us realise how little knowledge we have about anything. In the human real world, only true observation counts, not belief structure. The way for elation,

---

[21] http://www.ncbi.nlm.nih.gov/pmc/articles/PMC2092574/

fulfilment, and serenity relates to deep dreaming and imagination, which later appears to manifest.

> "The true soldier is he who fights not the external but the internal
> foes. Everything are one, both visible and the invisible."
>
> —Shabistari

By knowing yourself, you will know the universe. The more you know about life, the more you will become responsible, and the more balanced, peaceful, and joyful your life will become. Your life uncovers who you are, where you come from, and why you are here. Use your mind and eagerly explore your dearest chance of living. Life relies on a constant collection of information, understanding it, and using it. It is our never-ending destiny.

Get the wellness in your life by creating equilibrium and joy inside yourself, and between humans and nature. You are already there if you understand yourself.

> How are you?
> See it within yourself
>
> What do you want from life?
> What does life want from you?
>
> You are not imagination.
> You are in the now, and you create now.
> You are the sense of now.
> You are who you are now.
> You are conscious information.
> Conscious time is a precious life reward.
> Consciousness from the way of life
> Creates the universe and you.
> You are life.
> Life is energy-matter.
> You are the energy-information.
> You are in unity with everything;
> Evolution and creation are you.
> You are what you focus on.
> You are what you thankful for.

You are what you think you are.
Conquer yourself to know yourself.
Knowing yourself leads to the finesse of life.
By knowing yourself, you will know the universe.
Take the time to think deeply and beyond.

Inferiority is self-inflicted.
Genius is self-granted.

If suffering invalidates the pleasure of learning,
Then you are learning from the wrong source,
Or you are not using information at all.

The universe, consciousness, and information are one,
Formed by the mind into a settled purpose:
To elevate over the matter-body.
The nature of man calls to victory over himself.
Welcome the virtuosity of wisdom
In the mystery of the whole life.
You are the result of your enquiry,
The outcome of all that you learn.
Like intuition, you become the facts initially not seen.
All actions in your life create the evidence of who you are.
What you use from the essence of concern
Creates your future.
Changing the universe changes you.
Creating yourself is creating the universe.
Be a person with a conscience.
Know about polarity in everything,
Unity of all by quantum agreement,
Contradiction of good and evil.
Persevere to be part of creation,
Loving all that exists.

Our time is in no time.
Inconsistency becomes consistency.

Variation creates temporary balance.
Dissimilarity becomes similarity.

Learning, knowing, and understanding
Create your daily balanced steps in the universe.
Reflection, meditation, and enlightenment
Are the ways to know yourself
And are the highest self-expression.

Pure ecstasy of living with eternal leading—
The whole life you can find in your lifetime.

You are the conclusion of all ideas
About yourself and the world.
Rectify them to create your wellness,
Your relationship with mind-spirit-body.
Being mindful of your lifetime is your real power.
Now, enjoy the whole of your journey.
Whatever you are doing is the starting point.
Choose properly the next one for a worthy finish.
Remember that the end is another form of existence.

What Is the Most Important for You?

The most important for you is your change.
You ask where the way is.
The way is your change
Do not lose your time; become the change.
You know it already;
It is deeper in your heart, mind, body, spirit.
You must find it for yourself.

The true investigation and exploration
Everybody is doing, mostly alone.
Then you will find the truth of your life.
Change is the most powerful universal law.

Change creates change, life, and the universe.
Create you, your balance, and peace.
Change is around you and is in all of us.
Become a better change.

MY STORY

In life, the only real warranty is the certainty and necessity to complete our lives. In the universe, everything is connected. Therefore my story connects with yours. I was born at 7/6/1950 in Poland, in the centre of Europe. Poland was the centre of the ancient trade roads to different lands. Such a centre becomes a hub of enormous significance of European history. Many countries in the past tried to control such an important place, and many wars and many shifting boundaries affected Poland. There are also many advantages to being the hub of Europe. The new goods, art, music, ideas, and genes enriched my country.

Today, upon seeing the past, I think that I was fortunate to grow in a time where the natural world and natural food combine with a natural outdoor playground with limited restriction. Kids from five years old were running free. As a young child, I loved to read books. I dreamed about travelling around the world through exotic lands. I even read the novels with action in Australia, which described the red land very well. Such a daily life formulated my healthy mind and body, deep thinking with curiosity, and reflection. In addition, I was freer to compare it to today's norms.

Water is a very important environment for me. I spend my time on the water before my formal living. How did it happen? My parents lived and worked on the big barge, shifting goods on the Polish river systems. I was conceived on the river, and for the whole pregnancy I was cruising on the barge. More than five years later, I was living with my parents on the rivers to transport coal, cement, grain, and sand. I remember the different smells of cargo, as well as the gentle movement of the barge on the waves. One day before going shopping, my mom left me in the cargo-loading chamber, opened on the top with a sand pit at the bottom of the loading compartment, so I could play by myself. She also left a bottle of water and an apple, but the most important thing that she should have not left was the ladder. In addition, she asked a woman from the next barge to check on me from time to time. Then she went shopping.

After an hour or so, I tried to find something else to explore. I discovered the ladder leading straight to heaven. I climbed to the top and then walked on the plank connecting the barge with the riverbank. I remember walking on the plank and eating the apple. I was five years old then. The woman supervising me suddenly had a premonition that something was wrong with me. She ran and checked the loading chamber. After that, she realised what could have happened. She noticed the small bubbles coming from the bottom of the river. She grabbed the wooden pole with the hook to check the water between the barge and the riverbank. Immediately she probed the spot with the hooked pole, and miraculously she hooked me on my suspenders.

Two days after this accident, I was okay. This event did not scare me from the water. Later, I become one of the top four swimmers in my country between fourteen and seventeen years of age. I even became a lifesaver at twenty years of age. The love for water was so strong that I later obtained a scuba diving licence. At the next step, I attended the navy's deep diver school, diving up to ninety metres underwater.

Two other sports caught my attention: chess and tennis. Chess was first. After many years, I noticed the similarities of the tactics between them. Both connect mastery of the game to the inner mastery of the mind, which carries far beyond both activities. A mental aspect of all sports and life was revealed to my inner self. It is about the magical state of mind in ideal, relaxed concentration, thinking, and action. I found one day that tennis combines two worlds, the physical and the mental. The insights in both are about controlling my ego rather than letting my ego control me.

I also love sailing, which I started in Poland while studying veterinary science. I am continuing this passion in Australia to this day. For many years, I have been sailing around the Great Barrier Reef, and the Whitsunday became my home. The last voyage was from Darwin, Australia, to Indonesia. I'm close to nature, and I began to realise the importance of the ecosystem for humankind's survival. I researched for many years about life, the universe, and the human mind-body complex.

What might be described as a sinkhole experience in my life? I found myself in a sinkhole in the military for two years' compulsory training. I learned some skills, of course, but the majority of time was wasted. I saved that time to study life and nature.

The correct frontier of life is guaranteed by the right choice and approach towards everything. There are so many dreams that negotiate their existence within the universe. I try to live my dream and complete life with a passion for deep exploration of nature, events, other people's thoughts, experiences, and wisdom, along with a conscious appreciation of everything around me. I dream to see and comprehend the whole world and myself. I try to discover full meaning, which reveals the truth of the laws of life and nature. My passion is collecting information about nature, life, and myself through profound research, in order to understand more about an essential, useful, and successful lifespan. I try all the time to be an open-minded traveller who is not afraid of the truth. I am a seeker of the truth. Virtuousness of life is included in the universality of truth, and any kind of truth ultimately becomes the winner.

In the wide spectrum, we are all students and teachers of the mysterious universe. That is why I like conversations with different people, in order to exchange information about the meaning of life, individuals, humanity's goals, and our prospects.

I am grateful for my existence. Life is my greatest adventure, and I can still be amazed by the awesome mystery and wonder of life and nature. Many years ago, I decided to learn how to keep my mind, body, and spirit healthy in order to enjoy life. I realise that I need to be rich in knowledge to take proper care of my mind and body. I gradually started a fascinating, unique journey in my life, a new quest: researching and learning not only for myself. After a long time, I become hooked on finding a new and true knowledge that was usable for me and others. The collection of informative evidence became the main source for this book.

All of us are on the way to raising our personal consciousness, which is increasing the collective consciousness and awareness of humanity. Additionally, cooperating using interconnectivity with all people, the earth, and the whole environment will enhance our chances to survive as a civilization.

Today, with pleasure and gratification, I can face life with confidence, certainty, and fulfilment. I love the past and the present. In addition, I know I am creating a very good future through my consciousness. Life is about self-discovery versus the wide spectrum of life. One day I asked myself, "How can our outer world be orderly if our inner world is not?" Today, more people know that the inner world is more important that outer circumstances. We all are on the way to improving humanity and the world. The best way is to first improve ourselves and then become responsible for our civilization and the ecosystem.

You Are on the Way of Life

I wish you all wellness.
Everything wishes you wellness.
As you grow older, you notice
That you are in the process of realizing the meaning of life.
The more you are in balance within yourselves,
The more life becomes an awesome mystery,
Discovering conclusions with guidance from silence and reflection.
Remember that silence can become blesses or cursed.

Follow the wheel of life, living the way.
A lifetime's worth of being conscious with wisdom
means peace and joy in healthy mind-body-spirit.
It is the greatest achievement and an enormous privilege.
You are not looking for insignificant gratification,
Mistaking one thing for another.
It turns into pain and confusion.

You want to live a life with purpose,
Becoming a good human being
With a worthy life in the repetition of the good.
You can see now more without a doubt;
You understand what is important and pointless.
Truthful and useful information will make you
More liberated and developed.
Moreover, you see what is serviceable for life and for you.
With love and joy of all, in unity of all,
You are living with the whole.

FOR MY READERS

It will be a very rewarding experience for me if this book is useful to you, my dear readers, the seekers of a more fulfilling life. You are inquisitive and researching to understand more, and that will improve your conscious existence. I honour you, your enlightenment, and your contentment. Thank you for your part of the conscious creation. Be content while walking along with life and nature. I wish you all the joy of living. In the love of life within you, there are all sanctioned worlds. I wish for you to become a worthy human, acquiring the virtue of true knowledge and having a stimulating existence. By using your uniqueness, you will do remarkable things, so enjoy it every day. I wish you all wellness. Everything wishes you wellness.

Love your life, the world, and wisdom; then all will protect you, and you will protect all.

Tadeusz Nowicki

BIBLIOGRAPHY

A

Altschule, M. *Origin of Concept of Human Behavior.* New York: Wiley, 1977.

Argyle, M., *Social Psychology of Work.* Harmnodsworth: Penguin, 1989.

Aristotle. *The Basic Writing of Aristotle.* New York: Random House, 1941.

Ariola, Paavo. *Are You Confused?* Tenth edition. Phoenix: Health Plus Publisher, 1979.

Aron, R. *Main Currents in Sociological Thought.* Harmondsworth: Penguin Books, 1968.

Aronson, E. *The Social Animal.* San Francisco: W. H. Freeman, 1980.

Attali, Jacques. *A Brief History of the Future.* Allen & Unwin, 2011.

Attenborough, David. *Life on Earth.* London: British Broadcasting Corporation,1979.

B

Baddley, A. D. *The Psychology of Memory.* New York: Basic Books 1976.

Bandura, A., *Principles of Behavior Modification.* New York: Holt, Rinehart & Winston, 1969.

Banton, Michael. *Race Relations.* London: Camelot Press, 1970.

Baron, M., Gainer, J. D. "Molecular Genetics and Human Diseases." *British Journal of Psychiatry* (1988): 152.

Barlow, Maude. *Blue Covenant—The Global Water Crisis and the Coming Battle for the Right to Water.* Melbourne: Black Inc., 2007.

Batmanghelidj, F. *Your Body's Many Cries for Water.* Second edition. Global Health Solution, 1998.

Bergland, Richard. *The Fabric of Mind.* Australia: Penguin Books Ltd, 1985.

Berman, Louis, Evans, J. C. *Exploring the Cosmos.* Boston: Little Brown, 1980.

Bernstein, Jeremy, *Einstein.* New York, 1963.

Beveridge, W. I. B. *The Art of Scientific Investigation.* London: Heinemann, 1974.

Biggs, John B. *The Process of Learning.* Sydney: Prentice-Hall, 1981.

Blakney, R. B., translator and editor. *The Way of Life: Lao Tzu.* New York: Penguin Publisher, 1983.

Boughard, T., McGue, M. "Familial Studies of Intelligence." *Science* 212 (1981): 1055–1059.

Bragg, Paul C., Bragg, Patricia. *Water: The Shocking Truth That Can Save Your Life*. Revised and expanded twenty-eighth printing. Santa Barbara.

Birdsell, J. B. *Human Evolution*. Chicago: Rand Mcnally & Company, 1972.

Bunn, Mark. *Ancient Wisdom for Modern Health—Rediscover the Simple, Timeless Secrets of Health and Happiness*. Australia: Enlightened Health Publishing, 2010.

Byrne, Rhonda. *The Secret*. New York: Atria Books, 2006.

C

Cadoret, R. "Genotype—Environmental Interaction in Antisocial Behavior." *Psychological Medicine* (1982).

Campbell-McBride, Natasha. *Gut and Psychology Syndrome*. Medinform Publishing, 2014.

Carr, Nicholas. *The Shallows: How the Internet Is Changing the Way We Read, Think and Remember*. New York: W. W. Norton and Company, Inc., 2010.

Chisholm, Don. *Have You Got a Gut Really Healthy?* Fifth edition. Self-published, 2014.

Chopra, Deepak. *Power, Freedom, and Grace: Living from the Source of Lasting Happiness*. 2006

Chopra, Deepak. *The Seven Spiritual Laws of Success: A Practical Guide to the Fulfilment of Your Dreams*. San Rafael: Amber-Allen Publishing, 1994.

Cordain, Loren. *The Paleo Diet*. New York: Mifflin Harcourt, 2011.

D

Dan, Yu. *Confucius from the Heart: Ancient Wisdom for Today's World*. Esther Tyldesley, trans. Sydney: Pan Macmillan, 2009.

Davidson, G. C., Neale, J. M. *Abnormal Psychology*. Fourth edition. New York: Jon Wiley & Sons, 1986.

De Bono, E. *The Mechanism of the Mind*. Aylesbury, 1979.

Demos, Raphael, *The Philosophy of Plato*. New York: Octagon Books, 1966.

Diamond, Harvey, Diamond, Marilyn. *Fit for Life II: Living Health*. Great Britain: Bantam, 1990.

Dingle, Peter. *A Supplement a Day Keeps the Doctor Away: The Science of Why We Need to Supplement Our Diet*. Australia: Barker Deane Publishing, 2012.

Donaldson, Margaret. *Children's Mind*. Glasgow: Fontana, 1978.

Dossey, Larry. *The Extra-Ordinary Healing Power of Ordinary Things*. 2006.

Dyer, Wayne. *I Can See Clearly Now*. Australia: Hay House, 2013.

Dyer, Wayne. *Change Your Thoughts—Change Your Life*. Australia: Hay House, 2007.

Dyer, Wayne. *The Power of Intention.* Australia: Hay House, 2004.

Dyer, Wayne. *Pulling Your Own Strings.* New York: Harper Paperback, 1994.

E

Enders, Giulia. *Gut: The Inside Story of Our Body's Most Under-rated Organ.* Australia: Scribe, 2015.

Emoto, Masaru. *The Healing Power of Water.*Fourth edition. Hay House, 2012.

Emoto, Masaru. *The True Power of Water, Healing, and Discovering Ourselves.* New York: Atria Books, 2005.

F

Farrington, Benjamin. *Greek Science.* London: Penguin, 1953.

Fife, Bruce. *Coconut Cures.* Colorado Springs: Piccadilly Books, Ltd., 2005.

Forni, P. M. *The Thinking Life: How to Thrive in the Age of Distraction.* New York: St. Martin's Griffin, 2011.

G

Gelb, Michael J. *How to Think Like Leonardo da Vinci.* Delta Trade Paperback, 2004.

Gore, Al. *The Future.* W. H. Allen, 2014.

Grant, Michael. *The World of Rome.* London: Sphere Book Ltd., 1974.

H

Haldane, Elizabeth S., Ross, G. R. T. *The Philosophical Works of Descartes.* London: Cambridge University Press, 1973.

Harrar, Sari. *Sugar Solution.* Rodale, 2004.

Harrison, John. *Love Your Disease.* Australia: Angus & Robertson, 1984.

Hay, Louise L. *The Power Is Within You.* Australia: Specialist Publication, 1991.

Hay, Louise L. *You Can Heal Your Life.* Fourth edition. Australia: Hay House, 2004.

Hay, Louise L., Richardson, Cheryl. *You Can Create an Exceptional Life.* Third edition. Australia: Hay House, 2012.

Hemenway, Priya. *Eastern Wisdom.* Groningen, Netherlands: Elixiyz Desk Top Publishing, 2006.

Highet, Gilbert. *Man's Unconscious Mind.* New York: Colombia University Press, 1960.

Hollingsworth, Elaine. *Take Control of Your Health and Escape the Sickness Industry.* Australia: Empowerment Press International, 2010.

J

Junger, Alejandro. *Clean Gut: The Breakthrough Plan for Eliminating the Root Cause of Disease and Revolutionizing Your Health*. HarperCollins, 2014.

K

Kaku, Michio. *The Future of the Mind: The Scientific Quest to Understand, Enhance, and Empower the Mind*. New York: Doubleday, 2014.

King, Michael, Ziegler, Michael. *Research Projects in Social Psychology*. Monterey, CA: Brooks& Cole, 1975.

Krishnamurti, J. *The Impossible Question*. London: Penguin Books, 1972.

Krishnamurti, J. *The Second Penguin Krishnamurti Reader*. Mary Lutyens, ed. London: Penguin Books, 1979.

Krishnamurti, J. *The Way of Intelligence*. Madras: Krishnamurti Fundation India, 1985.

Kuhn T. S. *The Structure of Scientific Revolution*. Chicago: Chicago University Press, 1962.

L

Legge, James, translator. *The Wisdom of Confucius*. Australia: AXIOM Publisher, 2002.

Le Guin, Ursula K. *Lao-Tsy, Tao T Ching*. Warsaw: Wydawnictwo Sic, 2010.

Lad, Vasant. *Ayurveda*. Delhi: Motilal Banarsidass Publishers Private Limited, 1998.

Lao Tzu.*Tao Te Ching*. John H. McDonald, trans. London: Arcturus, 2009.

M

McWalters, Malcolm, ed. *Understanding Psychology*. Sydney: McGraw-Hill Book Company, 1990.

Malinowski, B. *The Dynamics of Culture Change*. New Haven: Yale University Press, 1945.

Maltz, Maxwell. *Psycho-cybernetics*. Prentice Hall, 1973.

Man-Ho, Kwok, Palmer, Martin, Ramsay, Jaj. *Tao Te Ching: The New Translation*. Brisbane: Element Books Limited, 1994.

Medina, John. *Brain Rules*. Melbourne: Scribe Publications, 2013.

Michener, James A. *The Quality of Life*. London: Secker& Warburg, 1970.

Morter, Jr., Ted M. *Health and Wellness*. Frederick Fell Publishers, 2000.

Murphy, Joseph. *The Amazing Law of Cosmic Mind Power*. New York: Parker Publishing Company, 1978.

N

Ni, Hua-Ching. *Entering the Tao*. Boston: Shambhala Publication, 1997.

O

O'Neill, William F. *Educational Ideologies: Contemporary Expressions of Educational Philosophy.* California: Goodyear Publishing Company Inc., 1981.

Orgel, I. *Origin of Life.* New York: Wiley, 1973.

Ormstein, R. E. *Psychology of Consciousness.* New York: Freeman, 1972.

O'Toole, James. *Creating the Good Life: How to Apply the Wisdom of Aristotle to the Pursuit of Happiness in Midlife and Beyond.* London: Rodale International Ltd, 2005.

P

Peter, Ryan, Pesek, I. *Solar System.* New York: Viking, 1979.

Phillips, David A. *New Dimension in Health.* Australia: Angus & Robertson, 1983.

Pitchford, Paul. *Healing with Whole Foods.* Third edition. Berkeley: North Atlantic Books, 2002.

Plato. *The Education of the Young in the Republic of Plato.* Bosanquet Bernard, ed. Cambridge: Cambridge University Press, 1908.

Popper, K. *The Logic of Scientific Discovery.* London: Hutchinson, 1972.

R

Rechtschaffen, Stephan. *Time Shifting.* London: Doubleday, 1996.

Rudinesco, Elisabeth. *Philosophy in the Turbulent Times.* William McCuaig, trans. New York: Colombia University Press, 2010.

Rumi, Jalal Ad-Din. 1898, *Rumi—Work of the Great Philosopher, Poet and Mystic.* E. H. Winfield, trans. Australia: AXIOM Publisher, 2006.

S

Sagan, Carl. *Broca's Brain.* New York: Random House, 1979.

Sagan, Carl. *Cosmos: The Story of Cosmic Evolution, Science and Civilization.* London: Futura Publication, 1983.

Schmidt, Erick, Cohen, Jared. *The New Digital Age.* London: John Murry, 2013.

Silvert, Kalman H. *Man's Power: A Biased Guide to Political Thought and Action.* New York: The Vicking Press, 1970.

Steiger, Brad. *Worlds Before Our Own.* New York: Barkley Publishing Corporation, 1978.

T

Tolle, Eckhart. *The Power of Now.* Sydney: Hachette, 2011.

Tzu Lao. *Tao Te Ching.* London: Arcturus Publishing, 2009.

V

Velikowsky, I. *Earth in Upheaval*. Aylesbury: Abacus, 1978.

Virtue, Doreen, Virtue, Grant. *Angel Words: Visual Evidence of How Words Can Be Angels in Your Life*. Hay House, 2010.

W

Walker, N. W. *Water Can Undermine Your Health*. Prescott, AZ: Norwalk Press, 1995.

Watson, P. C., Johnson-Laird, P. N. *Psychology of Reasoning: Structure and Content*. London: Batsword, 1972.

Wheldall. *Social Behaviour*. London: Methuen, 1975.

Y

Yytang, Lin, ed. *The Wisdom of Confucius*. New York: Modern Library, 1966.